A Popular Guide
Through the

A Popular Guide

Through the

Old Testament

Mary Reed Newland

Saint Mary's Press
Christian Brothers Publications
Winona, Minnesota

Mary Reed Newland

committed much of her life to the needy.
For this reason, her family wishes to dedicate this,
her final project, in her honor to those who suffer
for lack of shelter, nourishment, and human dignity.

The publishing team for this book included Barbara Allaire, Stephan Nagel, and Carl Koch, development editors; Mary Duerson and Laurie A. Berg, copy editors; James H. Gurley, production editor; Gary J. Boisvert, typesetter; Maurine R. Twait, art director; Stephan Nagel, cover designer; cover photo, Colin Samuels, Photonica; pre-press, printing, and binding by the graphics division of Saint Mary's Press.

The acknowledgments continue on page 275.

Printed in the United States of America

Printing: 9 8 7 6 5 4 3 2 1

Year: 2007 06 05 04 03 02 01 00 99

ISBN 0-88489-544-0

Contents

1

The Story of God's Boundless Love

To you, O LORD, I lift up my soul. . . .
Make me to know your ways, O LORD;
   teach me your paths.
Lead me in your truth, and teach me,
   for you are the God of my salvation;
   for you I wait all day long.

(Psalm 25:1–5)

The Bible can be thought of as the expression, through human words and ways of communicating, of God's boundless love for us and God's longing for our happiness.

The Bible tells the Story of God's love for us, but it is not only a human account. It is the **word of God**, inspired by the Holy Spirit. Thus the Scriptures can nourish and transform the life of those who approach them with an open heart. In the Bible we can encounter not just words on a page but the living God.

The Great Story

As you know, the Bible consists of both the Old Testament and the New Testament. *Testament* is another word for "covenant." Here, in the briefest outline of the Bible:

1. God created the world and humankind out of infinite love.
2. God offered hope and a promise of salvation when human beings rejected that love.

3. God chose a people and formed a covenant with them, a special relationship, and promised that through them the whole world would be saved.

4. God molded and fashioned this people, the Israelites, during the ups and downs of their history. God offered them liberation, challenged them to live justly and faithfully, took them back when they strayed, consoled them in sorrow, and saved them when they got into trouble. The people of Israel—eventually called the Jews—looked to a future day when God's Reign of justice and peace would fill the whole world.

5. God sent the divine Son, Jesus, the long-awaited Messiah, as the human expression of God's love and the fulfillment of God's promises to Israel. Jesus is the fullness of God's revelation.

6. By his life, death, and Resurrection, Jesus brought salvation to all the world.

7. The Holy Spirit was sent by Christ to nourish, sustain, and renew the followers of Christ, who carry on Christ's work and message until the end of time. In the end Christ will return in glory, and God's universal Reign of justice and peace will finally be complete.

This book considers the Old Testament, or Hebrew Scriptures—the first part of the Bible—which tells the great Story through the time just before Jesus.

A note on terminology: For Christians the word *old* in Old Testament does not imply "outdated" or "no longer in effect," and *new* in New Testament, or Christian Testament, does not imply that it replaces or substitutes for the Old Testament. Rather, Christians believe that the New Testament is the fulfillment of the Old Testament. Both form a unity that is the inspired word of God. We cannot understand the New Testament without understanding the Old Testament. Both are the sacred Scriptures.

The Inspired Word of God

To say that the Bible is inspired by God does not mean that God dictated the words to the writers, who simply recorded what was "whispered" to them! Nor does it mean that everything in the Bible is factually correct or scientifically valid.

Instead, to say that the sacred Scriptures are inspired means God ensured that they contain *all the truth that is necessary for our salvation.* This is the truth of who God is, who we are and how we must act in relation to God and all creation, and where we are going—the destiny meant for us, union with God forever. This is *religious truth,* which is not the same as historical accuracy or scientific explanation.

In inspiring the Bible, God worked through human beings who wrote the sacred Scriptures. They, like us today, were subject to the cultural and intellectual limitations of their own era; they had many customs and ways of thinking that are not our own, and they wrote in Hebrew, Greek, and Aramaic.

Furthermore, these authors used various literary forms in ways that met the needs of their audiences. The Old Testament includes ancient myths and legends, royal court histories, letters, poems, songs, genealogies, sermons, liturgical instructions, laws, accounts of visions, and stories passed down orally for generations before being written down. The process of writing the Old Testament spanned about a thousand years.

God inspired not only the writers themselves but the whole people as they told and retold the stories of their own past; handed them down through the centuries; wrote, edited, and combined their written accounts over time; and finally sifted through all this literature to select the Scriptures that they believed were inspired by God and thus carried the authority of God. The listing of those books is called the *canon* of the Scriptures. Just as Jesus is both divine and human, the Bible itself shows the hands of both God and human beings.

Why *Study* the Bible?

Some of the Bible can be quite puzzling to modern ears. We may not understand the circumstances in which the texts were written or the meaning originally intended by the authors. Some of it may seem contradictory.

Scripture scholars translate the ancient Hebrew and Greek into modern languages, but they also try to get at what the authors really meant. Scholars delve into the history, archaeology, literary forms, and culture surrounding the development of the texts to help us understand their intended meanings. Of course, even the best Scripture scholars disagree on their findings and theories, and many questions are still open to debate. By and large, though, Scripture scholarship has shed great light on modern understanding of the Bible.

The purpose of studying the Scriptures is not simply that we might know a lot of things about the Bible or even about its theological meaning. Knowledge is important and useful, but it is not enough. Rather, the deeper intent of Scripture study is that we might "fall in love" with the Bible, and with God, who is its source and inspiration.

Why the Old Testament?

Christians cannot understand the New Testament and Jesus without understanding the Old Testament. But in itself—and not just because it points to the New Testament—the Old Testament has permanent value. It contains profound teachings, beautiful prayers, and some of the greatest literature ever created. Most important, in the Old Testament we encounter God, its inspiration.

This book provides you with a "guided tour" of the Old Testament. It walks you through all the books, considering the circumstances in which they were composed, describing their contents, and offering insights into their meaning from the perspectives of contemporary Scripture scholarship and Catholic Tradition.

The book directs you to read key passages from each book of the Old Testament. No book can substitute for reading the word of God. So you are invited to plunge into the Scripture passages themselves, which have the power to touch our life in a way that summaries of them do not.

Once you are equipped with a Bible, this book, and a willing spirit, you are ready to discover the meaning of the Old Testament, and to encounter God in the process.

A God Who Acts in History

The God revealed in the Old Testament is not aloof or distant from human affairs; this God acts within human history. The Story of God's actions and the people's responses over many centuries is called **salvation history.** It will help to keep the big picture of that history in mind as we set out to discover the meaning of the Old Testament, because the history and the Scriptures of ancient Israel were intertwined.

About 3000 B.C.E. history as we know it began, with the development of early forms of writing. The biblical period—from the beginnings of Israel as a people through the time of Jesus and the earliest years of the church—was from about 1850 B.C.E. until about 100 C.E. It lasted almost two thousand years.

Note: The standard practice today is to use the abbreviations B.C.E. (before the common era) and C.E. (of the common era) in place of the traditional abbreviations B.C. and A.D.

The Founders and the Promise

The history and the religion of the Israelites began with Abraham. Abraham was a wandering herdsman who lived in the region now called Iraq, around 1850 B.C.E. According to the Book of Genesis, God promised to make Abraham's descendants a blessing to the world and to give them the land of Canaan, later known as Palestine. The Promise was that Abraham's descendants would reveal the one God to the world. Christians believe that this Promise reached its fulfillment in the coming of Christ.

Abraham's descendants and their families inherited the Promise. His son Isaac and grandson Jacob, like Abraham, would be called the patriarchs, or founders, of the Jewish faith. Their wives—Sarah, Rebekah, and Rachel—would be called the matriarchs.

The Exodus of the Israelites and the Covenant

At the close of the Book of Genesis, the descendants of Abraham are living in Egypt, having traveled there from Canaan in order to survive a famine. Yet as the Book of Exodus opens, we find them enslaved by the Egyptians. Practically nothing is known about the Israelites in Egypt from about 1700 to 1290 B.C.E.

About 1290 B.C.E. the understanding that one God was above all other gods came to Moses when God revealed God's name, Yahweh, meaning "I am the One who is always present." With God's power the Israelites, led by Moses, made a daring escape from Pharaoh's army through the sea—the Exodus—and were thus freed from slavery.

After a dramatic encounter between Moses and God on Mount Sinai, a Covenant between Yahweh and the Israelites was confirmed. The Israelites' part of the Covenant was to keep the Ten Commandments, which God had presented to Moses. God's part was to make the Israelites "the people of God" and to be with them as long as they kept the Covenant. Once again God promised that they would be given the land of Canaan. But before they entered Canaan, they wandered in the desert as they learned to trust God's care for them.

Taking Over the Promised Land

After Moses' time the Israelites, led by Joshua, entered Canaan. Over the next centuries—from about 1250 to 1000

B.C.E.—they fought against the people who lived in that region. In these battles the Israelites were led by military leaders called judges. During this time the Israelites abandoned their nomadic ways for the more settled agricultural life that was native to the region.

The Nation and the Temple

Around 1000 B.C.E. Israel became recognized as a nation, with David as its anointed king and Jerusalem as its capital city. God made a promise to David that his royal line would endure forever. Later Jews put their hope in a descendant of David to save them from oppression.

David's son Solomon built the Temple in Jerusalem, and it became the principal place of worship for the nation. As both a political and a religious capital, Jerusalem became a great and holy city.

The Kings and the Prophets

After Solomon's death in 922 B.C.E., the nation broke in two, with the kingdom of Israel in the north and the kingdom of Judah in the south. Heavy taxes and forced service in both kingdoms created hardships for the people. In addition, the kings often practiced idolatry, the worship of idols.

Prophets spoke out against both kingdoms' injustices to the people and infidelity to God. They questioned the behavior of the kings and called them and their people back to the Covenant. Yet the kingdoms continued to oppress the poor and worship pagan gods until eventually both kingdoms were crushed by powerful conquerors. The Assyrians obliterated the northern kingdom of Israel in 721 B.C.E. and took its people into exile. In 587 B.C.E. the Babylonians destroyed Judah, including the city of Jerusalem, and took its people to Babylon as captives.

The Babylonian Exile and the Jewish Dispersion

While the people were exiled in Babylon, other prophets encouraged them to repent of their sins and turn back to God. During this time the prophet known as Second Isaiah proclaimed that God was the one and only God. Monotheism, the belief in one God, was now the revelation of this people to the world, their blessing to the nations.

After fifty years in Babylon, the exiles were released from captivity by the conquering Persians and allowed to return home. Judah, no longer a politically independent kingdom, had become a district within the Persian Empire, and the returned exiles became known as Jews, from the word *Judah*. They rebuilt the Temple, and under Ezra and Nehemiah, they re-established the Law and restored Jerusalem. That city became the religious capital for the Jews who had resettled all over the world—that is, the Jews of the Dispersion.

During the exile the Jewish leaders had begun collecting and reflecting on their ancestral writings, forming the core of what would later become their Bible, known to Christians as the Old Testament.

More Oppressors

The Persian Empire was conquered in 330 B.C.E. by the armies of Alexander the Great. This made the Greeks overlords of the Jews for nearly three hundred years, with the exception of a brief period of independence after a revolt led by the Maccabees family. The Greeks were followed by the Romans, who captured Jerusalem in 63 B.C.E. Although tolerant of other cultures and religions, the Roman Empire severely punished revolutionaries.

It was a dark time for the people of the Promise, who longed for release from oppression and for the day when all their hopes for a good and peaceful life would be fulfilled. Many Jews looked toward the coming of a messiah, one sent by God to save them; some expected this messiah to be from the family line of David. It is at this point in the history of Israel that the Old Testament accounts end.

Jesus, the Savior

Into a situation of defeat and darkness for the people of Israel, Jesus was born—one of the house, or family line, of David. Christians see Jesus as the long-awaited Messiah, the fulfillment of all God's promises to Israel and the savior of the world. With his death and Resurrection, Jesus' followers recognized that he was the Son of God. The community of believers began to grow, first among Jews but later among Gentiles, or non-Jews. The story of Jesus and the growth of the early church is told in the New Testament.

Writing the Scriptures

Many of the books of the Old Testament were derived from earlier oral versions going back to the time when Israel was a people but not yet a nation. The written versions began later, when a simple system of writing Hebrew became available around 1000 B.C.E.—the time of David's and Solomon's reigns.

In a limited form, writing has been used for over thirty thousand years. In picture writing, realistically drawn figures represent an object, an event, or an idea. Many ancient societies developed writing systems based on picture writing. Over time the written characters became simpler, but each one still represented a word or a phrase. Ancient writers had to learn hundreds, even thousands, of written characters in order to record even brief reports or letters.

We associate the written characters called hieroglyphics with the Egyptians, who carved them on their temples and tombs beginning around 3000 B.C.E. Actually, the term *hieroglyphic,* meaning "of holy carvings," can refer to any system of highly stylized pictures—such as those once used by the Cretans in the Mediterranean or the Mayans in Central America.

The Egyptians added a special feature to writing by using some of their pictures to represent sounds. Egyptian writing

Judaism After the Biblical Period

Most of the Jews of the first century C.E. did not become Christian. Judaism went on, and it has carried the light of faith in the one God into our contemporary age.

The history of Judaism in the time after Jesus began with a crushing blow. A Jewish revolt against the Roman Empire led to the Roman destruction of Jerusalem and the second Temple in 70 C.E. The surviving Jews fled to Africa, Asia, and Europe. The Jewish Dispersion, the *Diaspora,* became a central fact of Jewish history.

That Jews were dispersed all over the Empire spurred the definition of an official set of scriptures to guide Jewish religious life. This would ensure the Jews' sense of identity as a

influenced the system that the Canaanites invented sometime before 1550 B.C.E. The Canaanites also used pictures, but eventually they adopted a set of simply written characters—all of which represented consonants. The written characters were linked to sounds, not words. Relatively few characters were needed; a couple of dozen could represent most of the sounds of speech. Now anyone who could learn a simple alphabet could write. Suddenly many more people could become professional writers, or scribes.

After the Israelites entered Canaan, they adopted both the language of the Canaanites and their alphabetic writing system. The ease of using an alphabet made it possible to preserve the ideas of common people, not just of royalty. In the Scriptures, then, the words of unpopular prophets stand alongside those of powerful kings.

The alphabet moved toward completion when the Greeks borrowed it from the Phoenicians, descendants of the Canaanites, around 800 B.C.E. Soon after, the Greeks took the final step of using some of the characters to represent vowel sounds. Hundreds of years later, the early Christian writers used the Greek alphabet and language to record the Gospels. A few of the books in the Catholic canon of the Old Testament were written in Greek, as well.

people set apart and bound by the Covenant with God; it would help them keep separate from the surrounding cultures that worshiped other gods and had immoral practices.

By the end of the first century C.E., this official set of the Hebrew Scriptures was defined. In 90 C.E. Jewish religious leaders met to agree on the *canon*—that is, the list of books recognized as divinely inspired and thus the primary source and guide for religious belief and practice. In translations this canon became known as the Bible, literally meaning "the book." The Jewish Bible was organized into three main parts: the Torah, the Prophets, and the Writings.

Catholic teaching is that Christians are forever linked with the Jewish people, who were the first to hear the word of God. God's Covenant and special relationship with the Jews still stand, "for the gifts and the calling of God are irrevocable" (Romans 11:29). The words of Saint Paul about the Jews express this: "To them belong the adoption, the glory, the covenants, the giving of the law, the worship, and the promises; to them belong the patriarchs, and from them, according to the flesh, comes the Messiah" (9:4–5).

In spite of great suffering and persecution, often at the hands of Christians, Jews have remained faithful to God through the centuries since biblical times. Like Christians, Jews work toward and await in hope the coming of God's Reign of peace and justice.

What Are the Scriptures of the Old Testament?

For the Jews: Letters from Home

The Old Testament, and the Bible as a whole, can be thought of as a "letter from God"—a message conveying God's truth that enables us to encounter God, who inspired it.

The Scriptures, though, can also be considered from their human aspect. They were written by flesh-and-blood human beings for real audiences who needed to hear what these writers had to say in their own time and place. And so for the Jews of the Dispersion, flung around the ancient world of the Mediterranean by war and persecution, their Hebrew Scriptures must have seemed like "letters from home."

Imagine what a letter from home might mean to a group of refugees. The Hebrew Scriptures were like that for the Jews of the Dispersion. They told the Jews in their own language how best to live a faithful life in unfamiliar surroundings. Most important, the Scriptures told them that the God of their people would be with them always.

These "letters from home" took the form of many types of writing: stories, legends, histories, oracles, conversations, letters, novels, lists, biographies, laws, speeches, poems, proverbs, and prayers.

The Catholic Canon of the Old Testament

Because Christianity's religious roots were in Judaism, Christians adopted the sacred writings of Judaism as their own. So the Bible of Judaism contains the same Scriptures as what Christians call the Old Testament, with the exception of a few more texts in the Catholic canon. These other texts—some of them originally written in Greek and others translated from Hebrew or Aramaic into Greek—often appear in Protestant Bibles under the category of apocryphal writings; they are not part of the Protestant or the Jewish canon.

The **Catholic canon** of the Old Testament consists of forty-six books, grouped in the following major sections:
- the Pentateuch
- the historical books
- the wisdom books
- the prophetic books

The Pentateuch

The heart of Israel's story is told in the first five books of the Bible, called the Pentateuch, which means "five books." The five books are Genesis, Exodus, Leviticus, Numbers, and Deuteronomy. The Jews refer to these books as the *Torah*, a Hebrew word that means "instruction" but is sometimes translated as "the Law." In the Jewish faith, these books are the primary scriptural authority in matters of belief and practice.

The Pentateuch's opening stories about the Creation, Adam and Eve, Cain and Abel, Noah, and the Tower of Babel show us God as a loving Creator and reveal the effects of disobedience. Following these stories are the tales of the patriarchs and the matriarchs—Abraham and Sarah, Isaac and Rebekah, Jacob and Rachel, and Joseph.

Next, we are told of Israel's slavery in Egypt, Israel's escape under the leadership of Moses, the Covenant at Mount Sinai, and the forty years in the wilderness, ending on the eve of Israel's entry into the Promised Land.

The Historical Books

The historical books tell of Israel's conquest of the land of Canaan—including stories of Joshua, the judges, and Israel's first kings (Saul, David, and Solomon). These books also describe the breakup of the nation of Israel, the reigns of the later kings, and the prophets' attempts to warn those kings of coming disaster.

In spite of the prophets' warnings, the kings disobey, disaster comes, and exile follows. Fifty years later a remnant of the people returns to Jerusalem, rebuilds the Temple, and struggles again with foreign powers and the people's own weaknesses. Through it all Israel's prophets remind the people of their Covenant with God and of their call to be a blessing to all the nations of the world. In addition to Joshua and Judges, the historical books include Ruth, 1 and 2 Samuel, 1 and 2 Kings, 1 and 2 Chronicles, Ezra, Nehemiah, Tobit, Judith, Esther, and 1 and 2 Maccabees.

The Wisdom Books

The wisdom books are usually listed as Job, Psalms, Proverbs, Ecclesiastes, Song of Songs, Wisdom, and Sirach (also called Ecclesiasticus).

- The Book of Job explores the age-old question of why bad things happen to good people. Job demands a reason from God for the calamities that overcome him, and God answers in a speech of matchless splendor.

- The Book of Psalms is a collection of religious songs once attributed solely to David but now to a number of authors. Some psalms were written for liturgical occasions, others for private prayer.
- The Book of Proverbs is a collection of writings filled with practical advice about living an ordinary life in the spirit of godliness.
- The author of the Book of Ecclesiastes was a questioner who, in the end, saw that life was a mystery for which he had no answers. It is wise to live life as well as possible and to enjoy it, he decided.
- The Song of Songs is a collection of love songs in the form of dialog, the speakers being bride, bridegroom, and attendants.
- The Book of Wisdom was meant to strengthen the faith of Israel, and spoke for the first time in Israel's history about life after death.
- The Book of Sirach was written to show that true wisdom had been revealed by God to Israel.

The Dead Sea Scrolls

Modern Scripture studies can be greatly affected by discoveries such as the Dead Sea Scrolls.

Possibly before the Roman invasion of Palestine in the first century C.E., a Jewish community called Qumran hid its library of scrolls in caves near the Dead Sea. There they remained until 1947, when shepherds discovered them.

Before the discovery of the Dead Sea Scrolls, the earliest manuscripts in Hebrew came from the ninth century C.E. The scrolls from Qumran date back almost a thousand years before that and serve as a check on the accuracy of later manuscripts. These scrolls confirm that Jewish scribes copied their manuscripts with great care and precision.

The Prophetic Books

The early prophets—such as Samuel and Nathan, Elijah and Elisha—are known for their life stories rather than for their recorded words. Often called the nonwriting prophets, these figures appear in the historical books.

The writing prophets, each of whose teachings are a book of the Bible, can be thought of in three groups, named in reference to the exile in Babylon:

- The *pre-exilic* prophets are Hosea and Amos (who spoke to the northern kingdom of Israel) and Isaiah, Jeremiah, Micah, Nahum, Habakkuk, and Zephaniah (all of whom spoke to the southern kingdom of Judah).
- The *exilic prophets* are Ezekiel (who went to Babylon with the deportees), Second Isaiah (the second part of the Book of Isaiah), and the unknown author of the Book of Lamentations.
- The *postexilic* prophets include Haggai, Zechariah, Malachi, Third Isaiah (the third part of the Book of Isaiah), Joel, Obadiah, and Baruch.

The prophetic books tell us about people who loved Israel and who warned it that to depart from fidelity to God would lead not only to moral blindness but to destruction as a nation—which is what happened. The Books of Jonah and Daniel are also listed with the prophetic writings.

This book covers all the books of the Old Testament (some only briefly). However, it does not treat the books in the same order that they appear in the Bible, which is by categories. This is so that the book can follow roughly the history of Israel. For example, historical and prophetic books are treated together in some chapters because they relate to the same biblical period.

Begin . . . at the Beginning

With all this in mind, open the first book of the Old Testament—the Book of Genesis, which tells the story of the Creation and of the first people on earth. As you proceed keep in mind the words of the great modern Jewish thinker

Martin Buber. Referring to the Hebrew Scriptures, Buber addressed these words to Christian readers:

> To you, the book is a forecourt;
> to us, it is the sanctuary.
> But in this place,
> we can dwell together,
> and together listen to the voice
> that speaks here.
>
> (*The Writings of Martin Buber,* p. 275)

Questions for Reflection and Discussion

1. What has been your experience with the Old Testament? Recall how you were taught to view it. What sort of influence has the Old Testament had on the growth of your spirituality?

2. Spend some time exploring your Bible. Find a passage in the Old Testament that you think is beautiful, powerful, or inspiring. Ponder why you chose it. What is the truth it offers you?

3. Who are the patriarchs and matriarchs in your family tree? What legacy have they left your family? What stories are told and retold in your family? Why is it important to preserve and pass on family stories?

4. Reflect on a time when you felt deep trust in God, or a time you faltered in your trust. In your own salvation history, how important has it been to remember these times?

5. What does Martin Buber's statement at the end of the chapter mean for you?

2

Stories of God's Creation and Promises

Praise the LORD! . . .

Praise him, sun and moon;
    praise him, all you shining stars!
Praise him, you highest heavens,
    and you waters above the heavens!

Let them praise the name of the LORD,
    for he commanded and they were created.
He established them forever and ever;
    he fixed their bounds, which cannot be passed. . . .

Mountains and all hills,
    fruit trees and all cedars!
Wild animals and all cattle,
    creeping things and flying birds! . . .

Let them praise the name of the LORD,
    for his name alone is exalted;
    his glory is above earth and heaven.

(Psalm 148:1–13)

Much of the Old Testament, including the **Book of Genesis,** was written down and put into final form around the period of the Babylonian exile, in the sixth century B.C.E.

The exile is a time of crisis for the Israelite people. They have lost their homeland, Judah. Their holy city, Jerusalem, has been conquered, and their sacred Temple, the center of their life, has been destroyed. Here they are, a defeated people forced to live among their captors in Babylon. Babylonian culture and religion, with their strange ways and their belief in many destructive, warring gods, feel like a horrendous assault on everything the exiles hold dear.

Disturbing questions gnaw at the exiles: Has God abandoned us? We thought we were the Chosen People of an all-powerful God. Or are the Babylonians right after all? Could the chaotic, competitive gods of the Babylonians really be superior to the one God we worship? Is that why we have been defeated, humiliated, and brought here to this strange, unfriendly land—because our God failed?

In the midst of their doubts and feelings of despair, the exiles desperately need to hear the liberating truth: Our God is in charge—of *everything in the world,* including the Babylonians! God is all good, and God creates only goodness. We can count on that. God can turn even our failures to good if we trust in God with all our heart. We are God's people, and God will never abandon us.

That message of hope and trust in God's goodness did reach the discouraged exiles and their offspring, who after about fifty years were released from Babylon to go back and build a new life in their home country, Judah. The Book of Genesis, put together in its final form during and after the exile, strengthened and lifted the hearts of the returning Israelites, by that time called the Jews. It helped remind them that from the beginning their God had been in charge, bringing forth goodness out of everything, even out of nothingness! Genesis helped them understand their origins—who they were and why they should have hope.

Stories of the Origins

The first part of Genesis (which means "beginning"), made up of chapters 1 to 11, is a kind of prehistory of Israel. Various versions of the stories in it were first told by folksingers and storytellers early in Israel's history, as they wove together accounts of "where we came from." The stories are filled with fragments of myths from the ancient Near East. But over the centuries and especially around the time of the exile, the stories were transformed by the scriptural writers.

The stories became powerful, God-inspired religious tales that expressed Israel's beliefs about God and the world's origins, in stark contrast to the beliefs of their Near East neighbors. In those eleven chapters of Genesis are the marvelous stories many of us recall from childhood:

- Creation (how the original goodness of Creation came from the one God)
- Adam and Eve and the Fall (how sin entered the world)
- Cain and Abel, Noah and the Flood (how the evil of sin spread)
- the Tower of Babel (how humanity, in terrible condition, was unable to save itself from its own sinfulness)

By the end of Genesis, chapter 11, the stage is set for the great drama that follows—the story of God's relationship with a special people through whom the world would be saved. The rest of Genesis tells of how one man, Abraham, and his descendants down to Joseph became that Chosen People, the Israelites.

But let's begin at the very beginning: "In the beginning . . ."

Creation: Original Goodness

Where did we come from? Why are we here at all? Are we meant to be happy or miserable? Ancient peoples turned these questions over in their minds, as human beings have continued to do right down to today.

Many people in the ancient Near East, including the Babylonians, had rather pessimistic answers to these questions. They were **polytheistic**, worshiping many gods, and believed that the world had come from those gods—self-serving, violent, and destructive deities that had made the earth for their own pleasure, and humankind for their slaves. This was a chaotic world where human beings were caught in the middle of the gods' wars, trying to please first one bad-tempered god, then another, to avoid their wrath.

The ancient Jews had quite a different answer to the question of why we are here at all. Contrast the Babylonians' frightening worldview with the Jewish view in the Book of Genesis of a wonderful world created by God: Out of chaos, the one God brings forth goodness—order, beauty, and abundant forms of marvelous life. It is all meant to be wondered at, enjoyed, and cared for by human beings, the last of God's creatures, who are made partners with God in loving all Creation.

In this first story, the sun and the moon and the stars are not gods that rule humans (as the Babylonians believed them to be) but are *created by* God as good and then are set calmly in their proper place in "the dome" (Genesis 1:7) of the sky. God is in charge! The great sea monsters, perceived as evil demons by many ancient peoples, are shown to be what they are—good, innocent creatures that God loves. Then God creates the first human ('*adam* in Hebrew, also meaning "earth creature"). This first human was understood to mean all of humanity, which was godlike, made in God's own image—full of dignity and beauty.

You can sense God's delight in such handiwork: "God saw everything that he had made, and indeed, it was very good" (Genesis 1:31).

Read Genesis 1:1–31; 2:1–4.

The story of Creation underlies a basic attitude in the Judeo-Christian heritage: God is good, we are good, and life is good. God cares about us and all Creation, and wants us to be happy. We are to uphold the inherent dignity and worth of each human being because all are created in God's image. And God has entrusted us with this amazing world, to be caretakers, not destroyers, of Creation. God wants full life for every person and intends for us to preserve and watch over the environment.

The Sabbath: A Gift of Rest

The Creation story tells of God "resting" on the seventh day after a flurry of creative work. This might seem a curious detail to include, but remember that the story was written down during the exile. In that time, keeping the **Sabbath** was a sacred custom the Jews had carried with them to the exile. It marked them as unique among their neighbors. In Babylon the Sabbath took on much importance as a constant reminder for the Jews that they were God's people, not the Babylonians' or their gods'. So the

Creation story writer included God's own resting on the seventh day to emphasize the importance of keeping the Sabbath holy as a day to rest, praise God, and be refreshed together—a gift from God not to be turned down.

Jews today celebrate the Sabbath from Friday sunset to Saturday sunset. For Christians the Sabbath is Sunday, recalling the day of the Resurrection of Jesus Christ.

Is It Science?

The Creation account in Genesis has stirred up controversy among believers, both Christian and Jewish, especially in the last century. **Creationists** insist that the account in Genesis is factually true—that is, God created the world in just seven days, in the order given in the story. **Evolutionists** argue that the universe has evolved over millions of years, with humankind as a late part of that evolutionary process. Evolutionists claim that the Bible's Creation account was never intended by its biblical writer to be a factual explanation. Developed in the literary form of a myth, it was meant to convey religious truth, not scientific fact.

The Catholic understanding of the Creation account is that no contradiction exists between the biblical story and the theory of evolution. The Genesis story is about the religious meaning of the origins of the universe, not the scientific facts of those origins. The church affirms that much scientific evidence supports the evolution theory. In no way does that shake the religious truth of the Creation account— the truth that God is the source of all goodness, including our own existence as human beings made in God's image.

In the story of Creation, we can see the magnificence of God's truth. It is expressed through the inspired poetic genius of its writer, probably a member of the priestly class of Jews, who with few words put everything in place.

Adam and Eve

Genesis moves on to another account of Creation, which focuses on the story of **Adam and Eve.** Do not be concerned if some of the details are inconsistent with the first account. The biblical writers had the job of weaving together a number of different strands from their oral tradition. Sometimes, when inconsistencies arose, they didn't worry about them but let both accounts stand. No doubt they figured that each one contributed some valuable religious truth that they did not want to leave out. From our vantage point, we can see God's inspiration at work in the writers' decisions about what to include.

In the story, Adam and Eve are created to enjoy the delightful garden and to be intimate companions for each other. They are also privileged to be on walking and talking terms with their Creator. But soon the man and the woman are caught up in disobedience and guilt. They have eaten the forbidden fruit, and feeling naked, they try to cover themselves. When they hear God approaching, they hide. God calls Adam, and his excuse for hiding is his nakedness. Yet earlier Adam was naked and unashamed. God asks if he has eaten the fruit of the tree of knowledge, and Adam, unwilling to take the blame, tries to shift it to Eve. Eve, just as unwilling, accuses the serpent of tricking her.

Thus sin has done its work and ruined Adam and Eve's relationships—with God, between themselves, and with Creation. Now God foretells the consequences of their sin: Man's work will not give him perfect pleasure but will be difficult and will weary him, and woman will be subject to her husband and will bear children in pain.

Read Genesis 2:4–25; 3:1–24.

This story of Creation tells of the **Fall**—that is, the first sin of humankind—termed by Christians **Original Sin.** The "knowledge of good and evil" (Genesis 2:17)—so alluring to Eve and Adam—is a knowledge that is God's alone. Adam and Eve are not satisfied with being what they are, humans made in God's own image, seen as "very good" by God, and destined for happiness. They looked at themselves and decided that their humanity was not good enough. Their sin was the denial of the goodness of Creation. Adam and Eve decided that they had to snatch divine likeness from God, when they had it already. Thus they damaged their relationship with God.

The ancient Jewish storytellers wanted us to understand that human beings, not God, destroyed life in the garden. Created with freedom, humans can choose to believe God and live in the divine image or to rebel against

God and reject their full humanity. The misery that follows results from human choice. Thus God does not create injustice in the world; human beings do so by their bad choices.

Sin's Spread: Cain and Abel

Like ripples in a pond, sin will spread out over the ages and touch everyone. Genesis describes sin's spread first with a story about hatred between brothers that ends in murder, then with a story about depravity in society, and finally with one about arrogance among the nations.

The story of **Cain and Abel** tells of two brothers, sons of Adam and Eve—the first a farmer, the second a shepherd—offering gifts to God in sacrifice. God blesses only Abel's sacrifice and encourages Cain to rise above his jealousy. Angry, Cain murders Abel. So the first sin has begun to affect the human family, in the form of another sin, murder. As if that were not enough, in response to God's inquiry about Abel's whereabouts, we hear Cain's insolent reply, "'Am I my brother's keeper?'" (Genesis 4:9). Those familiar words are echoed even today in the responses of people who want to deny that they have any responsibility toward others.

Read Genesis 4:1–16.

More Sin and a Promise: Noah and the Flood

The account of the **Flood** almost begins with "Once upon a time," so accustomed are we to hearing it as a nursery tale. The story tells of how bad things can get once sin spreads its ugliness. There is such depravity on the earth that God regrets creating the human race.

Only one man, **Noah**, finds favor with God and is instructed to build an ark to protect himself, his family, and some animals from destruction. Noah does as God commands, the Flood comes, and the ark safely rides the waters until they recede. All other creatures are destroyed.

Leaving the ark, Noah offers a sacrifice of thanksgiving. The story of Noah ends with God's first **covenant**, or solemn promise—with Noah because he obeyed.

Read Genesis, chapters 6; 7; 8; 9:1–17.

God's Word Saves Us

The story of Noah is probably related to other similar flood stories found in ancient literature. The tale's authors were not interested in figuring out historical causes of the flood, if indeed such a flood occurred, but in teaching the powerful truth that whoever hears and obeys God's word will be saved, and whoever does not will be lost.

"Saved from what?" is the question. We know that devout people are not necessarily saved from disaster. Even those who Jesus says will live forever are not saved from calamity in this life.

The answer is that hearing and keeping God's word saves us from forgetting how to love and serve. When we *do* forget how to love, something happens inside us, where it is unseen. We turn hard and cold, perhaps not instantly but gradually. Our warm, fleshy heart eventually turns to cold stone without our even being aware of it. *That* is the awful fate that God wants to save us from.

The Rainbow: A Sign of a Promise

The end of the Flood is marked with a rainbow as a sign of God's love for every creature on the earth, and a promise that the world will never again be destroyed by a flood. This promise is the first instance of a covenant between God and human beings, in the Bible. The next time you see a rainbow, remember how dearly God loves the earth.

An Arrogant World: The Tower of Babel

The last of the prehistory stories in Genesis is the tale of **Babel.** Once again humankind tries to carve out a destiny of its own making. Here the presumptuous ambition of Adam and Eve to be equal to God is projected on a grand scale when the nations try to build a tower with its summit in the heavens so they can "make a name for themselves." God comes down to see the tower, is appalled by the nations' arrogance, and stops them by confusing their language and dispersing the peoples.

Read Genesis 11:1–9.

The story of Babel shows how sin has spread to affect even the behavior of the nations, who seek glory in power, might, wealth, superiority, and dominance—without a thought for God. Today the nightly newscasts are filled with stories of such attempts, as well as stories of the pain, corruption, and devastation they beget.

Thus the first eleven chapters of Genesis tell about God's good purpose for the world, and then how things went. These prehistory chapters come to a close with the world desperately in need of God's salvation.

If the first part of Genesis explains why things went wrong in the world, the second part tells how God chose a people to start setting things right again. This latter part of Genesis tells stories about the founders of the Israelites, the people chosen as the instrument through whom God would save the world.

Abraham

Like the stories about Creation, the stories of the founders were remembered and told for centuries before they were written down. Unlike the stories of Creation, the stories of the patriarchs and the matriarchs take place in historical times. Their setting is a period about four thousand years ago (2000 to 1700 B.C.E.).

The first of these stories is about **Abraham** and his wife, **Sarah**. Through Abraham, Sarah, and their descendants, God would establish a people, a "nation," through which God would save the world. It all begins with the story of people who are willing to follow God's call wherever it leads them. Abraham and Sarah appear in the Book of Genesis first with the names **Abram** and **Sarai**.

The Call of Abram and God's Promise

Among the Semitic nomads wandering along the highlands of the Near East is a man named Abram. (The word *Semites* refers to a number of ancient peoples of the Near East, from whom the Israelites descended.) Abram travels from the city of Ur to the city of Haran, and it is in Haran that he hears God's call. God bids Abram to take his family away from all that is familiar and go to a land "'that I will show you'" (Genesis 12:1). And God promises that from Abram's offspring will come a great nation, a blessing for the world. This is the first mention of God's **Promise** to the people who would become Israel. Abram takes Sarai, his nephew **Lot,** and all his possessions, and goes, not knowing where God is leading him or what to expect. In faith he follows a God he does not yet know to the land called **Canaan.**

Read Genesis 12:1–9.

The story of Abram's call, written as though God is speaking directly to him, is about Abram's struggle to understand the mystery of the gods—until it comes to him that one God is above all other gods. Abram's call probably came the way that God's call comes to anyone: silently, subtly, during the search for answers that we call prayer.

Abram may not have understood God as the *only* God, but as the God he would worship above all others. Even though belief in the one God is the cornerstone of Judaism, it was not yet clear to the people of Abram's time. But from a later perspective, Jews recognized the God of Abram as *the* one and only God.

Abram, an old man whose wife is childless and beyond her childbearing years, lets God lead him—and becomes the father of the faith of the Jews, the Christians, and the Muslims. Recall the story of Babel, where human beings close themselves off to God in the illusion that they are "on top," in control. Their arrogance brings on disaster. Abram, on the other hand, is humble before God. He is open to God's purpose for his life, and is willing to leave behind all that is familiar to follow God's call. He knows he is not in control; God is. Thus God is able to accomplish great things through Abram.

Count the Stars if You Can

Years pass, and Abram and his family travel to other lands and arrive back in Canaan. But still there are no children. Having waited faithfully and grown older, Abram begins to doubt that he will have a son. He has no child; Sarai is barren, apparently unable to bear children.

God tells Abram to look up at the stars and count them if he can. God promises that Abram's descendants will outnumber the stars. And Abram believes, despite the apparent impossibility of it all. By *descendants* God refers to all who believe or will believe because Abram believes.

Read Genesis 15:1–6.

An Alternative Plan: Hagar

Sarai continues to be childless, and she finally proposes that Abram take her Egyptian maid, **Hagar**, as a concubine and beget a child by her, which would legally belong to Sarai. This idea works, but not without a lot of bad feeling between the two women. At one point the pregnant Hagar runs away to flee the harshness of her mistress. In the wilderness a messenger of God appears to her. At his command she returns to submit to Sarai, fortified by the promise that her unborn son, **Ishmael**, will grow to manhood wild and free.

Read Genesis 16:1–16.

The customs in early biblical times of taking concubines and of practicing **polygamy** need some explanation: If a wife was barren, a female servant might become a surrogate childbearer, a concubine to the husband. Or the husband might take a second wife in order to give the family children. Both of these practices helped to assure the survival of the tribe.

The Sign of the Covenant

God establishes with Abram a covenant, a solemn pledge on both sides. This repeats the covenant made previously with Abram—the Promise that he will bring forth a multitude of descendants, and that all the land of Canaan eventually will be his people's. The sign of the covenant between God and the people is a ritual for all males, **circumcision**, which identifies Abram's people as God's people. To reflect this new status and identity, Abram's name is changed to Abraham and Sarai's to Sarah.

Read Genesis 17:1–22.

Visited by Strangers

Abraham is sitting at the entrance to his tent in the heat of the day when he is approached by three strangers—who, we later learn, represent God. In a display of graciousness, Abraham offers them refreshment, water for bathing, and a place to rest.

According to the custom of the time, Sarah, as a woman, is not present in this scene, but she is listening behind the flap of the tent. When she hears one of the visitors say that in a year she will bear a son, she laughs out loud. The visitor answers her laugh with, "'Is anything too wonderful for the LORD?'" (Genesis 18:14). The story, rich in color and detail, repeats God's promise to Abraham that one day he will be a father of nations.

These verses (Genesis 17:17; 18:12) contain a bit of wordplay: **Isaac,** the name that God gives to their son-to-be, means "laugh" in Hebrew.

Read Genesis 18:1–15.

The story of the visit to Abraham highlights a solemn obligation of biblical times: the giving of **hospitality.** For a traveler in the wilderness, hospitality was a matter of survival, and to be refused hospitality was sometimes a death sentence.

Abraham and Sarah offer hospitality out of kindness, without any inkling that these mysterious guests represent God and have something marvelous to tell them. The Letter to the Hebrews in the New Testament hints at this story, which would have been quite familiar to readers of the letter, with these words: "Do not neglect to show hospitality to strangers, for by doing that some have entertained angels without knowing it" (13:2).

Pleading with God

As the story continues, God reveals to Abraham a plan to destroy the wicked cities of **Sodom and Gomorrah** if the complaints against their inhabitants are found to be true. Abraham pleads for the safety of his nephew Lot, who lives in Sodom. As Abraham again and again presses God not to destroy the just people along with the wicked in this infamous city—even if they number only a few—God graciously agrees.

In Sodom the wicked inhabitants propose the rape of some young men (or angels) to whom Lot has given shelter. Rape is evil at any time, but doubly heinous considering the life-giving hospitality required by guests. Lot offers his own daughters in order to protect his guests—to no avail. So the cities will be destroyed, except for Lot and his family, the only just people remaining in those wicked places. The angels rescue Lot and his family. In the well-known ending to the story, Lot's wife, curious about the fate of the cities, looks back to check out the destruction and turns into a pillar of salt—a famous but unimportant biblical detail.

Read Genesis 18:16–33; 19:1–29.

Enter Isaac, Exit Ishmael

Isaac is born, and now Sarah's laughter is of a joyful kind. Hagar is expelled because Sarah fears that Ishmael might threaten Isaac's inheritance. Again, we must admire Hagar's behavior. Alone in the wilderness with no water left and thinking that her boy will die, she walks some distance away from him because she cannot bear to watch his suffering. Then, aided by an angel of the Lord, Hagar finds a spring and saves her son. Ishmael goes on, with God's blessing, to live in the wilderness and eventually to take a wife. The story is a tribute to Hagar's perseverance and faith.

Read Genesis 21:1–21.

A God Who Chooses Imperfect People

Curiously, Hagar emerges from the Genesis story more noble than the ancestral heroes Abraham and Sarah. Hagar is portrayed sympathetically, even though Sarah's son, not Hagar's, is the one God intends to be the ancestor of the Chosen People.

The Jews did not try to whitewash their heroes, only to show that God had chosen a people far from perfect. Yet in spite of their faults, God was able to make them a light to the world. And that says something encouraging to all of us imperfect people.

What of Hagar? The story makes it clear that God holds her and her offspring in the most tender care. Being chosen does not necessarily mean being more worthy, as the Israelites will be reminded over and over in their checkered history with their God.

Tradition has made Ishmael a **bedouin**—that is, a nomadic Arab—and the **father of the Arab peoples. Islam** claims Abraham as their father in faith through the line of Ishmael. So Abraham is considered the ancestor of all three great **monotheistic** religions in the world today: Judaism, Christianity, and Islam.

Abraham's Sacrifice

The next story is often called **Abraham's test.** In it, God bids Abraham to take Isaac, the son he loves with all his heart, to a place on a mountain and sacrifice him as a holocaust—that is, a burnt offering. In anguish Abraham climbs the mountain with the boy. In answer to Isaac's question about what they will sacrifice, Abraham can only say, filled with faith, that God will provide a victim. At the last moment, an angel of God stops Abraham from killing his son, and instead a ram is provided for the sacrifice.

Read Genesis 22:1–19.

What Kind of God?

The biblical writer displayed only admiration for Abraham's obedience. Clearly the writer had no problem with this story, but how can we come to terms with a God who would ask such a thing, even if not intending to carry it out—to say nothing of a father who would acquiesce?

Abraham came from a culture that occasionally reverted to human sacrifice in times of national crisis, as a desperate attempt to secure divine help. We do not know for certain if this was the case with Abraham, but people have often thought that they knew what God wanted and have been mistaken. Only when the angel stayed his hand did Abraham know what his God expected of him. Many people have interpreted the story of Abraham's test as confirming that God forbids human sacrifice, something that seems obvious to us today.

Isaac and Rebekah: Best Biblical Romance

Abraham returns home, and at Sarah's death buys a field in which to bury her, the first piece of ground that his people possess in a land that will one day be theirs.

Isaac grows up, and Abraham, facing his own death, instructs his steward to find a bride for Isaac from among their tribe back in Haran. Now we have a novella—a little masterpiece of storytelling. Rich detail, exotic marriage customs, and the loveliness and generosity of **Rebekah** are woven together in the most beautiful of all the biblical romances. We glimpse Rebekah's adventurous spirit when she agrees to leave Haran immediately, over the protests of her kin. The story ends with the bride glimpsing Isaac as she approaches her new home and Isaac taking her to his tent, where he marries her. In Rebekah he finds comfort after the death of his mother.

Abraham marries again and has many children by another woman. When he dies—at the age of one hundred and seventy-five—Isaac and Ishmael bury him next to Sarah in the family's field.

Read Genesis 24:1–67.

World Happenings
Between 2000 and 1700 B.C.E.

Africa
The Egyptian pharaohs no longer build pyramids as their tombs. Instead they are buried in tombs deeply tunneled into the walls of the hills on the western side of the Nile River.

America
The Eskimo culture begins on the Bering Strait. Pottery is made in Mexican villages.

China
The potter's wheel is introduced. Pigs, dogs, oxen, goats, and sheep are domesticated.

Abraham's unbelievable age at his death is an exaggeration common in biblical stories. It is a way of saying that Abraham was wise and blessed.

And so the story unfolds. Through many ins and outs, heroic moments, laughter, sinfulness, and sadness, God is at work. First through Abraham and Sarah, then through Isaac and Rebekah, God is keeping the Promise to fashion a people who will be God's own and a blessing for all the nations. After the disaster of the Fall and the rampant spread of sin and depravity over the earth, it looks as though God is beginning to put the world back together again.

But the drama is just getting started. . . .

Jacob: A Man Named Israel

Once again, in the stories about Isaac and Rebekah's son Jacob, the biblical writer shows God at work building a people—making sure that the divine purposes are accomplished.

From the time of her pregnancy, Rebekah knows that the younger of the twins she will bear is destined to be the

Europe
Early cultures begin using bronze to make tools and weapons. The Stonehenge circle in England is used for religious and astronomical ceremonies. Culture on the island of Crete is at its height; the bull-god is worshiped at the city of Knossos.

India
Chickens and elephants are domesticated. Sacrifice is offered in the worship of a mother-goddess.

The Near East
Around 2000 B.C.E. the destruction of Ur, the Near East's major city, results in the decline of the dominant culture.

principal heir to Isaac's goods and, most important, heir to his leadership of the tribe. By rights, the elder, the firstborn of the twins, should succeed his father. But Rebekah is convinced that God's purpose is otherwise, and she devotes herself to maneuvering the younger twin into the position of heir. This move will entail some deception, which Rebekah seems quite ready to engage in.

The twins are born—first **Esau,** the shaggy redhead, and then **Jacob,** following close behind, grasping Esau's heel as if trying to get ahead of him! Clued in by his mother as a child about his destiny, the young man Jacob manages to trick Esau into swearing over his birthright to him.

In time, father Isaac, old and failing in his eyesight, wants to give his dear elder son, Esau, his blessing to seal Esau's right to head the clan. Rebekah, ever alert on Jacob's behalf, stages an elaborate deception of her husband so that Jacob, not Esau, will get Isaac's blessing. Jacob puts goatskin on his neck and wrists so as to feel like hairy Esau to his near-blind father. Sure enough, the little drama works, and Jacob gets the prized blessing. Aghast, Isaac realizes he has been deceived, but he cannot take back his blessing once given. The furious Esau vows to kill Jacob one day.

For all her presumption, Rebekah sincerely believes that the will of God in this affair is in her hands. She strives to obey it at great personal risk.

Read Genesis 27:1–41.

Jacob Journeys to Haran

To escape Esau's fury, Jacob suddenly must flee to Haran, where Abraham first heard his call from God so many years before. The young man can also find a suitable wife there, not a Canaanite that his mother would frown upon. Jacob—young, feisty, and self-satisfied—sets off with Isaac's blessing. Camping the first night, he dreams of angels ascending and descending from heaven. He hears the voice of God repeat the Promise made to Abraham, and names the place **Bethel,** meaning "the house or abode of God."

In the final scene of this episode, Jacob seems to choose the terms of the relationship with God (Genesis

28:20–21), but God, not people, initiates covenants. Jacob sounds like a brash young man, who feels that it is his right to bargain with God.

Read Genesis 27:42–46; 28:1–5,10–22.

Life in Haran

Arriving in Haran, Jacob stays at the home of his uncle **Laban.** He is so good at helping with the flocks that Laban would like to keep him there, and marry off both of his daughters to Jacob as well. Jacob is in love with the younger daughter, **Rachel.** But Laban tricks him into marrying the older sister, **Leah,** after seven years, and then has him wait seven more years before giving him Rachel in marriage.

The years pass, and Jacob is older and wiser, although no less conniving. He has two wives, two concubines, and many children, and is totally fed up with Laban. In a kind of midlife crisis, he remembers the land of Canaan and God's Promise and wants to return home. So he and his substantial household of wives, slaves, and flocks set off for Canaan.

Midway to Canaan, Jacob remembers Esau. Fearful of his brother's anger, Jacob sends herdsmen ahead with large flocks of animals to be given as gifts to placate him. In his fright Jacob reminds God of the promise of protection, which he now desperately needs.

Reaching the border of Canaan, Jacob shepherds his family and flocks across a river and, staying alone on the other side, has a strange encounter, the meaning of which continues to puzzle scriptural commentators.

The mysterious being who meets Jacob in this story has been called by translators a stranger, a man, an angel— some even suggest a demon. This "someone" wrestles with Jacob until the break of day, when Jacob, refusing to let go, asks for a blessing. In reply the stranger asks his name, and when he says that it is Jacob, he is told that from now on he will be known as **Israel,** meaning "one who has contended with divine and human beings." Left alone as the sun rises, Jacob marvels that he has seen God face-to-face and has not died.

Read Genesis 32:23–32.

The interpretations of this episode are so numerous that we are almost free to interpret it for ourselves. Was it a night of prayer? Was it a struggle with conscience? Was it a dream? Jacob—separated for fourteen years from his ancestral home and faced with Esau's possible rage—could well have been terrified and torn between going on and turning back. In the context of biblical history, this is a curtain-raising story. Jacob is returning to the destiny long ago promised, to the land of Canaan, and to his place among the people chosen to be a blessing to the nations. He has been named Israel by God, and his descendants, God's chosen ones, will be known as the Israelites.

Family Worship of God

Jacob continues on to meet and make peace with Esau. He then goes to Bethel and builds an altar on the spot where he heard God's promise on his outward journey. He orders his family to rid themselves of the trappings of their pagan religion—not only the household gods but also their ornaments, earrings, even clothing—in a purification rite that initiates the family into the worship of the God of Israel. Again God transfers to Jacob the blessing given to Abraham and Isaac, the Promise of the land of Canaan and a royal line that is to be a blessing to the nations.

In a short passage, we are told of the death of Rachel at the birth of her second son, **Benjamin.** Jacob returns home and finds Isaac still alive. At his death Jacob and Esau bury their father in the field where Abraham and Sarah lie.

Read Genesis 35:1–29.

Joseph: Treachery, Triumph, and Forgiveness

The stories about Joseph are also about his father, Jacob, because God is not finished with Jacob yet. These famous tales also drive home the message that keeping God's word brings rewards far beyond anything imaginable—and that God can bring good out of even the most wicked of deeds and desperate of circumstances.

Sold into Slavery

Joseph, Rachel's first son, is seventeen years old and Jacob's favorite, but not his brothers'. Dan, Naphtali, Gad, and Asher dislike Joseph because after he tended flocks with them, he told his father tales about their behavior. The others resent him for being their father's favorite, the son of Jacob's beloved Rachel. Jacob has had a long, flowing tunic made for Joseph—the garb of tent dwellers, not shepherds, and unlike the short, coarse garments that his brothers wear. Worse, Joseph's dreams contain portents that one day he will lord it over his family. When he rashly recounts these dreams, even Jacob rebukes him. The scene is set for his undoing.

One day the brothers are tending the flocks some distance away from home, and Jacob sends Joseph to see if things are well with them. As the brothers watch him approach wearing his long, flowing coat—hardly the clothing for a hike in the country—they plot to kill him and throw his body down a well. But **Reuben** has no heart for such a deed and suggests that instead they put Joseph into a dry well, for Reuben plans to return later to rescue him. The brothers do this and then sit down to eat—the writer's comment on their callousness.

Seeing traders on the way to Egypt, **Judah** suggests that they sell Joseph instead and avoid having his blood on their hands. The deed is done, and the brothers hide it by showing Joseph's coat, which they have dipped in goat's blood, to Jacob. Seeing the bloody coat, Jacob believes that Joseph has been killed by a wild animal, tears his own garments, and mourns the loss of Joseph for many days.

Here are all the elements of a family saga. Consider the parts of this melodrama:
- Jacob's favoritism
- Joseph's talebearing and boastfulness
- the brothers' envy and betrayal
- the brothers' deception of their father, Jacob (they seem to have inherited some of his traits)

The wonder is that, sinful and guilty as they are, God will lead these men to self-knowledge and remorse, some even to heroism and holiness.

Read Genesis 37:1–35.

Joseph's Fate in Egypt

Once in Egypt Joseph does quite well for himself. Though a slave, he is given considerable responsibility under the pharaoh's chief steward. But Joseph lands in prison, falsely accused of rape by the steward's lustful wife, who has tried unsuccessfully to seduce the handsome young man.

Even in prison, though, Joseph is singled out as special. The knack for interpreting dreams that got him in such trouble with his brothers comes in handy when Joseph is asked to explain the pharaoh's dreams to him. He does so well at it that he gains the pharaoh's favor.

By the age of thirty, Joseph has been made governor of Egypt, second only to the pharaoh in power. He has married a beautiful Egyptian woman, and they have two sons, Manasseh and Ephraim.

Then severe famine strikes the whole Near East, including Egypt. But years earlier Joseph had predicted the famine through the pharaoh's dreams, and fortunately he has been storing up grain supplies for just such a disaster.

The Founders' Journeys

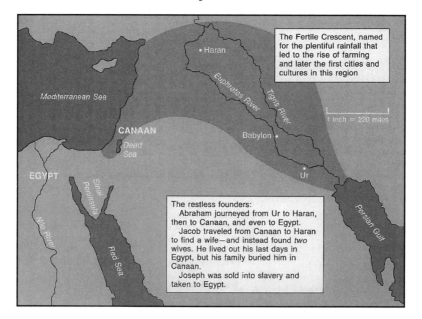

The Fertile Crescent, named for the plentiful rainfall that led to the rise of farming and later the first cities and cultures in this region

1 inch = 220 miles

The restless founders:
Abraham journeyed from Ur to Haran, then to Canaan, and even to Egypt.
Jacob traveled from Canaan to Haran to find a wife—and instead found *two* wives. He lived out his last days in Egypt, but his family buried him in Canaan.
Joseph was sold into slavery and taken to Egypt.

People from all over the Near East go to Egypt to buy grain from the Egyptian surplus.

Read Genesis, chapters 39, 40, 41.

The Brothers on Joseph's Turf

Back in Canaan, Jacob sends ten of his sons to Egypt to buy grain for the family's survival. And who is in charge of grain sales? Joseph.

Joseph's brothers, however, do not recognize him, and so Joseph takes the opportunity to toy with them a bit. He pretends to think they are spies and puts them in prison, refusing to sell them grain. Then he decides to let them go with the grain on condition they will return with their younger brother, Benjamin. As Jacob's dearest child after Joseph, Benjamin has not been allowed to come along on the trip. And they must leave one of the brothers, Simeon, as a pledge until they return!

Back home, the brothers plead with Jacob to let them take Benjamin back to Egypt so they can rescue the brother they left behind. Reuben even offers his own sons as a pledge for Benjamin's safety. But Jacob is adamant: they may not take his beloved Benjamin!

Read Genesis 42:1–38.

Jacob's Sacrifice

Eventually Jacob's clan needs grain again, but without Benjamin the brothers cannot go back to Egypt for it. After bemoaning the terrible price he must pay, Jacob finally consents to part with Benjamin because his people must live. The sacrifice will take him to his grave, he cries, but he will do it.

Read Genesis 43:1–14.

Up until this point, we have not seen a lot to admire in Jacob's character. Consider his lifelong deceit, craft, and greed. Not until the moment when he agrees to sacrifice Benjamin (as Abraham was willing to do with his own son generations before) does Jacob become one of the great saints of the Scriptures.

Return, Reunion, Reconciliation

Back the brothers go to Egypt, and on arriving they are invited to Joseph's house for a banquet—still unaware that he is the brother they sold into slavery. When Joseph sees Benjamin, he leaves the room to weep. Later, when Joseph sits down to eat, he sends tidbits from his own plate to share with Benjamin as a gesture of royal favor.

When the brothers prepare at last to leave with their grain, the steward hides Joseph's own goblet in Benjamin's sack as a plant. Once they are on their way, Joseph sends servants after them. The cup is found, and Joseph orders Benjamin to stay behind as a slave. Now Judah steps forward and, in a beautiful speech, pleads with Joseph to consider the aged father who will die if Benjamin fails to return. Judah pledges his own life in Benjamin's place, and Joseph, close to tears, sends everyone but the brothers from the room.

Weeping so loudly that the others hear him in the hall, Joseph finally reveals his identity, forbidding his brothers to blame themselves for their past misdeeds. Everything was allowed to happen, he says, so that when they were in danger of starving, someone would be there to feed them. Joseph's story is a tale of reconciliation and redemption.

Read Genesis 43:15–34; 44:1–34; 45:1–28.

Not only does Jacob get a bigger heart in this story, so do Joseph and his brothers. Joseph, who in his youth was boastful and proud, has the heart to forgive his brothers their wicked deed of selling him into slavery. The brothers have grown, becoming ready to make sacrifices for the well-being of those they love. The whole family has developed from bitterness and hate to tender appreciation of one another.

Happy Ending

So all ends happily. The brothers return home, fetch Jacob and his family, journey back to Egypt, and settle there. Jacob is rewarded for his sacrifice of Benjamin by seeing all his sons reunited. In his old age, Jacob adopts Joseph's two sons, Manasseh and Ephraim—which is why they are listed as two of the twelve tribes of Israel. When Jacob dies, Joseph takes his body back to Canaan for burial. Joseph also lives to old age, and makes his brothers swear that whenever their people return to the land of God's Promise, his bones will be taken there to be buried in the field where Abraham, Sarah, Isaac, and Jacob lie.

The stories of the patriarchs are all tales with happy endings—astonishingly so. Joseph's last request reveals, however, that the saga of ancient Israel is not over.

Nourished Spirits

Imagine how the Genesis stories must have bolstered the spirits of the exiled Israelites in Babylon. They could see in these stories the pattern of God's work: *God worked with simple, flawed human beings to bring about God's Promise, that the people of Israel would become a "light to the nations," the people through whom God will save the world. Our all-powerful God makes good happen, in spite of our sin and weakness.* This hopeful message reached the exiles, who needed to recognize God's loving hand at work in the midst of their tragic failure.

By the end of the Book of Genesis, the descendants of Jacob Israel are living in Egypt. The stage is set for telling the story of the greatest event in the unfolding of God's plan among the Israelites—the Exodus.

Questions for Reflection and Discussion

1. What difference do a people's beliefs about their origins make to their attitudes about life? What does the Old Testament story of Creation tell you about your own worth and dignity?

2. "[God] rested on the seventh day" (Genesis 2:2). Create a chart of your typical week, noting how much time is given to work, social activities, family, friends, sleep,

and other things you're involved with. How would you evaluate your need for a *sabbath?*

3. "Am I my brother's keeper?" What does it mean to be responsible for another person? Who have been your "keepers" during your life?

4. Considering your experience, how have you encountered one act of sin leading to another and another.

5. "Is anything too wonderful for the Lord?" Sarah laughs when she hears she will have a child in her old age. But with God nothing is impossible, nothing is too wonderful! Reflect on wonderful events from your life. What were the circumstances?

6. Usually we associate hospitality with physical needs being met, like the desert travelers welcomed by Abraham and Sarah. But more than offering food, drink, or rest, hospitality is about offering friendship and a safe presence. Think about the simple ways that you can show warmth, safety, and care—hospitality—to the people who make up the fabric of your life.

7. In the Israelites' understanding, things would work out the way God wanted them to—no matter what or who tried to get in the way. God could bring good out of situations that were weird, puzzling, unfair, or evil. Reflect on this idea, recalling examples from your own life.

8. Joseph forgives his brothers for selling him into slavery and abandoning him. Who needs your forgiveness? Are there any obstacles to forgiving? What might happen if forgiveness is withheld?

3

The Exodus and the Covenant of Sinai

As a deer longs for flowing streams,
    so my soul longs for you, O God.
My soul thirsts for God,
    for the living God.
When shall I come and behold
    the face of God?

. . . . . .

Why are you cast down, O my soul,
    and why are you disquieted within me?
Hope in God; for I shall again praise him,
    my help and my God.

(Psalm 42:1–6)

The **Book of Exodus** is at the heart of the Old Testament. It proclaims the great truth that God freed the descendants of Abraham, Isaac, and Jacob from oppression and slavery in Egypt, then formed them into a chosen nation, Israel, and created an everlasting bond with them through the Covenant of Sinai.

The Exodus stories, like those of Genesis and the other books of the Torah, were collected and edited into the Book of Exodus around the time of the exile in Babylon (seven hundred or so years after the Exodus took place). These accounts were close to the hearts of the exilic and postexilic Jews for many reasons:

- At the beginning of the story of the Exodus, the Israelites were living as slaves in a foreign land, Egypt. The Jews of the exile had a similar experience, living in Babylon as captive subjects of a mighty empire.

- The people of the Exodus struggled in a frightening and hostile wilderness. Similarly, the exiled Jews made a long, painful journey to Babylon, and back again to Judah some fifty years later.
- Most important for the Jews was God's revelation to their ancestors in the wilderness. Through Moses the people of Israel discovered the identity of their God, and through the Covenant, they found their own identity as God's people. Similarly, in Babylon, after repenting of their sins, the exiles rediscovered their true identity as God's beloved.

The Exodus: Freed from Slavery

The Book of Exodus begins about four hundred and fifty years after the death of Joseph. The reigning pharaoh of Egypt, unlike the Semitic pharaohs of Joseph's time, hates and fears the people of Israel and orders them enslaved. Then comes the royal command: All Israelite males must be slain at birth.

Young Moses

The story of **Moses** begins when his mother, to save her infant son from being slain by Pharaoh's orders, puts him in a basket and floats it on the Nile River, where he is discovered by Pharaoh's daughter. A little girl darts out of the reeds with the information that a Hebrew woman nearby could nurse the baby. The princess hires the woman to care for the child among the Hebrews until he is old enough to be returned to the royal household. Because the little girl and the nursing woman are Moses' sister, **Miriam**, and his mother, he grows up knowing that he is really an Israelite—although he is raised by Pharaoh's daughter as an Egyptian prince.

Reaching manhood, Moses sees an Egyptian slave driver beating a Hebrew one day. He is outraged at the injustice done to one of his own kinsfolk, so he attacks the slave driver, kills him, and buries his body in the sand. When he finds out the next day that the murder is known to others, Moses fears Pharaoh's anger and flees Egypt eastward to the land of the nomadic Midians. There he meets a priest, marries one of his daughters, and becomes a shepherd.

Read Exodus 1:6–22; 2:1–15.

The Burning Bush: In the Presence of the Holy

Life goes on miserably for the Israelite slaves; one cruel pharaoh replaces another. Though the Israelites have forgotten about the God of their ancestors Abraham, Isaac, and Jacob, they cry out in agony, and God is mindful of their suffering.

One day while tending sheep in Midian, Moses sees a strange sight—a bush aflame but not consumed. Drawing near, he hears God telling him to remove his sandals, for he is standing on holy ground. Moses is awed by the mysterious presence, then alarmed to hear the command that he return to Egypt and order **Pharaoh** to let the Israelites go. Moses protests that he is unsuited for such a task, but God insists. Again Moses protests: he does not know God's name. Who will he tell the people that their God is? God reveals the sacred name to be **Yahweh**—interpreted within the scriptural text as "I am who am" or "I am who I am." Once again Moses excuses himself: the people will not believe him. God gives him two miraculous signs by which to convince the people—or at least himself. Still Moses argues: he is slow of speech and tongue, suggesting a speech impediment. Finally, God becomes angry and says that Moses' brother, **Aaron**, will accompany him and do the talking—but Moses is to go.

Read Exodus 3:1–22; 4:1–17.

Scholars suggest that the worship of the God named Yahweh was, in fact, unknown before the time of Moses. Although the early Israelites began to worship Yahweh within their own group, they did not necessarily see their people's God as the one and only God or as the God of all the nations. This belief came later. The concerns of Moses' people probably did not extend much beyond their own families and tribes.

For Jews the name Yahweh stresses the unutterable mystery of God, and out of reverence they have preferred not to pronounce it. Instead they substitute titles such as Adonai, meaning "the Lord." Many Christian versions of the Bible have adopted the word *Lord* in their translations, meaning "divine sovereignty." This book will follow the same practice.

"Let My People Go!"

In Egypt Moses and Aaron give God's message to the Israelites, who exult because the Lord has seen their affliction. Yet Pharaoh, when told of God's command to "'let my people go'" (Exodus 5:1), is unmoved: Why should he heed a God of slaves? Isn't he, Pharaoh, a god also—son of the great god Ra? Besides, freeing his workforce would upset the system. Accusing Moses of luring the Israelites from their work, Pharaoh doubles their burden. The people cry out that Moses' promise of the Lord's protection has not freed them but only increased their sufferings. They want no more to do with the Lord. Now God promises to take action.

Notice that the Israelites have to be convinced of God's presence by miracles. They have been in Egypt for over four hundred years, and they no longer know their God. Yet God knows them.

Read Exodus 4:27–31; 5:1–23; 6:1.

Pharaoh: Plagued by Plagues

Moses and Aaron return to Pharaoh and repeat their demand, Pharaoh ignores them, and then the ten plagues begin. Water turns to blood, frogs overrun the land, and gnats and flies torment the Egyptians. Sickness afflicts their cattle, boils plague the people, hail destroys the crops, and locusts eat what is left. Darkness covers the land, and Moses proclaims the final plague—death for the firstborn of Egypt. Pharaoh will beg them to leave, Moses says—but still Pharaoh is adamant.

Read Exodus 6:28–30; 7:1–25; 8:1–11; 11:1–10.

Were the plagues miracles or natural phenomena? As natural disasters they were not unknown to Egypt. But the point is that God freed Israel from Egypt—whether through miracles or natural occurrences.

Pharaoh's performance reads like that of a character in a TV soap opera. Note the following passages in Exodus:
- Pharaoh's arrogance in 7:22–23
- his bargaining and going back on his word in 8:4–15
- his wavering in 8:21–28
- his pretended repentance in 9:27–28
- his craftiness in 9:33–35
- his ransom plan in 10:8–11
- his hypocrisy in 10:16

Did God harden Pharaoh's heart, or was he naturally stubborn? The Scriptures say both things, ten times each, and both may be true. The human heart is hardened by flinging itself against the will of the loving God, and proud, powerful rulers do not give in easily, especially to slaves. The God of the lowly Israelites was in Pharaoh's way.

Preparation for the Passover

God gives Moses instructions in preparation for the journey out of Egypt. Every family is to slay and roast a yearling lamb or kid, eat it with unleavened bread—a yeast dough would take too long to rise—and be ready to leave. Then they are to smear the top and posts of their doorway with the blood of the lamb so that the angel of God will *pass over* their home when striking down the firstborn of Egypt. The Israelites are to celebrate this meal every year as a perpetual reminder of the **Pesach,** or **Passover.**

At subsequent Passovers the Israelites rid their households of all leaven—that is, fermented dough kept from one baking to another, a form of yeast—and all leavened bread. Starting afresh with new dough symbolized a new life of freedom. Jewish families today do this during the Passover season and serve only unleavened bread, called matzo. From this custom came the Catholic use of unleavened bread in Communion.

Read Exodus 12:1–14.

The memorial meal of the Israelites became the Passover **seder,** or ritual meal, of the Jewish people. Although we do not know for sure, the **Last Supper,** Jesus' meal with his disciples the night before he died, was likely a seder. We do know that Jesus used the language, food, and ritual of the Passover to help his disciples understand the meaning of his own death in the context of their history. The Jewish seder celebrates freedom from slavery in Egypt and the longing for freedom everywhere in the world. The Last Supper has become the Christian Eucharist, which celebrates freedom from the power of sin and death through Jesus' life, death, and Resurrection.

"Go, and Good Riddance!"

At midnight a loud cry rises up over Egypt as the firstborn of every household is discovered dead. As Moses has foretold, Pharaoh summons him and cries out that Moses and his people must go, that it will be a blessing to be rid of them.

At last the people of Israel leave—a ragtag crowd of slaves, foreigners, men, women, and children, unarmed and on foot, leading their milking animals, and carrying all their belongings—including the bones of their ancestor Joseph, who wanted to be buried in the **Promised Land,** the land of Canaan first promised to Abraham.

Read Exodus 12:29–39.

Again, the point of the story is *that* God freed the Israelites, not *how* God freed them. The slaying of the Egyptians' firstborn is not described.

The Great Escape: Crossing the Sea of Reeds

God, in a pillar of cloud by day and a pillar of fire by night, leads the Israelites. Hardly have they left when Pharaoh, in a rage, starts after them. The Israelites see his chariots in pursuit, are terrified, and cry out to Moses accusingly: "Were there not enough graves in Egypt? Is that why you brought us out to the desert to die?" (adapted from Exodus 14:11). Moses bids them to wait to see what the Lord will do. The cloud moves to the rear of their camp and hides them from the Egyptians. Then the wind blows all night, parting the Sea of Reeds, and in the morning the Israelites cross safely—just ahead of the Egyptians. The water returns, and Pharaoh's troops drown. Moses and his sister, Miriam, together with their people, sing a *canticle* praising God for the victory. Scholars believe that the oldest parts of the Old Testament might be found in two verses of Moses and Miriam's canticle (15:1,21).

Read Exodus 13:17–22; 14:1–31; 15:1–21.

Murmuring and Grumbling in the Wilderness

The people of Israel have hardly finished celebrating their new freedom when they begin to complain about the hardships of the journey. When the water is bitter, the Lord sweetens it. When they lack food, the Lord sends manna and quail. When again they need water, Moses strikes a rock and water gushes out.

Read Exodus 15:22–27; 16:1–36; 17:1–6.

Scholars are not sure what the food was that the Israelites called manna. One possibility is the sweet sap that forms on one variety of desert tree. Whatever it was, the Israelites depended on it as their "daily bread" throughout the forty years of their wandering in the wilderness.

An Exodus Perspective for the Exiles

The Israelites were freed from slavery and oppression by the power of God and then led into the wilderness, where they had to learn over and over to keep trusting in God's care for them. Reflecting on that reality centuries later, the Jewish exiles in Babylon understood what that meant for them in their oppressed situation: "The Lord will save us. The Lord will free us. And when we are tempted to give up in despair, the Lord will go on looking after us, giving us everything we need to keep going. *Trust the Lord.*"

The Covenant of Sinai: An Offering from God

When the Israelites arrive at Mount Sinai, Moses goes up the mountain. There God bids him to tell the people that the Lord has brought them safely to this place and that if they will keep the Covenant, they will be the Lord's holy nation, dearer than all other peoples. Moses returns to the people and repeats this message, and the people say they will do everything the Lord asks of them.

On the third day, as the people prepare themselves for God's coming, a great storm breaks out on the mountain. Lightning flashes, thunder peals, and dense clouds cover the peaks. Moses leaves the people behind to go up the holy mountain and receive God's message. Then the Lord gives Moses the Ten Commandments.

Read Exodus 19:1–11,16–19.

Some scholars speculate that the writer may have embellished this account of divine visitation with details from Israel's later liturgical celebrations. The trumpet blasts and clouds of smoke that were included to symbolize the Lord's arrival could have been part of the celebration of the great event in the centuries that followed it.

The Ten Commandments

The **Ten Commandments,** or the **Decalogue,** had a long history of development beginning in the time of Moses (1250 B.C.E.). Many other laws were added to them over the years and are included in Exodus—as well as in the Books of Leviticus, Numbers, and Deuteronomy. These later laws will be treated in the next chapter. Here we will look at the Ten Commandments in their historical context.

Read Exodus 20:1–26.

No Other Gods

The first commandment did not say that no other gods existed, but it did declare that there was only one God of the Israelites and that they should worship no other.

This commandment also prohibited idolatry. In the Near East at the time, people commonly worshiped idols that represented gods—for example, a statue of a bull or a sun symbol. The first commandment stated that such human efforts to depict God were bound to fail and should not be attempted. At another level idolatry can be understood as "making a god" out of something that is *not* God—for instance, treating social status or money or even school grades like God, as deserving our total allegiance and "worship." An addiction—to alcohol or other drugs, to gambling or smoking—can also be a form of idolatry.

God's Name

The second commandment forbade the use of God's name in irreverent, sacrilegious ways. As mentioned earlier, devout persons rarely spoke God's name, but those less devout sometimes abused it in the belief that using the name Yahweh in prayer or when swearing an oath would magically force God to do their will. This commandment speaks to the great reverence that is owed to God, and thus to God's name.

The Sabbath

The third commandment called upon the Israelites to keep Saturday, their seventh day, as the Sabbath—free for worship in honor of God's rest on the seventh day in the story of the Creation. Later, by contrast, Christians chose Sunday as their holy day in honor of the Resurrection, which they believed signaled the first day of the New Creation. For the Israelites, keeping the Sabbath holy and restful was one way of saying, "We belong to God, not to any human authority." The Sabbath helped them remember *who* they were, and *whose* they were. This was especially important for the Jews in exile, when, as a powerless minority in a strange land, they were trying to preserve their religious identity.

Parents

Today we associate the fourth commandment, "Honor your father and your mother" (Exodus 20:12), with children and obedience. Originally the law addressed adults and sought to protect aging parents, who needed their adult children to care for them. The humanity of a society, it has been said, can be judged by how that society treats its youngest and its oldest citizens.

Murder

The fifth commandment, sometimes translated as "You shall not kill" (Exodus 20:13), is more accurately translated as "You shall not murder." In nomadic groups a person's life and dignity were protected only by the assurance that kinsfolk would revenge any injury or insult. Acts of revenge often escalated to bloody feuds and sometimes resulted in the extinction of entire family groups. At the time of the Exodus, the purpose of the fifth commandment was to lessen the violence arising from hatred, malice, and the taking of the law into one's hands. Much later, in speaking of this commandment, Jesus denounced other forms of destructiveness—for example, anger, contempt, slaying with words, and vicious gossip. Today this commandment speaks to a variety of threats to human life that were not obvious to the Israelites.

Adultery

The sixth commandment, "You shall not commit adultery" (Exodus 20:14), had as its purpose the protection of marriage and the family. In ancient times the well-being of the family took precedence over the individual's desires because the stability and even the survival of the community depended on it. A married person's having sexual relations with someone other than the marriage partner often led to vengeance and feuds. It was held in great horror among the Israelites, and its punishment was death. Later laws of ancient times addressed other wrongful sexual relationships.

Stealing

"You shall not steal" (Exodus 20:15), says the seventh commandment. Stealing of goods that rightfully belong to someone else breaks down the trust necessary for a community.

False Witness

The eighth commandment forbids giving false testimony, especially in cases being judged by elders or in courts. At the time the Commandments were given, when a liar intended to bring about a sentence of death for an accused person, the penalty for false witness could also be death. Today the commandment against "false witness" is understood to forbid gratuitous lying.

Coveting a Married Woman

The ninth commandment given was later divided, and the second half was made into the tenth commandment—which is how they are treated here. Both commandments have to do with covetousness, or greediness, and both reveal a profound understanding of the path of sin. Sin begins in the mind and in the heart. Setting our heart obsessively on someone or something—and not on the ways of God—is part of the sin of covetousness, and entertaining the idea of a sin often leads to the act. Coveting a neighbor's spouse can be the first step toward adultery. Today this commandment reminds us that the intent in our heart is important.

Greed for a Neighbor's Property

The tenth commandment relates to coveting a neighbor's goods, an envious craving that is the first step to injuring one's neighbor. Such greed leads not only to "keeping up with the Joneses" but also to trying to surpass them, and life can become a nightmare in which people are possessed by their possessions.

Other Laws of Israel

The Book of the Covenant, which follows the Ten Commandments in Exodus, treats laws of worship, civil laws, and laws controlling morality. Many of these laws were radical steps forward for the time, creating a relative degree of fairness in situations where previously violence or greed held sway. Other laws in The Book of the Covenant strike us today as clearly unjust, such as the law that was quoted at one time to justify owning slaves. This law said that if the owner of a slave struck the slave but did not kill him or her, that person would go unpunished because the slave was property.

Read Exodus 21:20–21.

A Law That Frees

The Israelites perceived the Ten Commandments and the other laws not as burdens that dragged them down but as mutual understandings that enabled them to live in freedom and peace with one another. For instance, once vengeful killing is ruled out in a community and everyone agrees to follow that law, people no longer have to live in fear.

For the Israelites, keeping the Commandments was a sacred pact with one another as well as with God. They recognized that rules can actually free people by giving them lines or boundaries that everyone in a community pledges not to cross.

Sealing the Covenant

In preparation for ratifying the **Covenant of Sinai,** Moses builds an altar with twelve pillars representing the twelve tribes of Israel. He has young bulls sacrificed for offerings, dividing their blood into two bowls. Half of the blood he splashes on the altar as a symbol of the Lord's presence, and the other half he sprinkles on the people as a sign of the binding of God and the people in a kind of marriage. Doing so, Moses proclaims the Covenant of Sinai. Then God bids Moses to ascend the mountain again to receive the stone tablets on which the Law has been written.

Read Exodus 24:3–8.

Blood was the sign of life itself. In fact, laws of the time prohibited the consumption of animal blood because life was God's dominion, not humans'. In the ancient world, blood rituals such as the one described above were practiced as a way to seal covenants or agreements between kings.

The Covenant of Covenants

The sealing of the Covenant of Sinai is a high point of Israel's story. You have read about other blessings, promises, and covenants that God made with Adam, Noah, Abraham, and Jacob. Other covenants made between human parties are also mentioned in the Old Testament. The Covenant of Sinai, however, surpassed all others in the minds of the biblical editors. At Sinai the Lord proclaimed for all time that the people of Israel were the people of God. In Judaism the Covenant of Sinai is a never-to-be-repeated event—the testament that gave its name to what Christians now call the Old Testament. This event is also of profound importance to Christians, who as believers in God are also children of Abraham and the people of Israel.

Something else is worth remembering: By the time the finishing touches were put to their Scriptures, the Jews better understood what it meant to be the people of God. Theirs was a privileged role but not an easy one. To be called as witnesses to the one God for all the world was an extraordinarily difficult mission.

Infidelity, Then Forgiveness

The story of Exodus continues with an account of immediate and shocking infidelity. When Moses returns to the mountaintop and remains for forty days and nights with God, the people think that he has left them. They grow bored and hunger for diversion, and astonishingly, they ask Aaron to make them an idol. More astonishingly, he does. Gathering the gold ornaments of the people, Aaron melts them, fashions a golden calf, and proclaims that it is the Lord, the God who brought them out of Egypt (or, some scholars surmise, the animal on whose back God's throne rests). The people offer sacrifices to the golden calf, deluding themselves into thinking this is not a problem.

Read Exodus 32:1–6.

The Tablets Destroyed

The Lord, knowing what the people have done, vows to destroy them, but Moses intercedes. Moses descends the mountain, discovers their revelry, and breaks the tablets of the Law, which has already been broken by the people. Angrily, Moses confronts Aaron, orders the idolators slain, and returns to beg God's forgiveness for the rest of the people.

At first the Lord refuses to accompany the Israelites, but orders them to continue on their way to the land flowing with milk and honey. However, upon further pleading by Moses, God agrees to be present in a pillar of cloud before the **tent of the meeting** (a portable tent where Moses meets God in prayer throughout the journey), but only when they halt.

Read Exodus 32:7–20; 33:1–11.

The Love Between Moses and God

One of the most moving passages in the Scriptures is a conversation between the Lord and Moses that is like two lovers talking. Moses begs the Lord to go with the Israelites so that all the world will know that they are God's people. The Lord agrees. Then in a burst of longing, Moses begs, "'Show me your glory, I pray'" (Exodus 33:18). The Lord replies that no one can look upon the glory of God's face and live, but that the Lord will pass by and shield Moses so that he can safely see God from the back.

Read Exodus 33:12–23.

The Covenant Renewed, the Tablets Rewritten

The Lord tells Moses to bring new tablets, and before engraving the Commandments on them, the Lord reveals what God is like. The Jewish teachers called this scriptural passage "The Thirteen Attributes of God." God then renews the Covenant, promising to work marvels for Israel that the world has never seen before—if Israel keeps God's word.

Descending from the mountain, Moses is radiant with the glory of God. Because the people are afraid to approach him, Moses covers his face with a cloth, removing it only when he goes to speak with the Lord.

Following God's instructions, the people fashion a dwelling place for the **ark of the Covenant**—the container for the stone tablets of the Law. Aaron and his sons are ordained as priests—those who may offer sacrifice to God on behalf of the people. The cloud indicating the presence of the Lord settles down over the ark's dwelling place (the tent of the meeting) and fills it. When the Lord moves, as a cloud by day and as fire by night, the people of Israel follow. Where the Lord stays, the people stay. Thus the Israelites resume their journey.

Read Exodus 34:1–35; 40:1–38.

According to the Exodus account, the ark of the Covenant, which contained the stone tablets of the Law, was a small wooden box, about the size of an orange crate, kept within a tent sanctuary while the people of Israel were in the wilderness. On top of the ark was a plate of gold called the mercy seat, the throne where God met the people of Israel. Thus the sanctuary itself was called the tent of the meeting. The ark was carried at the head of the column when the people traveled through the desert, and before the army in battle.

Later, when King Solomon built the Temple in Jerusalem, he established the sanctuary within it. In English versions of the Bible, the sanctuary is called the **tabernacle,** which simply means "tent."

Jews still celebrate the **feast of Tabernacles,** known as **Sukkoth,** commemorating God's providence during the time in the wilderness. During this weeklong autumnal feast, many Jewish families put up simple booths, decorate them with harvest fruits, eat their meals there, and sleep under the stars.

What Is God Like?

The thirteen attributes of God are briefly described in the following list of phrases drawn from Exodus 34:6–7:

- *1, 2. "The* LORD, *the* LORD." This repetition indicates that the Lord is the God of all things and all creatures and is the beginning and end of all time.

- *3. "A God"*
- *4. "Merciful."* The Hebrew word for *merciful* is the same as that for *womb,* which suggests that God possesses a mother's tender understanding of her children.
- *5. "Gracious."* The Hebrew word for *gracious* suggests kindness for its own sake, not as a means to some other goal.
- *6. "Slow to anger"*
- *7. "Abounding in steadfast love."* This phrase refers to God's fidelity to the Covenant even when Israel has disobeyed.
- *8. "Faithfulness."* God is not only present but is always offering love to us. In the New Testament, the term that comes closest in meaning is probably *grace.*
- *9. "For the thousandth generation."* The word *thousand* implies endless.
- *10, 11, and 12. "Forgiving iniquity and transgression and sin."* The literal translation of these attributes is "bearing crookedness and rebellion and failure." The implication is that God's love and goodness are stronger than evil.
- *13. "Yet by no means clearing the guilty, / but visiting the iniquity of the parents / upon the children / and the children's children, / to the third and fourth generation."* God forgives those who want forgiveness.

    This attribute sounds extremely harsh, but it needs to be considered in light of the ninth attribute, describing God's graciousness to the "thousandth generation." The intention of the thirteenth attribute is to suggest that God does not let wrongs go unpunished. Remember that belief in personal punishment in an afterlife developed later in Jewish history. So if an individual died without being punished for injustices, it was believed that the punishment must then have fallen on his or her children.

    People who see "the God of the Old Testament" as angry and vengeful should ponder Exodus 34:6–7 in order to see in it the God whose attributes are made present to us in Jesus. God's self-revelation to Moses in this portrait matches well the Gospel portrait of the father in the story of the prodigal son, the parable told by Jesus in Luke 15:11–32.

More Than Miles to Go

You have completed the Book of Exodus, but the people of Israel have only half completed their journey to the Promised Land. The rest of the journey is more than simply a matter of miles. The Israelites cannot enter the land of Canaan until they comprehend more fully the Law and the Covenant. So the people have more to learn in the wilderness.

Questions for Reflection and Discussion

1. Consider the "unutterable mystery of God." What image of God is strongest for you right now?

2. No matter how long we stay away from God, God never forgets us. Is there a hymn, a song, or a poem that speaks of God's abiding presence to you?

3. On their journey the Israelites were protected by God in the pillars of cloud and fire. Reflect on how you have experienced God's direction in your life. God also fed and protected the people. Ponder the many gifts that God gives you each day.

4. A relationship is understood as a covenant when both parties promise to be faithful to each other and genuine love and care is shared between them. What covenants are you in? What are the blessings and responsibilities of these covenants?

5. Examine and try to summarize your own practice of the first three commandments.

6. Which of the last seven commandments are most challenging for you? for our society?

7. Choose one of the thirteen attributes of God that strikes you as somehow particularly significant or appealing. Try to understand why this attribute is important.

4

Living Out the Covenant

> Hear, O Israel: The LORD is our God, the LORD alone. You shall love the LORD your God with all your heart, and with all your soul, and with all your might. Keep these words that I am commanding you today in your heart. Recite them to your children and talk about them when you are at home and when you are away, when you lie down and when you rise. Bind them as a sign on your hand, fix them as an emblem on your forehead, and write them on the doorposts of your house and on your gates. (Deuteronomy 6:4–9)

The keystone to the Book of Exodus is the Ten Commandments, which establish the terms of the Covenant of Sinai. The next three books—Leviticus, Numbers, and Deuteronomy—tell of other laws that spell out more precisely how Israel is to keep the Covenant. These laws, expressing the spirit of the Ten Commandments, deal with relationships, rituals, and matters of daily life.

Many of the laws in these three books address situations that the Israelites would not experience until long after their period of wandering in the desert. Laws about land ownership, houses, vineyards, and how to perform Temple rituals probably grew out of their life in the Promised Land. But the biblical writers and editors set these laws within the great story of Moses leading the Israelites through the desert for forty years, thus emphasizing how important the laws were. So significant were they to the people, that taken together, the whole collection of laws from Exodus through Deuteronomy is called the **Law of Moses**, the **Mosaic Law**, or simply **the Law.**

Leviticus: Holiness and Ritual

The writer of the **Book of Leviticus** was probably an Israelite priest in the time after the exile, when the Temple was rebuilt in Jerusalem. **Priests** were members of the tribe of **Levi**, who led worship in the Temple. The Book of Leviticus can be thought of as a handbook of instructions for Israel's worship.

Community worship was central in the life of the Israelites: it expressed *who they were*—God's own beloved people—and bound them together as one family pouring out its faith and trust in God. Therefore, ritual had to be done with great reverence and care, according to precise instructions. To stress the solemnity, the writer presented the regulations for rituals in the form of direct statements from God to Moses or the Israelites in the wilderness, in the style of the Covenant

Out of Egypt into the Wilderness

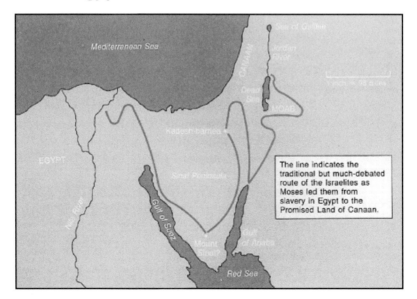

The line indicates the traditional but much-debated route of the Israelites as Moses led them from slavery in Egypt to the Promised Land of Canaan.

of Sinai. Scripture scholars point out that these instructions were written centuries after the wilderness period and were meant for worship in the second Temple.

For the writer of Leviticus, the grateful, reverent, humble attitude toward God that characterizes true worship was meant to be woven together with everyday concerns and actions to form one whole, holy life. So besides ritual instructions, the Book of Leviticus includes teachings and directives on how to live out the holiness of their worship in their relationships. Leviticus encourages its readers to honesty, reverence, respect, tolerance, compassion, and generosity—virtues that are as needed now as they were at the time of its writing.

Sacrifices of Atonement

Leviticus treats the rituals of the Temple, which included different kinds of prayer and sacrifice. Like many other ancient peoples who offered sacrifices to their gods, the Israelites believed that when they sinned against God, they needed to do something to atone for it, to repair the damaged relationship. So they sacrificed an animal as an atonement. The blood of the animal, poured out on the altar, signified life itself given to express the offerer's sorrow; the altar signified the presence of God.

The rituals described in the first half of Leviticus are **sacrifices of atonement** that took place in the Temple. In addition, once a year, on the **Day of Atonement**—called **Yom Kippur**—the high priest entered the Temple sanctuary called the holy of holies, where God was believed to dwell, and offered incense, then the blood of a bull and the blood of a goat. The sacrifice of blood was meant to represent the life of the people, offered to God to reconcile them with God.

During the **Dispersion,** Jews continued, as they do today, to celebrate Yom Kippur as their holiest day of the year, a day to atone for the sins of the past year.

The Sacrifice of Jesus

The author of the New Testament's Epistle to the Hebrews, writing to Jewish Christians, used the familiar sacrificial rituals of atonement to give meaning to the death and Resurrection of Jesus. He called Christ the true high priest—who offers the victim, who is also the victim, whose blood is spilled for the people, and who reconciles humankind to God with his perfect sacrifice. It is enlightening to see that much of the vocabulary that Christians have used to describe how Jesus Christ redeemed the world comes from the Book of Leviticus.

Read Hebrews 8:1–2; 9:11–15.

The Holiness Code

A section of Leviticus—chapters 17 to 26—contains the **Holiness Code.** These teachings were collected and put in the book by the priest-writer not because they focus on worship in itself but because they show how true worship is expressed in a person's everyday life, in just and compassionate relationships. For example, Israel is told the following:

* Leave some of the harvest for gleaning by the poor.
* Do not withhold the wages of a laborer until the next day.
* Do not curse the deaf or put a stumbling block in the way of the blind.
* Do not take vengeance or bear a grudge; "love your neighbor as yourself" (19:17).
* Do not oppress foreigners; treat them as you would your own people.
* Do not fashion dishonest weights and measures.
* Every fifty years there will be a **jubilee**—that is, debts are to be canceled, and those who have lost their property are to have the opportunity to redeem it.

Read Leviticus 19:9–18,33–35; 25:1–23.

Leviticus reminds us that holiness is not simply a matter of going through all the right prayers and rituals, although those are important. Love for God, the essence of true worship, is shown in love for one's neighbor.

Numbers: Priestly Regulations and Inspiring Stories

The **Book of Numbers** is a complex work by many authors and editors. Its present title comes from the census mentioned in the first part of the book, which reports exaggerated numbers of Israelites as well as lists of priestly

World Happenings
Between 1700 and 1250 B.C.E.

Africa
The Egyptians extend their empire eastward into Asia and southward into the Sudan. By 1600 B.C.E. the cat has taken up residence in Egyptian homes.

America
Agricultural villages, which grow corn and other crops, become numerous in Central America.

China
A system of writing, in which each word is a picture, is used to communicate with the spirit world. Armies use chariots and wooden bows, reinforced by horn and sinew.

Europe
The Greeks lay siege to the city of Troy in what is now modern Turkey, giving rise to the legend of the Trojan War.

India
Hindu priests collect the religious hymns of the Rig-Veda. One of these hymns praises "the unknown god," who is lord of all that exists.

The Near East
After 1500 B.C.E. the warlike Assyrians from northern Iraq become a leading power in the region. Their kings trade gifts with the pharaohs of Egypt.

regulations. The original Hebrew title, "In the Wilderness," describes the second part of the book, which tells of Israel's wandering in the wilderness on the way to Canaan.

More Complaining and Grumbling

The second part of Numbers begins with another version of the tales in Exodus of the people's grumbling. Here the people complain about the food in the wilderness, lamenting loudly for the cucumbers, melons, onions, and garlic they had in Egypt rather than "'nothing at all but this manna'" (11:6). When Moses, distraught, asks God to let him die, God promises that the people will eat all the meat that they want. A strong wind drives flocks of quail in from the sea, and the people gorge themselves so greedily that some of them die.

The lesson for the Israelites is that *God will provide,* especially when things look bleak. God will give us far more than we ever dreamed of.

Read Numbers 11:1–23,31–34.

Jealousy and Rebellion

Even though God provides for the people in the wilderness, jealousy raises its ugly head, and some challenge Moses' authority. First Moses' own sister and brother, Miriam and Aaron, claim that they have authority equal to Moses'. "Does Moses think he's the only prophet around? What about us?" they imply. Angrily, God rebukes them, saying that other prophets have visions and dreams of God, but only Moses sees the Lord face-to-face, that is, intimately. At the end of God's denunciation, Miriam's skin has turned white with leprosy. A week spent outside the camp for purification is required for her healing. The people cannot start out again until she is brought back.

In another story someone challenges Moses and Aaron's authority, and others incite a political rebellion, accusing Moses of leading Israel out of Egypt on a wild-goose chase. But the rebels, with their families, are all destroyed. Then God gives a sign—almond blossoms growing from

Aaron's staff—to confirm that Aaron's tribe has been chosen for the priesthood and is not to be challenged.

*Read Numbers 12:1–16; 16:1–35; 17:1–11 (or 17:16–26
in NAB or NJB).*

The story of Israel is about the beginnings of the community that Christians call the church. That community
was made up of people who were, like people today, weak
and sinful, and sin took its toll. In the same way today, sin
hinders the journey of the church, yet repentance and
God's healing forgiveness get it back on its way.

Also, it horrifies us to think that God might destroy
whole families as punishment for one member's sin. However, we need to understand that the destruction may have
been the result of some natural disaster. In the Israelite culture, such disasters were commonly assumed to be punishment from God.

Exploring the Land of Canaan

At one point, as the people draw nearer to the Promised
Land, God has Moses send a man from each tribe to cross
the border and explore Canaan. They return with tales of a
land flowing with milk and honey but, they fearfully add,
occupied by giants, next to whom the Israelites would seem
like grasshoppers. Two of the scouts, Caleb and Joshua, want
to enter the land nevertheless, but the people begin to
mutter. Forgetting that God has broken the might of Egypt
for them, the people complain that it would be better to
have died in Egypt or to die now in the desert than to go
into Canaan and be slaughtered.

God takes the people at their word and declares that
for each of the forty days spent scouting Canaan, they will
spend a year in the wilderness, until every member of the
generation brought from Egypt has perished. Only Caleb
and Joshua, who trusted in the power of God to protect
them in Canaan, will live to see the land, along with the
offspring of the first generation. Immediately the people
change their tune. They will enter Canaan. Moses warns
them not to disobey God; but the people go anyway, are
defeated, and return disheartened.

Read Numbers 13:1–3,17–33; 14:1–45.

The story above is about faith and risk taking. Here a frightened Israel again forgets the generosity and mercy of God. The people choose instead the fragile security of the desert—and they get to stay there. They will be lost and will wander for forty years because they did not trust in God's care for them.

Water from a Rock

In the next story, the people settle at a place in the wilderness called Kadesh, more often called Kadesh-barnea. Again they quarrel with Moses, complaining about the hardship of the wilderness compared to the lush life in Egypt. God bids Moses to strike a rock with his staff so the rock will produce water for the parched Israelites and their livestock. Moses and Aaron gather the people, but sarcastically berate them as rebels before striking the rock. Water gushes forth from the rock, but the Lord is angry about the brothers' outburst at the people. God punishes Moses and Aaron, saying they will die without entering Canaan because they have not shown forth God's holiness in their treatment of the people.

Read Numbers 20:1–13.

Why do Moses and Aaron deserve such a harsh penalty? The explanation seems to be that time and again, when the people's faith has weakened, God has shown unfailing care and has inspired them through a mastery of nature. This time Moses and Aaron have resorted to angry sarcasm, changing the people's experience from one of renewed faith to one of fear. They have not dealt with the people in a reverent way, conveying God's sanctity.

A Soothsayer Predicts Victory for Israel

As the Israelites journey through lands occupied by others, they are forced to detour, bypass, or sometimes do battle with other peoples—at which they are successful. So the king of Moab, desiring to protect the Moabites from being overcome by the Israelites, asks for the services of a soothsayer, Balaam, to tell him what to do. But to the king's horror, the words that come from Balaam's mouth in the form of an oracle are actually blessings for Israel. A final blessing lists the nations that Israel will overcome and includes a passage referring to a star that will come from Jacob.

Read Numbers 24:14–17.

The passage about the star coming from Jacob was probably interpreted by Jews of the exile as a prediction of the reign of David or of the great destiny of Jacob's descendants. For the early Christians, however, the oracle was seen as a prophecy of Christ's coming. The nativity story in Matthew's Gospel also mentions a star that the wise men followed to find the child who was king of the Jews. No doubt Matthew's reference to the star and the wise men helped the first Jewish Christians understand that Jesus was the Promised One.

A Summary of Numbers

Saint Paul provided a Christian interpretation of the Book of Numbers in his First Letter to the Corinthians. Once again we see how much is missing for Christians if, in reading the Gospels and the epistles, they do not have an acquaintance with the writings in the Old Testament.

Read 1 Corinthians 10:1–13.

Deuteronomy: The Law and Love

As you are reading from the **Book of Deuteronomy**, you may wonder, Haven't I heard all this before? And the answer is yes. In some fashion you have heard much of this before, in the Books of Exodus and Numbers. But the writer or editor of Deuteronomy used a different device to tell the story of Israel's liberation, Covenant with Yahweh, and wanderings in the desert. He set the story into the framework of three sermons by Moses to the Israelites as they stand on the plains of Moab poised to cross the Jordan River and enter the Promised Land. ("The hill country of the Amorites" is often used to describe Canaan, the Promised Land.)

So the opening of Deuteronomy sets the scene for Moses' sermons. The book closes with Moses climbing a mountain to take a final look at Canaan, which he will not be able to enter. He blesses the tribes of Israel, dies, and is buried and mourned by the people. Moses' assistant, **Joshua**, filled with wisdom because of his great love for God and his long apprenticeship under Moses, becomes Israel's new leader as they prepare to cross the Jordan and take the land of Canaan.

Read Deuteronomy 1:1–8; 34:1–12.

Moses' Passionate Message to His People

The sermons that make up most of Deuteronomy give a kind of last will and testament of Moses. They are Moses' passionate, often touching messages to the people he has loved and guided. He tries to inspire them to be faithful to God in this new land where many temptations await them—temptations to idolatry, to wealth, to trusting in their own power instead of God's.

These sermons retrace the wilderness journey of the Israelites in several retellings, reminding the people over and over of how God has been with them all along. Even though they have complained, rebelled, and not trusted, God has loved them and cared for them in their journey from slavery in Egypt, to the sealing of the Covenant at Horeb (another name for Sinai), through the forty years in the wilderness, and to the brink of entering the Promised Land.

Read Deuteronomy 1:22–33.

Did Moses actually preach the sermons that make up most of the Book of Deuteronomy? Probably not. In biblical times it was common for followers of a great leader, even centuries after his death, to compose speeches or writings and attribute them to that leader. They could do this because their leader's authority had been passed down to them and they could speak for him to people of their own era, in the spirit of his teaching if not in the details.

So the sermons of Moses probably were composed and edited by later teachers who, under God's inspiration, relied on various sources in Israelite tradition. This explains why the sermons contain many references to events or customs that came long after Moses.

Keeping the Law

In the midst of the storytelling and retelling, Moses' sermons repeatedly urge the people to keep the Law, the terms of the Covenant, faithfully and diligently. Moses recounts the giving of the Law, including a somewhat different version of the Ten Commandments than in the Exodus account. (*Deuteronomy,* incidentally, is a Greek word meaning "second law.")

Read Deuteronomy 5:1–21.

Deuteronomy gives many other refinements of the Law, with applications to daily life as varied as what to eat, how to treat slaves justly, how to ensure that the poor are not trapped in their poverty, what festivals to celebrate, and how to carry out war so that the Israelites are not tainted by the idolatrous nations they rub shoulders with.

Here are some examples of laws having to do with justice:

• Every seven years debts must be forgiven, although the approach of the "release year" must not deter one from lending money to a poor neighbor.
• Slaves who have served six years must be released in the seventh.
• Interest on a loan may be demanded of a foreigner but not of an Israelite.
• Israelites may not be sold into slavery. Anyone who does so can be punished by death.
• Millstones owned by the poor may not be taken in pledge for a loan, for without their millstones they cannot grind flour.
• Parents and children may not be punished for one another's crime.

Josiah's Reform Movement

Those who composed the Book of Deuteronomy, called the **Deuteronomists** by modern scholars, were probably part of a vigorous reform movement in Judah that began about thirty years before the exile—**Josiah's reform.** Josiah, king of Judah, began the reform after an old "Book of the Law" was discovered in the Temple during repair work. Its scrolls contained a code of religious laws that forbade the corrupt, unjust, and idolatrous practices that had become rampant in Judah as the people polluted their Yahwistic religion with their neighbors' worship of false gods.

King Josiah was determined to call the people back to the Covenant they had broken by insisting on strict adherence to the extensive code of laws. This newly discovered code was probably the principal source for the Deuteronomists in composing the Book of Deuteronomy.

Josiah's reform movement did not succeed in heading off the disastrous exile, which came about twenty years after Josiah's death. In the Deuteronomists' view, the exile was inevitable because of the people's continuing idolatry, hardheartedness, and confidence in their own might, not God's. The Deuteronomists believed that God's people prosper on the land when they are good and obey the Law, but their life and land is doomed to failure when they defy God.

The Deuteronomists, before and during the exile, had a profound effect on the formation of the Bible and on the future of Judaism. Along with the Book of Deuteronomy, a number of the historical books of the Bible were written or edited by the Deuteronomists.

Love at the Core of the Law

At the heart of all the laws in Deuteronomy is the great prayer called the **Shema** (from the Hebrew word that begins the prayer, meaning "hear"). This prayer has been called the essence of Judaism. Repeated daily by Jews from biblical times up to the present, this profession of faith constantly reminds them that God is one, and that they are to love the one God with their entire being—heart, soul, and strength. In the time before the exile, the unfaithful Judahites desperately needed to hear that wake-up call, to remember the essence of the Covenant with Yahweh: God loves us, and we must love God above all else. After the exile and ever since, Jews have cherished the Shema as a prayer expressing what their life as God's people is all about.

The Shema includes the beautiful plea to the people to keep the command of love in their hearts wherever they are, to teach it to their children over and over, and to bind it to themselves so they will never forget it.

Read Deuteronomy 6:4–9.

Rabbis of biblical times interpreted the words of the Shema quite literally. So it is customary for many Jews to fasten to the doorpost of their dwelling place a scroll on which are inscribed the verses of the Shema. This scroll, called the **mezuzah** (meaning "doorpost"), reminds Jews of God's holy presence as they enter and leave their home.

In addition, the verses of the Shema are kept in two small square leather boxes called **phylacteries.** In the Orthodox observance of Judaism, these boxes are strapped onto a person's forehead and left arm when the verses are recited. A Jew's daily act of binding the boxes to head and arm and wearing them heightens the awareness of God's nearness in all the thoughts and actions of daily life.

Jesus and the Great Commandment

Being thoroughly Jewish, Jesus and his parents would have recited the Shema daily. He quoted Deuteronomy 6:5, about love of God, to the Pharisees who tried to trip him up with their question about which commandment of the Law was the greatest. Knowing that love of God cannot be separated from love of others, Jesus also added the command from Leviticus 19:18, "You shall love your neighbor as yourself."

In another Gospel passage, the story of Jesus' being tempted in the desert, Jesus likewise used verses from Deuteronomy three times to respond to the devil's temptations. He was obviously formed and inspired by God's word in the Book of Deuteronomy.

Read Matthew 22:34–39; 4:1–11.

On the Brink of the Promised Land

At the closing of the Book of Deuteronomy, the Israelites are poised to enter Canaan, the abundant land promised by God to their father, Abraham, and his descendants. Moses has died, and now Joshua will lead them as they take over the land.

The Jews of the exile must have delighted in hearing about how their ancestors finally reached the Promised Land, with God's love and power protecting them all along the way. The exiles must have imagined that, like their ancestors, they would some day make it back home to their own land, if they would only stay faithful to God.

With the end of Deuteronomy, the Torah, the five books that Jews consider the most essential of the Jewish Bible, comes to a close.

- The first book, Genesis, taught us about the origins of the people of Israel.
- Exodus showed us how God freed them from slavery in Egypt and made the Covenant of Sinai with them.
- Leviticus showed us the great concern that the Jews held for reverent worship and holiness.
- Numbers took us on the journey with the Israelites through the wilderness in search of the Promised Land.
- And Deuteronomy gave us insight into the essential spirit of Judaism, which is wholehearted love for God. This last book of the Pentateuch also brought the story of Israel to the brink of the Promised Land, with Joshua as God's chosen one in charge of the Israelites.

Now we, and the Israelites, are ready to launch into the Promised Land.

Questions for Reflection and Discussion

1. Looking at your way of life, describe your own "holiness code." Name at least six "musts" for expressing love of neighbor. How might you apply the concept of jubilee to your holiness code?

2. Providence means that God provides us with what we need, when we need it—sometimes through an event or a person. What experiences of providence have you had?

3. In the Shema the Jews attempt to express and pass on their burning love for God. Who has done this for you? How do you pass on your love of God to others?

4. How does the Old Testament sense of the Law inform your own sense of the value of code and creed in your spirituality?

5

The Promised Land

"Choose this day whom you will serve; . . . but as for me and my household, we will serve the LORD."

Then the people answered, "Far be it from us that we should forsake the LORD to serve other gods; for it is the LORD our God who brought us and our ancestors up from the land of Egypt, out of the house of slavery, and who did those great signs in our sight. He protected us all along the way that we went, and among all the peoples through whom we passed; and the LORD drove out before us all the peoples, the Amorites who lived in the land. Therefore we also will serve the LORD, for he is our God." (Joshua 24:15–18)

The Books of Joshua, Judges, and Ruth tell stories about the beginnings of the Israelites' life in the Promised Land, covering the period from Moses' death to just before Israel became a nation with a king.

A History in the Midst of Exile

Recall again that much of the Old Testament was edited and rewritten during the exile in Babylon. The Jews had suffered a terrible disaster, losing their homeland and their freedom. They had thought they could never be defeated, but here they were, humiliated subjects of a foreign king. Their self-assurance evaporated as they came face-to-face with their own failure. They wondered, "What went wrong? How did we end up here?"

During this period the Deuteronomists tried to answer that question by composing a history of the Israelites from their entry into the Promised Land (about 1250 B.C.E.) up through the monarchy to the time of the exile (587 B.C.E.), a span of almost seven hundred years. They used many old oral and written sources, compiling, editing, and rewriting them into several books of the Bible, which are now called the **Deuteronomic history:** Joshua, Judges, the First and Second Books of Samuel, and the First and Second Books of Kings. The Book of Deuteronomy was a kind of introduction to that history, laying out the story of God's Covenant with Israel before they reached the Promised Land.

This history served as a **self-examination** for the people of Israel. They had gotten themselves into this terrible state of affairs, the exile, through their unfaithfulness to God and their self-delusion that they would never be overcome. The Deuteronomists knew that the people would need to own up to the mistakes of their past if they were to have any hope for the future. The people could not blame the Babylonian Empire or God or bad fortune for their plight. Their hope lay in recognizing all they had been given by God, how they had betrayed that relationship, and the call God was offering them to commit themselves to a new, faithful way of life.

So the Deuteronomists helped the people of Israel turn the disaster of the exile into a time of reflection and transformation that would ready them for the return one day to their homeland, full of hope in their hearts.

The Books of Joshua and Judges can be read as part of the "examination of conscience" that is the Deuteronomic history.

Joshua:
Sweeping into the Promised Land

The **Book of Joshua** tells about one of Israel's greatest heroes, the man chosen by Moses to lead the Israelites into Canaan. It offers wondrous accounts of how Israel enters and takes the land under Joshua's command and settles there. This book, as well as the Book of Judges, contains accounts of battles and victories in which the Israelites pillage whole cities and slaughter their inhabitants. This may surprise or even shock us. Our study may help give perspective on why these accounts are included, and what meaning they could have for us today.

Joshua Is Sent

The book opens with God's sending Joshua to take the land of Canaan, urging him to be brave and steadfast, and reminding him to keep the Law and that God will be with him. Joshua says that in three days the Israelites will cross the Jordan River from the east, an ideal position from which to launch an invasion of Canaan.

Read Joshua 1:1–18.

The story of Joshua reminded the exiled Jews in Babylon centuries later of their need to turn to God again. Joshua represented everything that Israel was supposed to be—completely faithful and trusting in God. As these verses remind the reader, Israel's exile was the result of ignoring the Law of Moses and rejecting the love of God.

Rahab and the Spies

Joshua sends two spies to scout Jericho, the first city across the Jordan. Entering it without trouble, they go to a lodging house run by a prostitute named **Rahab**, who recognizes that they are Israelites. When the king's men come to question her about the visitors, she sends the spies to hide under the flax drying on her roof and misdirects the search party to the countryside. After dark Rahab bargains with the spies. She will help them escape if they will promise safety for her family when Jericho is invaded. The men give her a red cord to hang in the window of her house, which is built into the city wall, and they promise not to harm anyone in the house marked by the cord. The spies return to Joshua with news of the city's terror as it awaits invasion.

Read Joshua 2:1–24.

We might criticize Rahab for her betrayal of the city. Is she a traitor in choosing the survival of herself and her family? The biblical writers seem undivided in their opinion that she is doing the will of God.

Rahab reappears in a surprising passage in the Christian writings. The biblical writers, including those of the New Testament, had no trouble acknowledging the worthiness of this woman who was not only a prostitute but a Canaanite. They saw her divinely given role in the history of Israel, and even in the ancestry of Jesus. God's way, it seems, is to choose the most unlikely persons to accomplish God's purposes in the world.

Read Matthew 1:1–6; James 2:24–25.

Crossing the Jordan River

Now comes another story of a miraculous crossing, reminding us of Moses leading the Israelites through the Sea of Reeds. Joshua orders the march; and as soon as the feet of the priests touch the riverbed of the **Jordan**, the waters cease to flow—piling up to the north and disappearing to the south. The people cross over, and one man from each of the twelve tribes carries a stone from the riverbed to build a memorial at the new camp. They call it Gilgal, meaning "circle" and referring to a circle of stones.

Read Joshua 3:1–17; 4:1–24.

We could certainly offer all kinds of natural explanations of how the crossing of the Jordan took place, and scholars have tried to come up with some. The important point, though, is not exactly how the crossing happened but that *it was God's doing.*

The ancient stories of the crossing, worked into the Deuteronomic history, were intended to impress on the Israelites that their arrival in Canaan was a gift from God, not something they had accomplished on their own. This theme comes through again and again in the Book of Joshua's accounts of amazing victories.

Israel in the Promised Land

Once in Canaan the people eat for the first time the produce of the Promised Land. The manna—the breadlike sub-
stance from the heavens that had sustained them through
their years in the wilderness—disappears. They have their
first celebration of the Passover in the land of the Promise.

In a mysterious encounter, Joshua meets the captain of
the army of the Lord (captain of a host of angels), and like
Moses in Exodus 3:5, Joshua is told to remove his sandals because he stands on holy ground. This encounter is a sign
that God will be with Joshua in the coming battle at Jericho.
Read Joshua 5:10–15.

No longer wilderness people, sustained by miraculous
manna, the Israelites were able to eat from the abundance of
the land God had given them. They now had a place to call
their own. From here on, their happiness and well-being
would be associated with the land. For them, the land was
not just a place to live but, as God's gift to them, the source
of life, blessing, joy, and security. Here they would know
shalom, the deep peace of God. There would be struggles
ahead to attain the land from the local inhabitants. But the
Israelites never doubted that God wanted them to have that
land as the place where they would grow and prosper.

Jericho: "And the Walls Came Tumblin' Down"

Joshua's soldiers lay siege to **Jericho**, surround the city, and
cut off its supplies. Then early each morning for six days,
seven priests carrying rams' horns lead the Israelites out of
camp. Behind these priests come other priests carrying the
ark of the Covenant. Troops march before and behind the
priests. The entire company, silent except for the blaring of
the rams' horns, marches once around the city. At dawn on
the seventh day, the Israelites circle the city seven times,
and at a signal they begin to shout and storm the walls. Jericho falls, and only Rahab and those in her house are saved
from the slaughter of the people and animals in the city.
Read Joshua 6:1–21.

We do not know if the walls of Jericho literally fell down, or how that might have occurred. Modern archaeology shows no evidence of a wall at Jericho in that period. Whatever happened, the biblical writers believed that God had helped Israel take Jericho.

The details of the procession to Jericho, the circling of the city seven times, the blowing of horns, the shouting as the people storm the walls, sound much like a liturgical ritual. Some scholars think that these descriptions may have been instructions for regular rituals of commemoration at the ruins of Jericho years after the Israelites' victory there. These instructions could have then found their way into the written account of the battle.

In the Jericho account, we also read of a practice called **the ban**, in some translations termed "devotion to God for destruction." The practice first comes up as God's command in the Book of Deuteronomy. It was essentially an order to destroy everything in a conquered town—all its inhabitants, their possessions, and their animals—and to take nothing for one's own. It is worth considering why such apparently savage behavior was written into the accounts as fulfilling God's command.

What About Those Battles?

The violent imagery of the battles in the Book of Joshua, and especially the practice of the ban, is hard to understand in light of our concept of God as compassionate and merciful, as the one who commands us not to kill. How can this type of warfare, which aims at total destruction, be justified by the scriptural writers as God's will, even as a sort of devotion to God?

First of all, we need to recognize that stories of such destruction were not intended to give us moral direction about war. Nor is it likely that the ban was ever really carried out in the total way that the Book of Joshua describes it. However, we know that ancient warfare involved much brutality, as it often does today, and the scriptural accounts reflect that.

One way to look at these accounts is to see them as having a theological purpose, teaching the people how totally and exclusively they were to devote themselves to God. The Deuteronomists, living among their fellow Jews in Babylon at the time of the exile, knew that Israel's history through the centuries before the exile was full of infidelity to God. This took the form of worshiping the idols of the Canaanites and engaging in horrible practices as a way of trying to get the Canaanites' gods to do what the Israelites wanted.

These Canaanite practices included fertility rites, which involved the use of male and female prostitutes at the Canaanite temples. The Canaanites imagined that this would encourage their fertility gods, **Baal** and Ashtarte, to produce a good crop on the land. The Israelites, trying to master the techniques of farming, often gave in to the temptation to do whatever the successful locals did to ensure a plentiful harvest—so they, too, would visit the temple prostitutes. Another practice was that of child sacrifice to the gods as a way of appeasing them when they were angry. Even that atrocity some Israelites practiced, including some of their kings through the centuries.

The Deuteronomists knew that God wanted the Israelites to have nothing to do with such immorality. If it meant they must get rid of everything Canaanite, so be it. Thus the ban was a practice included in the scriptural accounts partly as a warning to later Jews against having anything to do with other religions and their terrible practices.

Beyond the theological point of the ban, we have to acknowledge that the Israelites' taking over the land did probably involve much brutality, and that this was the reality of warfare. But was God truly in favor of that? Was God really on the side of the Israelites as they slaughtered their enemies?

We must answer that God would never will the destruction of innocent people, in ancient times or today. However, God's will was that the Israelites possess the land. Their claiming the land was accomplished partly through the methods the people of that time knew—warfare. The people may have thought their means of warfare were God's will, but they were conditioned by the prevailing practices of the time. God, however, can bring good out of the strangest circumstances, even at times, situations of great evil.

In the accounts of Jericho and other battles, the overriding message is that when the people put their trust entirely in God, they are victorious. Pride in one's own power and disobedience to God will bring disaster, as is illustrated in the next story.

Breaking the Ban: Defeat at Ai

After Jericho's destruction Joshua's men scout the town of **Ai** and predict an easy conquest. Yet Israel is defeated. Demoralized, Joshua prays to God, who tells him that someone has broken the ban by taking loot from Jericho. Assembling the tribes Joshua discovers that a man named Achan is the culprit.

Achan is executed by stoning, and his loot is burned and buried. He failed to trust in God by honoring the ban. His disobedience and greed, shown in his taking loot from Jericho, brought defeat to Israel at Ai. The point of the story is that the Israelites must hold nothing back, giving their obedient devotion entirely to God.

Read Joshua 7:1–26.

The Sun Standing Still

Local Canaanite kings become terrified of the Israelites. One group some distance away, the Gibeonites, makes a protective alliance with Israel. When the five local kings learn that the Gibeonites are allied with Israel, they put Gibeon under siege. Its citizens cry to Joshua for help. Joshua's army marches under cover of darkness, takes the besiegers by surprise, and routs them. In the midst of battle the next day, Joshua asks God to stop the sun in the sky, and the storyteller marvels at God's obeying a human. The attacking kings—lumped together as "the Amorites" in some versions of the Bible—are found by Joshua and executed.

Read Joshua 10:12–14.

Joshua's request that the sun stop in the sky is a fragment of an ancient song of victory from the lost Book of

Jashar—apparently a book of poems celebrating Israel's heroes.

Did the sun really stand still? Undoubtedly the sun did not set until Joshua had overcome the local kings—which is to say that God helped him to victory before sundown. We do not need to puzzle over whether the sun actually "stood still," though believers have debated this over the centuries. We can recognize this curious detail as a poetic figure of speech and concentrate on the point of the story—that the victory of Joshua and the Israelites that day was a gift from God.

Conquests, Tribal Divisions, and Cities of Refuge

The remainder of the Book of Joshua offers a simplified account of the conquest of Canaan, claiming that Joshua captures all the land and subdues all Israel's enemies. The division of the land among the tribes of Israel is reported— along with the setting aside of the cities of refuge, or asylum. *Read Joshua 20:1–6; Deuteronomy 19:1–13.*

Twelve, the number of the tribes, became symbolic for the Israelites—and later for Christians. In Acts of the Apostles 1:15–26, for example, we read that the Apostles choose Matthias to replace Judas in order to complete "the Twelve," whom Jesus said would sit on twelve thrones to judge the twelve tribes of Israel.

Joshua's Military Successes

The writer's claim of a quick conquest of Canaan cannot be accurate because in the next book, Judges, we will see Israel living side by side with Canaanite tribes—sometimes dominating them, sometimes as their vassals, and even intermarrying with them.

The Deuteronomists do not seem troubled about telling the story inconsistently in the two books. That is because the purpose of the Joshua account is theological, not historical. It is meant to show that God was with Joshua, the faithful, obedient leader.

The Cities of Refuge

Places of refuge probably came later than the time of Joshua, perhaps during the time of King David. The idea behind them was to protect people guilty of accidental or unintentional killing from being attacked by the victims' families for blood vengeance. Down through the centuries, Egyptians, Jews, Greeks, Romans, and Christians all have followed similar practices of **sanctuary**—so called because the refuge was often at a religious shrine. Sanctuary remains a universal custom, offering aid to the persecuted and the homeless.

The Death of Joshua

In a solemn farewell, Joshua begs his people never to forget the one God who has done so much for them, and he warns them of the consequences if they do forget. The Israelites renew the Covenant at a place called **Shechem**, and Joshua's work is done. He dies and is buried in his tribal land.

Read Joshua 24:1–33.

Joshua was one of Israel's greatest leaders—strong, courageous, careful, honest, unshaken by failure, a keeper of treaties, and an upholder of the Law. An inspiration to his people, Joshua's heart was on fire with love for God, and by obeying God, he brought Israel into the Promised Land.

For the Deuteronomists, who constructed their history of Israel centuries after Joshua's time, Joshua was an ideal figure. Their portrayal of Joshua gave the exiles a model to follow. After the wondrous era of Joshua's divinely given victories, however, the story of the Israelites in the Promised Land takes a downward slide, as we will see in the Book of Judges.

Judges: Saving Israel from Itself

The **Book of Judges,** which has nothing to do with legal matters, might be better called the Book of Deliverers because its stories tell how God raises up deliverers to save

Israel when, after settling in Canaan, the Israelites are unfaithful and overwhelmed by enemies.

The book spans the years between the death of Joshua and the beginning of the First Book of Samuel (about 1200 to 1025 B.C.E.), but was put together long afterward during the exile as part of the Deuteronomic history.

With Joshua gone the tribes fall into self-indulgence and idol worship, which leads to their downfall. When Israel forgets its call to reveal the one God to the nations, it becomes selfish, timid, and self-delusional, and ends up dominated by idol-worshiping neighbors. However, each time this happens, the people eventually repent of their infidelity, and then God brings forward a hero, a tribal leader called a **judge**, through whom God delivers the people from destruction. Here is how the pattern goes with each story of a judge:

1. The Israelites fall into sin, worshiping idols and abandoning God.
2. Their sin leads to their own calamity. They are assaulted and persecuted by their enemies, the Canaanites.
3. The Israelites repent of their sin and cry to God for help.
4. God has mercy on the people and raises up a judge to deliver them from disaster, and they triumph over their enemies.

After the victory the people are faithful to God and live in peace for a time, but soon the **cycle of sin, disaster, repentance, and deliverance** starts up again.

The stories of the judges are derived from early songs and poems—much like the tales of King Arthur and Queen Guinevere. These heroes, however, are not nobles but peasants. Nor is their behavior particularly noble. Rather, they are people called by God to deliver Israel—regardless of their personal weaknesses.

Twelve judges are mentioned in the Book of Judges itself: six minor judges, barely mentioned, and six major judges—**Othniel, Ehud, Deborah, Gideon, Jephthah,** and **Samson.** Their stories are full of adventure, trickery, betrayal, and courage. Like the Book of Joshua, they are full of violence. We will study three of the major judges: Deborah, Gideon, and Samson.

Israel Settles in with the Canaanites

The Book of Judges opens with a description of Israel in Canaan that is very different from the picture given in the Book of Joshua. In Joshua we read that all Canaan was captured and its people overpowered. But in Judges, Israel has not only settled down among the Canaanites but even intermarried and worshiped with them.

Read Joshua 21:43–45; Judges 1:21–36; 3:1–7.

Deborah: Victory with a Gruesome Touch

Deborah, referred to as both a judge and a prophet, is a magistrate of the tribe of Naphtali, deciding local disputes for her people. Her tribe has done "what was evil in the sight of the LORD" (Judges 4:1). As is the pattern in the stories of the judges, the tribe thus has fallen under the domination of the Canaanite king Jabin, whose army, with its nine hundred iron chariots, has kept the people subject for twenty years. The people cry out for help to the Lord, and God chooses Deborah as an instrument of the divine rescue. Deborah reveals to Barak, the commander of the Israelite militia, that God wants him to lead an army against Jabin's general Sisera. Barak fearfully agrees to go if Deborah will accompany him, and she consents but says that he will lose the credit for the victory.

When the Canaanite Sisera assembles his army in the valley, torrential rains render his chariots useless, and he and his troops are routed. Sisera deserts his troops and flees to the tent of his friend, whose wife Jael welcomes him, serves him refreshment, and bids him to rest while she stands guard.

Though she behaves hospitably, Jael is actually outraged at Sisera's desertion of his troops. So while he sleeps, she hammers a tent peg through his skull. Ever after Jael is glorified in the savagely triumphant **Canticle of Deborah.** Defeat at the hands of a woman—even in this case a woman who breaks her word and betrays the sacred law of hospitality—is the ultimate disgrace for a warrior. A final sarcastic touch to the story is the glimpse of Sisera's mother and wives waiting in the harem to divide the spoils that he will never bring.

Read Judges 4:1–24; 5:1–31.

A Bit of Gloating and Glee

The purpose of the story of Deborah and Jael is to recount the many ways that God helped Israel become free of its enemies. The Jewish exiles who later listened to this story certainly needed a victory to gloat over—needed to believe that someday, somehow, they too would be freed.

When the story of Deborah and Jael was in its early form, it was probably told at gatherings as great entertainment. It is not terribly different from some films and TV shows today that use violence to capture their audience and build to a violent climax in which the "good guys" convincingly beat the "bad guys." Such violence in entertainment may not be very admirable, but it is not so different from the stories of the judges.

For all the gruesomeness of the tale of Deborah and Jael, the story surely nurtured hope in the exiles' hearts that they too, with God fighting for them, would one day overcome their oppressors.

Deborah's canticle is one of the oldest writings in the Bible, dating back almost to the time of the events it describes.

Gideon the Lowly

After forty years of "rest" for the land—that is, peace—the Israelites again fall into the evil practices of worshiping Canaanite gods. Gideon's tribe, Manasseh, together with all Israel, then comes under oppression by Midianite desert dwellers, who raid the tribe's land and ruin its crops. The Israelites cry to God for mercy, and God, though clearly unhappy with their disobedience, decides to save the people through the young man Gideon.

We first glimpse Gideon threshing wheat in his family's winepress, when an angel calls him to save his people. Gideon protests that as the youngest of the lowliest family in Manasseh, he is hardly a candidate for such a heroic task. Yet God assures Gideon of a victory and consumes Gideon's sacrificial offering with fire as a sign of favor.

Read Judges 6:1–24.

In fairy tales a repeated theme has the youngest child first scorned as good-for-nothing and then vindicated as a savior. Help comes disguised as a fairy godmother or a friendly genie, timidity gives way to confidence, and marvelous things happen. The stories of the judges have this same quality.

Gideon Destroys the Altar of Baal

In a dream Gideon is told to destroy the altar of the Canaanite god Baal, built by unfaithful Israelites. When he does so, the outraged townspeople order Gideon's father, Joash, to slay Gideon. Joash cunningly suggests that if Baal is a god, Baal should kill Gideon himself. No doubt to mock the god, Gideon is given the nickname **Jerubbaal**, meaning "Let Baal contend against him."

Gideon asks for another sign that God has chosen him to save Israel: Placing a sheepskin outdoors on the threshing floor, he asks God to have dew fall on it and not on the ground—which it does. When Gideon reverses the request, the wool remains dry overnight, though the ground becomes dewy.

Read Judges 6:25–40.

The worship of Baal needs to be wiped out among Gideon's people before he can expect a victory over the Midianites. But even after he has accomplished that by tearing down the altar to Baal, Gideon still is not confident. The sign with the sheepskin assures him. Insecurity and fear were frequent companions of the judges, and later the prophets, when answering God's call.

Gideon's Victory Is God's

Gideon gathers a large army, but is rebuked by God for doing so. God points out that with such a huge force, the Israelites would probably credit any victory they win to their own might, not to God's power. Under God's direction Gideon whittles down his troops to three hundred men. He divides these into companies, and each man is given a horn and an empty water jar in which is hidden a lighted torch. On a dark, moonless night, the three hundred Israelites surround the Midianite camp, break their water jars, reveal the torches, and blow their horns. The Midianites believe Israel's attack force to be much larger than it is because in the Midianite army, only the officers (each officer commanding ten men) carry torches. In the dark the Midianites begin fighting each other, and the survivors flee in terror. Gideon's men seize the Jordan ford and slay all of the enemy who attempt to cross.

The grateful Israelites beg Gideon to be their king, but he insists that God alone is their king. However, he will erect a cultic object to celebrate the victory. Collecting the Israelites' golden ornaments, he creates an ephod—a receptacle for use in seeking oracles. Unfortunately, the people slip back into their old ways and begin to worship the object as an idol; in the end it spells the ruin of Gideon's family. Following Gideon's death his son Abimelech murders all but one of his own brothers.

Read Judges 7:1–8,16–22; 8:22–35; 9:1–6.

God inspired Gideon to execute the brilliant bit of psychological warfare that brought him victory. But Gideon's scheme to erect the ephod—without consulting God—was his undoing.

Although Gideon's son Abimelech was proclaimed king, the biblical writers did not recognize him as such. His savage behavior excludes him from most lists of the judges as well.

Samson: Foe of the Philistines

The stories about Samson are thought to be folktales by some scholars and history by others, though in highly exaggerated form. History or not, what matters is that the stories convey the religious truth that God was with the Israelites. The stories were probably first told around campfires in the days when the Philistines dominated the Israelite tribes of Dan.

The **Philistines** were one of the sea peoples who had invaded Canaan from the Mediterranean Sea and were expanding into the interior, where they clashed with the

Israelites. With their metalworking skills and their superior iron weaponry, the Philistines posed a severe threat to everyone in the region.

As time went on and Israel lost even more territory to Philistia, the people found comfort in these tales of Samson, a village hero and one-man war machine who had started the Israelites' resistance to the dreaded Philistines. In both life and death, Samson proved to be too much for the hated enemies of his people—but he did not ultimately conquer them.

When the story of Samson opens, the Philistines have dominated Israel, which had again fallen into unfaithfulness to God, for forty years. Samson's birth to a barren woman is foretold by an angel, who says that Samson is to be a **Nazirite**—a man consecrated to God from birth, never to touch strong drink or cut his hair or his beard.

Read Judges 13:1–25.

Notice that the angel advises Samson's mother not to consume wine or strong drink during her pregnancy—a recommendation that we think of as quite modern.

Samson: Strong Man and Victim of Himself

Several stories tell of Samson's exploits against the Philistines, all of which involve amazing strength and disastrous relationships with women. Samson falls in love with a Philistine woman, and there follow the famous tales of his great strength. He kills a lion barehanded, slaughters thirty Philistines, discovers that his wife has been given to another, and in a rage sets three hundred foxes afire in the Philistines' fields. Captured, Samson breaks his bonds and kills a thousand Philistines with the jawbone of a donkey.

Eventually Samson becomes infatuated with Delilah, a woman bribed by the Philistines to find out the secret of his strength. Ever unable to resist the enticements of women, Samson finally tells her of his consecration to God and that the secret of his strength is the length of his hair. He falls asleep, she has the Philistines enter and cut his hair, and he is captured.

Samson's eyes are gouged out, and he is put to grinding grain like a beast at the mill wheel. But his hair grows again, and his strength returns. When the Philistines make sport of him in the temple of their chief god, Samson stands between two pillars and pushes them over. The temple collapses, killing Samson and all the Philistines at the scene.

Read Judges 14:1–20; 15:1–20; 16:1–31.

Samson has little to recommend him. He is a violent man with an uncontrolled passion for women. His story is the tragedy of a physically strong, morally weak man who might have been great if he had used his gifts for good.

The details of Samson's birth—including the angel and the Nazirite calling—are probably late additions to justify how such an unsavory character could be a judge.

Even if Samson the judge were not a historical person, such rages and lusts often appear in real life. When finally he is the cause of his own downfall, the story becomes a classic yet familiar human tragedy. No wonder Samson has inspired so many operas, writings, movies, and paintings.

Given Samson's character, why did the Deuteronomists list him among the judges? Perhaps their purpose was to marvel at the kind of people God can make use of, and that may be why God inspired the Deuteronomists to include Samson as a judge. Then too the wild adventure of the stories would have delighted the exiles, who needed to hear of larger-than-life exploits to boost their flagging spirits.

Perhaps Samson also reminded the exiles of how their nation, blessed by God with land and wealth and God's favor, had also become deluded and morally weak. Israel had brought ruin upon itself. It was plain to the exiles that Samson as a leader fell far below the ideal of Joshua. The Deuteronomists, and God, could use Samson to bring the point home strongly: Be like Joshua, not like Samson.

Ruth: An Israelite Foreigner with a Great Destiny

The story in the **Book of Ruth** is set in the time of the judges, and so it is included in this chapter. However, this story could not sound more different from the tales of the judges. In it we find no battles, but selflessness, patience, loyalty, and gentle kindness. In addition, within the story is the notion that a foreign woman could become a devoted member of the Israelites, not a theme found in Judges.

The Book of Ruth had its beginnings in Israel's oral tradition in the period of the early kings (about 800 B.C.E.) and was probably told by storytellers who appeared in villages and towns at the popular festivals. Its final written version was from the period after the exile; it is not part of the Deuteronomic history. Its purpose was twofold:

- to teach how God could create a blessed ending out of a difficult situation
- to tell how it came about that Israel's noble King David had a Gentile (a non-Jew) as his great-grandmother

In Ruth's concern for the survival of her mother-in-law, her strength of character far exceeds that of some of the judges.

A Family Faces Calamity

When famine strikes Israel during the period of the judges, a man from Bethlehem journeys with his wife, **Naomi,** and their two sons to start life again on the plain of Moab, a foreign land. Soon after their arrival, the man dies and leaves Naomi to raise their sons alone. When the sons are grown, each of them marries a Moabite woman—one named Orpah and the other **Ruth.** After ten years the young men die, and Naomi, grief stricken, plans to return to her homeland because she has heard that the famine is over.

Naomi starts out, and the two young widows accompany her for a distance. Then she stops, bids them good-bye, and asking God's blessing on each one, urges them to return home to find new husbands. But Ruth and Orpah want to stay with her. Naomi tries to convince them not to throw in their lot with her because her life will be miserable back in Israel. All three women weep, and after affectionate farewells Orpah returns to Moab, but Ruth remains with Naomi.

Naomi's love for the young women is evident in her insistence that they return to Moab, marry, and bear children. She resigns herself to seeing the end of her husband's family line, an unhappy possibility for any Israelite to face. She could have urged the young widows to come with her to Israel and marry members of her dead husband's clan, but she knows that would be a great sacrifice for them.

The Book of Ruth is most famous for its portrait of the beautiful relationship between Ruth and Naomi. Ruth's magnificent speech (1:16–17) pledges and binds her not only to Naomi but to God. In her selfless commitment to Naomi, her God, and her people, Ruth makes a covenant with the God of Israel. She is a foreigner who is as worthy of the Covenant as any Israelite.

Read Ruth 1:1–18.

Destitution and Generosity

As Naomi anticipated, she and Ruth face destitution when they get back to Israel. As widows they are unprovided for, and Naomi expresses her bitterness to God.

However, it is the time of the barley harvest, and Ruth decides to glean the barley fields because the two women need food. By chance Ruth goes to the field of a farmer named **Boaz**, who is a kinsman of Naomi's late husband and a man of wealth and influence.

Boaz has already noticed Ruth and learns that through Ruth's marriage to Naomi's son, he is distantly related to her. He invites Ruth to glean in his field, instructs the young men not to bother her, and bids her to follow close to the women as they harvest. Ruth, astonished, throws herself on the ground and asks why a foreigner should be treated so generously. Boaz reveals that he knows of her, and he praises her loyalty to Naomi. When he asks the blessing of the God of Israel upon her, he reveals his knowledge of her conversion.

Boaz continues his kindness, offering Ruth special attention and help throughout the harvest season and asking his workers to treat her respectfully. When Naomi becomes aware of Boaz's concern for Ruth, she is delighted. Perhaps there is hope for Ruth's future after all, because by Israelite law, this generous man, being kin to Naomi's husband, may be claimed for marriage by the widowed Ruth.

Read Ruth 1:19–22; 2:1–23.

Ruth and Naomi are examples of "the poor and the alien," of whom the Law, and later the prophetic and wisdom books, speak. Gleaning is not theft, nor is it begging. Ruth has a right to glean because the Law requires that gleanings be left for the poor.

Read Leviticus 23:22.

Naomi Makes a Match

Naomi, seeing what good things God has in store, does a bit of matchmaking. She bids Ruth to bathe, perfume, and dress herself in her best attire. Then Ruth is to go to the threshing floor, where Boaz and his men are working late into the evening, and stay out of sight. When the men have eaten and drunk and lain down to sleep, Ruth is to go where Boaz lies, uncover a place beside his feet, lie there, and wait for Boaz to tell her what to do.

Ruth does as Naomi bids, and when Boaz awakens and finds her, she asks him to cover her with his cloak. Boaz understands that by this request, Ruth is proposing to him, invoking the claim to marry him under Israelite law, and he blesses her. He will do all he can to arrange the marriage, although first a kinsman with closer ties to Ruth must be consulted. If this man does not want her, Boaz does. He tells her to sleep but to rise before the workers awaken so that there is no suspicion of scandal.

In the morning when Ruth returns and tells Naomi what happened, Naomi assures her that Boaz will not rest until he has settled the matter.

Read Ruth 3:1–18.

Up to now Boaz has viewed Ruth as praiseworthy but not as a potential wife. Naomi's plan is for Boaz to see Ruth as a wife. Naomi must be sure of his character; someone less honorable might take advantage of Ruth. But Boaz takes precautions to protect Ruth's reputation and, aware of the meaning of her actions, plans to marry Ruth in a way that is proper and legal.

Boaz Marries Ruth

Boaz clears his right to marry Ruth with a man who is a closer kin to her. That man gives up his right, and so Ruth and Boaz marry. In time Ruth bears a son, whom they name Obed, who becomes the father of Jesse, who in turn becomes the father of David, king of Israel.

Read Ruth 4:1–22.

That Ruth eventually becomes great-grandmother to David is highly significant. Being Moabite, Ruth is one of a foreign nationality that is expressly excluded from membership among the Israelite community, according to a law in Deuteronomy 23:3–6. Yet here is a Moabite woman, according to this story, who is recognized as an honored ancestor of the greatest king in the history of Israel. The postexilic author of Ruth evidently wrote to answer the question about whether it was right or good that a Gentile be welcomed by marriage into the community of Israel. The question was long debated among the Jews and controversial after the exile. But this story of the famous and much-loved Moabite Ruth reveals the Lord's choice of a Gentile as forebear to their great King David—and a far nobler person she was than some of the Israelites.

A God of Surprises

A reader of the Scriptures might wonder how books like Joshua and Judges wind up in the same Bible with Ruth. What do these books share in common? What is the core biblical message present in these quite different books?

Despite their apparent differences, these books all speak a message of total trust in and fidelity to God. God is the one who brings about good, turning disastrous situations into opportunities for fullness of life, peace, and abundance on the land. In Joshua, God miraculously clears the way for the Israelites to take over the land promised to Abraham. God can do anything, even using the apparently unworthy to accomplish God's purposes. So a Canaanite prostitute, Rahab, is God's instrument for the first victory in the Promised Land. In Judges, God turns around the Israelites' infidelity and failure, raising up leaders—some of them rather unsavory characters—to fight the oppressors and bring a measure of security to the Israelites on the land. And in Ruth, God blesses the simple faith and loyalty of a foreign woman, giving her a line of descendants that includes the revered King David.

Again and again God surprises. God overturns merely human plans in order to bring about something more wonderful through God's power to transform for the good even the darkest of times and dimmest of characters. What a message of hope for the exiles, for Jews and Christians down through the ages, and for us today.

Questions for Reflection and Discussion

1. God offers unlimited chances to turn from our mistakes—no matter what we have done—and to start over. It's always our choice, however, to make a fresh start. What second or even third chances have you needed in your life? How was the action of God's grace apparent to you?

2. Morality, far from being something we must do to please God, is meant to protect us. How have you experienced morality in this way?

3. What does shalom mean to you? What challenges does it present those of us living at this time in history?

4. In today's culture, worshiping idols takes on various forms, such as spending excessive time and energy to accumulate wealth. What are some other kinds of idol worship around us that could interfere with a person's devotion to God?

5. What is constructive, dignified obedience? How does this relate to the Israelites' understanding of obedience?

6. Providing sanctuary dates back to our Israelite ancestors. It was a holy obligation in the medieval church. Do we have a moral obligation to offer sanctuary?

7. Would Joshua be a fitting model for leadership in our time?

8. Gideon destroyed the altar of Baal because it symbolized the worst offenses of the surrounding culture. If you could eliminate something that represented evil in our society—something that would cause people to be outraged at you—what would it be?

9. Why has Samson generated so much more art, music, and drama than Joshua? Who are some modern Joshuas who are overshadowed by Samsons?

10. How is Ruth an exemplar of friendship, and how does she challenge us in our treatment of strangers?

6

Becoming a Nation

Have mercy on me, O God,
  according to your steadfast love;
according to your abundant mercy
  blot out my transgressions.
Wash me thoroughly from my iniquity,
  and cleanse me from my sin.

·   ·   ·   ·   ·   ·   ·   ·   ·   ·   ·

Create in me a clean heart, O God,
  and put a new and right spirit within me.
Do not cast me away from your presence,
  and do not take your holy spirit from me.
Restore to me the joy of your salvation,
  and sustain in me a willing spirit.

(Psalm 51:1–2,10–12)

The two Books of Samuel and the beginning of the First Book of Kings are part of the history edited by the Deuteronomists during the Babylonian exile. Recall that the Deuteronomic history attempted to answer the questions gnawing at the exiled Jews: How did we end up captured by our enemies, forced into exile far from home with our Temple and our beloved city destroyed? Has God abandoned us? Is there any hope for the future? What have we learned from this disaster?

Stories of Transition to Nationhood

To answer the exiles' disturbing questions, the Deuteronomists had to explain how, after the era of the Judges in the Promised Land, the Israelite people became a nation "'like other nations'" (1 Samuel 8:20). How did they come to have a king, a capital city, wealth, military power, a palace, and a magnificent Temple to their God? And even more important, what effect did nationhood have on them?

The Need for Unity

The Book of Judges, considered in the previous chapter, ends with this simple statement: "In those days there was no king in Israel; all the people did what was right in their own eyes" (21:25). In other words, by the end of the era of the judges, no central leader like Moses or Joshua had been able to unite the tribes into one people under God's Law. Judges like Deborah, Gideon, and Samson had risen among the tribes as they were needed. Filled with God's spirit, they had won victories in the struggles with the Canaanites for the land. However, that temporary kind of leadership was not stable or strong enough to build unity across the tribes. It could not keep the people from disintegrating into separate groups and clans that simply went their own way. Morally and spiritually, things were going rapidly downhill. This state of affairs was far from the ideal of God's Chosen People united in keeping the Covenant faithfully.

The lack of unity also threatened the very existence of the Israelites: The tribes of Israel, fragmented, did not stand a chance against the onslaught of the mighty Philistines. These "sea people" with their chariots and iron weapons were pressing eastward from the seacoast regions to threaten Israelite territories. Without the security of nationhood, it appeared that the Israelites were doomed.

Mixed Feelings About Nationhood

The **Books of Samuel** and the beginning of the **First Book of Kings** describe the time of transition to nationhood—in the decades around 1000 B.C.E. They tell stories of Israel's first three kings—**Saul, David,** and **Solomon.** The accounts show the new nation of Israel not only surviving the Philistine onslaught but growing in success and power.

The Deuteronomists, though, saw the whole process of becoming a nation from the perspective of four hundred or so years later. They understood that some features of being "'like other nations'" (1 Samuel 8:20), though attractive, were the seeds of destruction that had led to the nation's downfall. So they had mixed feelings about Israel's being a nation with a king.

The story of David, Israel's greatest king, introduces God's promise that David's line of descendants, the royal house of David, would endure forever as leaders of Israel. Eventually, as we will see in other books of the Bible, this became the basis for the prophecy that from the line of David would come a great leader, the Messiah, who would save the Jews from oppression and bring in a reign of peace and justice. Christians believe that this promise of a Messiah is fulfilled in Jesus Christ.

In putting together the history of Israel's transition to nationhood, the Deuteronomists used sections of the ancient Court History of David (no longer in existence). Dated at about 1000 B.C.E., the court history may have been the oldest written history in the world. David is at the center of that history, but as we now have the story in the First Book of Samuel, it begins with the great judge and prophet for whom two Old Testament books are named—**Samuel.**

Samuel: Anointer of Kings

The baby Samuel, like a number of other important figures in the Bible, is born to a woman who had not before been able to bear a child. Once Hannah weans the child, in joy and gratitude she offers him to God as a Nazirite (a special dedicated status like Samson the judge had) and leaves him in the care of the priest Eli at the shrine at Shiloh.

Samuel grows up serving God faithfully. Eli's two sons, however, are a different story. As priests they behave sacrilegiously—in spite of Eli's warnings. God announces through a holy man that Eli's family line will end.

One night, while sleeping in the sanctuary near the ark of the Covenant, Samuel hears his name called. He goes to Eli, who merely sends him back to bed. A second and third time this happens. Finally, Eli realizes that God is calling Samuel, and he tells Samuel to respond, "'Speak, for your servant is listening'" (1 Samuel 3:10). God tells Samuel of the coming fall of Eli's family. Samuel reluctantly tells Eli God's message, and Eli accepts this news. Eventually this and other prophecies reveal to the people of Israel that Samuel is a prophet to whom God speaks.

Read 1 Samuel 3:1–21.

The Cry for a King

As priest and judge, Samuel goes on to lead the Israelites for many years, rebuking them when they follow false gods and promising them victory over the Philistines if they obey God. The Philistines are finally defeated, and Israel lives in peace as long as Samuel is its leader.

The sons of Samuel are unfit to take his place as judge when he grows old, so the people cry out to Samuel to "'appoint for us, then, a king to govern us, like other nations'" (1 Samuel 8:5). God tells a displeased Samuel that "'they have not rejected you, but they have rejected me from being king over them'" (8:7).

Even though the people are preferring in some way to put their trust in a king rather than God, God tells Samuel to go ahead and give them what they want. But Samuel must warn the people of what trouble lies ahead if they have a king: A king will draft their sons to make arms, build chariots, and reap harvests; their daughters to make perfumes, cook, and bake. A king will also take their fields, vineyards, olive groves, and a tithe of their grain—that is, one-tenth of it. He will then take their menservants, maidservants, donkeys, and sheep. Finally, a king will make the Israelites into slaves. When at last they cry out to God, it will be to no avail.

Even with Samuel's warning, the people insist that they want to be "'like other nations'" (8:5) and have a king who will "'go out before us and fight our battles'" (8:20). Samuel has no choice but to follow God's command and give the people what they are clamoring for.

Read 1 Samuel 8:1–22.

In this exchange over whether to have a king, we can see the view of the Deuteronomists. For them and for the prophets, only God is the king of Israel. From the hindsight of four hundred years after Samuel, the Deuteronomists knew what would happen with most of the kings: they would be disasters. In fact the oppressive king described in Samuel's speech sounds much like Solomon, the third king.

The Israelites felt pulled toward the success-and-power model of other nations, with their kings, huge armies, and vast territories. Yet the question for them always was whether to follow that model or to be a nation apart, a different kind of nation that would be a light to all the others. This question still confronts Jews today as they struggle with the meaning of the modern state of Israel.

The term *Israel* has already been used in several ways. This summary can clarify its meaning and development:

Worlð Happenings
Between 1250 and 900 B.C.E.

Africa
Poverty and decadence plague the declining Egyptian Empire.

America
By 1000 B.C.E. the Olmecs in Mexico and the Chavin in Peru establish states with populations in the tens of thousands, along with priesthoods, civil services, and classes of traders and artisans.

China
The first Chinese dictionary is written, including over forty thousand written characters.

- The Hebrew meaning of the word *Israel,* though uncertain, is probably "may God rule."
- After his nightlong struggle with the stranger, Jacob is given the name Israel.
- Later, the people who claim descent from Jacob and the other founders call themselves the people of Israel.
- In the Second Book of Samuel, the ten tribes in the north are called Israel. The two tribes in the south are called Judah.
- When David unites the tribes, the nation is called Israel.
- When the kingdom is divided after Solomon's death, Israel is the formal name given to the northern kingdom. This kingdom is the first one to be conquered, and it is conquered by the Assyrians.
- When the exiles return from Babylon to the province of Judah, they are called Jews; the nation is called Israel.
- From that time on, *Israel* means the land and the people as a nation.
- To some Jews the modern state called Israel is a religious continuation of the ancient nation. To others the state is primarily a political entity.

Europe
Classical paganism blooms in Greece. A temple to Hera—worshiped as queen of heaven, goddess of women and marriage, and wife of Zeus (king of the gods)—is built in the tenth century B.C.E. at Olympia.

India
Basic elements of Hinduism develop, including a belief in a cosmic order and also a class system of priests, nobles, merchants, and workers.

The Near East
The Creation Epic confirms the position of the Babylonian god Marduk as the maker of the universe. The city of Babylon becomes the spiritual capital of the region.

Saul Is Anointed

Samuel is guided by God to find a king for the Israelites. He meets Saul, an unassuming farmworker searching for his father's donkeys. Samuel anoints Saul king and presents him to the tribes—even though Saul, a shy man for all his tall stature and good looks, tries to hide at the last minute.

Read 1 Samuel 9:1–27; 10:1–27.

The theme of this story about Saul is familiar: God chooses the lowliest and least. Although tall and handsome, Saul is hardly the regal type. He is from an ordinary family background, and is afraid of attention. Yet God chooses him.

Saul and David in Conflict

Once he is king, Saul pulls himself together and wins a stunning victory for Israel over the Ammonites. Afterward Samuel warns both the king and the people that the key to their success will be fidelity to God.

Yet Saul soon breaks faith with God. He disobeys God's Law twice. First, under pressure from his frightened soldiers who are about to be attacked by the Philistines, he offers a prebattle sacrifice instead of waiting for Samuel to do so (only priests are allowed to offer sacrifice). Then, in another battle, Saul fails to carry out the ban against a defeated enemy: he takes the enemy king and the best livestock as spoils of war instead of destroying them for God. Saul shows himself to be unfaithful, swayed by his own anxieties, and subject to the pressures of those around him. He does not truly trust in God and follow God's commands.

Samuel declares that Saul will now be rejected by God as king of Israel. The crown will be given to a more faithful, constant man. As the scriptural passage notes, "And the LORD was sorry that he had made Saul king over Israel" (1 Samuel 15:35).

Read 1 Samuel 11:11–15; 12:13–18; 13:5–14; 15:1–35.

The Empire That David Built

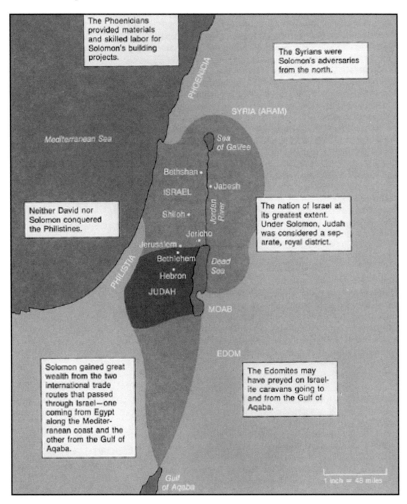

The Phoenicians provided materials and skilled labor for Solomon's building projects.

The Syrians were Solomon's adversaries from the north.

PHOENICIA

SYRIA (ARAM)

Mediterranean Sea

Sea of Galilee

Bethshan •

• Jabesh

ISRAEL

Jordan River

Shiloh •

Neither David nor Solomon conquered the Philistines.

Jericho

The nation of Israel at its greatest extent. Under Solomon, Judah was considered a separate, royal district.

Jerusalem •

PHILISTIA

Bethlehem •

Dead Sea

• Hebron

JUDAH

MOAB

EDOM

Solomon gained great wealth from the two international trade routes that passed through Israel—one coming from Egypt along the Mediterranean coast and the other from the Gulf of Aqaba.

The Edomites may have preyed on Israelite caravans going to and from the Gulf of Aqaba.

Gulf of Aqaba

1 inch = 48 miles

Another Choice for King

Samuel is led by God to search for another king for Israel. The theme of God's choice of the weakest and lowest is repeated in the story of David. God sends Samuel to Bethlehem, where he meets Jesse's sons. God instructs Samuel to overlook the older, taller sons that seem to have obvious regal potential—"'for the LORD does not see as mortals see; they look on the outward appearance, but the LORD looks on the heart'" (1 Samuel 16:7). Samuel chooses the youngest son, David, and secretly anoints him king. David will not be publicly declared king until later.

Two biblical traditions tell of Saul's meeting David. In one David is brought to play the harp for Saul to lighten his dark moods. In the other, the well-known, marvelously told story of David and Goliath, young David, armed only with a slingshot, prevails against the Philistine giant. In both stories Saul likes David, finds him gifted, and decides to keep him at court. But of course Saul does not realize that David has secretly been anointed king by Samuel and is destined to take his place.

Read 1 Samuel 16:1–23; 17:1–58.

Recall from the account of Jesus' birth in Luke's Gospel that Joseph and his pregnant wife, Mary, make a journey to Joseph's hometown for the census ordered by the Roman emperor. Because Joseph is of the house of David—one of David's line—the couple must go to David's place of origin, Bethlehem. And that is where Jesus is born.

Read Luke 1:26–33; 2:1–5.

Saul's Jealousy of David

David's popularity, attractiveness, and skill begin to arouse jealousy in the insecure and emotionally unstable Saul, until at last he tries to kill David. Both Saul's son **Jonathan** and his daughter **Michal**—who is also David's wife—help David escape Saul's murderous traps. Convinced of the king's irrational hatred, David finally bids farewell to Jonathan and Michal. He leaves the court as a fugitive, knowing that he is God's choice to be king but also that he must not rub it in to Saul, who is just beginning to realize the inevitable.

Read 1 Samuel 18:1–16; 19:1–18; 20:24–35,41–42.

As Samuel prophesied, God is no longer with Saul and everything he does goes wrong. Twice when he tries to kill David, his spear misses. When Saul sends David to the battlefront, David's prowess wins the love of the people. Even Saul's children give their loyalty to David. Saul realizes that nothing he can do will stop David from becoming king.

The story of David and Jonathan is one of the world's greatest tales of friendship. Notice how Jonathan's love for David is described, by his loyalty and the risks he takes for David.

David: The Loyal Outlaw

David flees to the shrine at Nob, which is near Jerusalem. There he contrives to get food from the priest by lying to him, saying that Saul has sent him on an errand. The priest gives David not only bread from the altar but the sword of Goliath as well. When Saul finds out, he orders the entire city of Nob destroyed, and the only survivor is one of the priest's sons. David, contrite, admits his guilt to the surviving son and offers him protection.

Still loyal to his people, David next rescues an Israelite town from the Philistines. Then he and his troops, a band of several hundred followers, flee to the desert, where David takes refuge in a cave. Pursuing him, Saul stops in the cave to relieve himself and apparently falls asleep. David could kill Saul at that point, but instead he cuts off a piece of his cloak and leaves him sleeping. When Saul emerges, David calls from a distance and tells Saul that he means him no harm. As proof David waves the cloth to show Saul that he was close enough to kill him but has instead spared his life. Saul then understands how righteous David is, how deserving he is to be king.

Read 1 Samuel 21:1–10; 22:18–23; 23:1–5; 24:1–22.

The destruction of the city of Nob at Saul's command is a bad moment in David's rise to kingship. After all, David has had a part in the terrible deed—having deceived the priest within the hearing of one of Saul's men. Innocent people die because of David's lie. As we will see, David is far from perfect, and the biblical writers let us know about his sins. But despite his human failings, David is still the one chosen to accomplish the divine purposes, and the writers repeatedly hold him up as a model of faithfulness to God.

As David spares Saul, we see in a touching and beautiful speech that his affection for Saul remains in spite of the king's attempts to kill him. After Saul acknowledges David's goodness and his right to be king, David swears he will never harm Saul's descendants. He keeps this promise even though the unstable Saul continues to hunt him down to destroy him. Loyalty to friends and family proves to be one of David's strongest and most admirable character traits.

Another Outlaw Story

David and his band survive by offering protection to the local inhabitants for a price—food and other provisions. But a wealthy herdsman whose shepherds have enjoyed David's protection refuses to pay up. When David angrily moves to confront him, the herdsman's wife, **Abigail**, intercepts David with supplies of food and wine, hoping to keep him from annihilating her family and her people. David is appeased, and later, when the herdsman dies, he marries Abigail. Saul has already given David's wife Michal to another man.

Read 1 Samuel 25:18–43.

David's marriage to Abigail is prompted by his gratitude and his admiration for her character. By contrast, Michal's remarriage was a political move by Saul, pure and simple. By having Michal marry another man, Saul hoped to weaken David's claim to the throne. Later, David will demand Michal back to strengthen his claim. David, as we will see, uses power effectively to further his own purposes. Even as God's chosen one, his trust in God is mixed with some heavy-handed tactics.

The Philistines Versus David and Saul

David decides to seek refuge from Saul, who is still out to get him, by staying with the Philistines. To ingratiate himself with their king, he pretends to attack Israelite towns—something the loyal David would never do to his own people. In reality he is raiding Canaanite villages for their livestock.

Threatened by the Philistines, a desperate, even deranged Saul seeks out a witch to conjure up the spirit of the dead Samuel (earlier he had outlawed such fortune-telling in the land). The ghost of Samuel reveals only that Saul and his sons will perish in battle the next day.

Meanwhile, at the Philistine camp, David is trying to outwit these enemies of Israel. His men, about to march into battle at the rear of the Philistine army, are apparently planning to attack the Philistines from behind during the battle.

But the Philistine chiefs distrust David and instead send his troops back to the village where they have been staying. Finding it sacked by Canaanite marauders, with all the women and children kidnapped, David rescues the captives and slays their captors. He then distributes the spoils to other towns where he and his troops were best known—a move that was not just generous but politically smart.

Read 1 Samuel 27:1–12; 28:4–20; 29:1–11.

A Tragic End for Saul

Israel's battle goes as prophesied by the ghost of Samuel, and in a tragic end to a career that was once bright with promise, Saul kills himself rather than be captured. The Philistines fasten his body and those of his sons—including Jonathan—to the walls of one of their cities. But the Jabeshites, who were once rescued by Saul, march all night, rescue the corpses, and take them to their own town.

Read 1 Samuel 31:1–13.

The First Book of Samuel completes the first of the major themes in Samuel—namely, the **reign of Saul**. The other theme, the **rise of David to his kingship**, follows in the Second Book of Samuel.

King David: Nation Builder

The Second Book of Samuel opens with a different version of Saul's death. A young soldier from the front of Israel's battle reports to David that Saul is dead. The wounded Saul persuaded the soldier to strike him a deathblow, lest Saul be captured by the Philistines. David is furious that the young man would violate "'the LORD's anointed'" (1:14), even though Saul asked him to finish his life. David has the young soldier killed, and then mourns the death of Saul and Jonathan in beautiful and passionate words.

Read 2 Samuel 1:17–27.

At First, King of Judah

Israel is now without a king, but has two rival leaders: Saul's general **Abner** in the north and David in the south. Abner makes Saul's eldest son, **Ishbaal,** king over the northern tribes, although Abner himself really wants to rule. David, with a power base already in the south, is anointed king of the southern tribes of Judah in Hebron.

Read 2 Samuel 2:8–11.

Actually, David is now *publicly* anointed king, because Samuel has already secretly anointed him.

Abner tries to move Ishbaal into the lead over David, but his plan fails. So, aware that David's star is rising, Abner betrays Ishbaal, returns Michal to David, and persuades the northern tribes to choose David for their king. The northerners remember David's loyal service to Saul, assemble together with Judah, and anoint David king over *all* Israel. He is thirty years old.

Murder and Mayhem

Sandwiched between these events is a series of murders and betrayals that sound like they could have come from a contemporary corporate-thriller movie. The plot would go like this:

Abner, the powerful and ruthless vice president of Israel, Inc., promotes to president the weak son (Ishbaal) of the deceased president (Saul). Abner also takes over the deceased president's mistress and tries to eliminate the lawfully designated president (David) by violence, but fails.

Insulted by Ishbaal, Abner next abandons his candidate for president of the company (Ishbaal) and persuades the stockholders whom he controls (the northern tribes) to vote for the lawfully designated president (David).

Returning from a business trip, Abner is waylaid and murdered by the new vice president (Joab, one of David's generals), whose brother was slain by Abner. The new president (David) is horrified and mourns Abner's death.

In the meantime two hit men from the north, certain that the president (David) will be pleased if his rival (Ishbaal) is removed, murder him. When the appalled president discovers the crime, the hit men are executed.

In short, David's reign begins with a bloodbath.

Read 2 Samuel 2:12–16; 3:6–13; 5:1–5.

David could be caught up in trying to destroy his rivals—Saul, Abner, Ishbaal—or at least he could rejoice when they are killed by others. But his response to their deaths is not even relief; it is deep anger at their murderers and profound mourning at the losses. Once David decides he is loyal to Saul, he never turns against him or those close to him.

United at Jerusalem

Alarmed at Israel's unity, the Philistines force David into battle, and his victories drive them down to the coastal plain. The Philistines are never again a serious threat.

David's next move is inspired. He captures **Jerusalem**, a Canaanite city that has boasted that even the lame and the blind could defend it, and makes it his capital.

Read 2 Samuel 5:17–25; 5:6–16.

David's two great feats were ending the Philistine threat and unifying the Israelite tribes. Making Jerusalem his capital was a stroke of genius. Because Jerusalem had never belonged to any one of the twelve tribes, David could not be accused of playing favorites by bringing his court there. Jerusalem was ideally located in territory between the northern and the southern tribes.

History has proven that David's decision was of much greater import than he would ever know. In Jerusalem David established what would become a holy city for Jews, Christians, and Muslims—more than half of all religious believers in the world today.

The Ark Comes to Jerusalem

Aware that the ark of the Covenant is a powerful symbol of God's presence to the people, David brings it to Jerusalem, where it will be housed in a tent. When David joyfully enters the city, dancing before the ark, his wife Michal berates him for acting like a fool. He replies that if to give God praise he must look a fool, he will. The story ends with the note that Michal never bears a child.

Read 2 Samuel 6:1–5,12–23.

David is so devoted to God that he dances exuberantly before God's ark, without concern for how he looks to the people (no one seems to mind his ecstatic dancing except Michal). As Michal's contempt toward David shows, she does not see or value his love for God. Apparently no bond of love remains between them; their remarriage was purely political. The text implies that David never makes love to Michal again—a sad ending to a young love for which they had risked so much.

The Davidic Covenant

David reflects that while he is living in a house of cedar, God has only a tent as a dwelling place. So David plans to build a house for the Lord. But the prophet **Nathan** says no to David's plan. Nathan tells David of God's greater plan for him—that God will instead build a different kind of "house" for David. This house of David will not be a building but a royal dynasty, a line of David's descendants that will endure forever. Scripture scholars call this promise by God the **Davidic Covenant.**

Read 2 Samuel 7:1–17.

The prophet Nathan, one of the nonwriting prophets, plays an important role in the lives of David and Solomon. In this first prophecy, Nathan reveals God's wish that the temple David is planning be postponed until his future son (Solomon) can build it.

The Messianic Promise

God promised that David's line would endure forever. In fact David's line endured unbroken for four hundred years; then it dropped into obscurity. Afterward devout Jews remembered this promise and waited for the reappearance of a leader from this royal line to be Israel's **Messiah.** The Hebrew word *messiah* means "the anointed," referring to the anointing of a king. By the time of Jesus, the belief in the coming Messiah was widespread among Jews in Palestine. The early Christians believed the Messiah to be Jesus, who was from the line of David. The Gospel writers referred to Jesus using the Greek word for *messiah—christos,* meaning "the anointed," from which the name Christ comes.

Read Matthew 1:1,12–17; Mark 15:2,26.

David and Bathsheba

As king, David is powerful, wealthy, and undefeated. But after years of war, he is tired, and one spring he stays home from battle. As he strolls on the roof of his house, he sees a beautiful woman bathing nearby. She is **Bathsheba**, whose husband is **Uriah**, a warrior at the battlefront. David sends for her and makes love to her, apparently with no qualms about breaking the commandment "You shall not commit adultery."

David gets nervous, though, when he finds out from Bathsheba that she is pregnant with his child. He tries to cover up his adultery by bringing her husband, Uriah, back from the battlefront, and telling him he can go home and stay with Bathsheba for a couple of nights. However, the plan fails because Uriah, a man of high principles, refuses to go home and enjoy himself while God's ark is out in the battlefield encamped with the other soldiers.

Desperate to cover up his sin, David has Uriah killed. He does this by directing his general at the front to place Uriah where he will be killed in battle—and this happens. Bathsheba mourns the loss of her husband, but then David sends for her to become his own wife, and she bears him a son.

Read 2 Samuel 11:1–27.

Despite his devotion to God and his persisting loyalty to family and friends, David has grave flaws. Having given in to his lust for Bathsheba, David then lies and manipulates others to cover up his mistake. But his sins only multiply, turning to murder. In arranging Uriah's death, David shows his willingness to betray a good and honorable man so as to keep the whole affair secret.

A Lesson and Repentance for David

David, however, is forced to confront the evil of what he has done, with the help of Nathan the prophet. Nathan presents the king with a parable, asking him to judge this case: A poor man had one ewe lamb that he loved very much, and a rich man had a flock of sheep. When the rich man had a guest over for dinner, he stole the poor man's ewe instead of slaughtering one of his own for the meal. "What should happen to such a man?" asks Nathan. "The fellow should die," cries David angrily. And Nathan says, "You are the man."

Through the parable David recognizes his sin and repents. He has been reminded that though he is a powerful king, he is subject to God and he must follow God's Law. When David pours out his sorrow, Nathan assures him that God forgives him and will not ask his life—but David will pay for his acts with much trouble and grief in his family. Sure enough, the son of David and Bathsheba, who was conceived in the adulterous incident, becomes sickly as a child and dies. Later, Bathsheba conceives and bears another son, named Jedidiah but in his adulthood called Solomon.

Read 2 Samuel 12:1–25.

The Deuteronomists who put the history together centuries after David were inspired to leave in the account of his acts of adultery and murder. They did not choose to idealize David by ignoring his sinful behavior. They make it clear that David is not above God's Law; he must repent for his sins, and he will suffer greatly for them. The message for us is that God works through limited and sinful persons, with David as a prime example of that. Perhaps that realization can give hope to all of us far-from-perfect human beings—hope that God somehow brings about the divine purposes even through our flaws and weaknesses.

Rivalry and Treachery in the Family

Nathan's prophecy of evil for David's family is fulfilled in a series of tragedies and treacheries. David has had a number of sons by various wives (polygamy was a common practice, especially among royalty). The obvious heir to the throne is his firstborn, **Amnon**. But the family is wrecked by incest, rivalries, hatreds, murders, and rebellions among the sons. Here is a brief summary of what is told with marvelous detail in the Second Book of Samuel:

- Amnon desires his half sister **Tamar** and rapes her, then turns on her and drives her away. Though angry, David does not punish Amnon because he is his heir to the throne.
- **Absalom**, another of David's sons and the full brother of Tamar, is enraged at Amnon for his horrible deed and has him slain two years later, then escapes to stay away from the angry David for three years.
- David loves Absalom and longs to have him return. After Absalom does come back, he finally reconciles with his father. But his intentions are evil: he begins to subtly undermine the people's respect for David as he plots to take over the kingship.
- Absalom attracts a following among the people, leaves Jerusalem with them, and then declares himself king instead of his father. David weeps for Absalom.
- In the midst of Absalom's rebellion, David is told of the disloyalty of **Mephibosheth** (Meribbaal, in some translations). This man is the surviving son of David's dear friend Jonathan and the grandson of Saul. It is reported that Mephibosheth is trying to take away the throne from David. This is especially hurtful to David because years earlier, after Jonathan's death, he had taken the young man into his court and treated him like a son.
- Absalom proceeds to attack Jerusalem, but David implores his men to protect his enemy Absalom from harm in the battle. But after Absalom is defeated, he is killed in trying to escape. David is heartbroken and mourns him piteously.

Read 2 Samuel 13:1–39; 14:28–33; 15:1–18; 17:7–13; 18:1–17,31–33; 19:1–4.

Notice that David's loyalty to family is so strong that he refuses to punish Amnon for raping Tamar, he trusts Absalom to come back into his court after killing Amnon, and he fails to recognize Absalom's treacherous intentions. His devotion to his sons seems to make him abandon good sense.

The Ending Years of David's Reign

After the failed revolts, David moves to reconcile the disgruntled tribes in both the north and the south. He refuses to punish Saul's family—even Mephibosheth.

David is enthroned once more in Jerusalem, and the kingdom is restored to a semblance of order. Yet the popularity of the aging king is not what it was. Animosity among the tribes is beginning to surface. And David—worn out, his judgment not always fair—has such bias toward his favorites that it is bound to fuel resentments and rivalries.

By the end of David's reign, Israel is indeed a nation like other nations, with a king and a capital. David has established his kingship over all the tribes of Israel, built a strong nation that can resist the Philistines, and set up its center in Jerusalem, a city that will embody the hopes and dreams of Israel for centuries to come, even to the present.

The Deuteronomists, who during the exile edited the history of David's times, may have looked back and wondered about the wisdom of Israel's becoming a nation with a king. They knew that the illusions and temptations of power and wealth corrupted most of the kings after David and ultimately led to Israel's downfall at the hands of the Babylonians. Yet they saw in David a model of what the kings, and all Israel, should have been—devoted to God.

Above all else David trusted in God and tried to serve God. When his enemies plotted against him and his own sons became his enemies, David continued to be devoted to God, placing himself in God's care. When he sinned grievously, he threw himself on God's mercy and did not despair. He must have been a hopeful example for the exiles, a sign that Israel could be forgiven its many failures and could go on to live faithfully in the service of God, if only Israel would keep God at the center.

Recall, too, God's promise to David that his royal line would endure forever. This Davidic Covenant became the source of hope among Jews of later times—and even to-day—that a messiah would be born from David's descendants to deliver the people from oppression. The early Christians saw this promise to David as fulfilled in Jesus.

King Solomon: Temple Builder

For the rest of the story of the monarchy, we turn to the two Books of Kings, the last part of the Deuteronomic history edited during the Babylonian exile. They tell of David's son Solomon, then the breakup of the nation into the kingdoms of Israel and Judah, the infidelity of their kings, the prophets Elijah and Elisha, and all the events that led finally to the exile. The Books of Kings show how the nation was mostly unfaithful despite warnings from its prophets. They were written to remind the disheartened exiles in Babylon that it was the people, not God, who broke the Covenant. Yet the restoration of their nation in the future would be possible if they would repent and turn to God again.

Passing the Torch to Solomon

As the First Book of Kings opens, David is close to death. His eldest son, **Adonijah**, is trying to take over the throne and even throws himself a party to celebrate. But Nathan the prophet manages to have David promise the throne to Solomon, David's son by Bathsheba. Solomon is then anointed king before his father dies.

On his deathbed David assures Solomon that if he and his line will remain faithful to God, they will always sit on the throne. Then, in what seems to be a bloody reversal of David's merciful attitudes toward his enemies, David counsels Solomon to settle the old scores. Upon David's death Solomon does so, killing off several known "troublemakers" and assuring himself of total control of the kingdom.
Read 1 Kings 1:1–22,28–40,49–53; 2:1–25.

Solomon Asks for Wisdom

To build an alliance with Egypt, Solomon marries the daughter of the Egyptian pharaoh. He also worships at one of the "high places," meaning an outdoor sanctuary.

In a dream Solomon asks God for an understanding heart to distinguish right from wrong. Pleased, God promises Solomon not only the wisdom to judge rightly but riches, glory, and a long life as well—if he is faithful.

Read 1 Kings 3:1–14.

The Deuteronomists frowned on outdoor sanctuaries because the Canaanites used them in fertility rites and in the worship of Baal. Although Solomon's worship seems genuine, the story is hinting of evil things to come, in its references to the high places—and to Solomon's Egyptian wife.

Solomon's Judgment

Solomon's understanding heart is immediately put to the test. Two prostitutes come before the king—one with a child, one without. The childless woman tells Solomon that each of them bore a child and that the other woman smothered hers in her sleep. Then she exchanged the dead infant for the live one and now claims him. The woman with the child denies this. The king calls for a sword and suggests that the child be divided and half given to each woman. The true mother, in anguish, cries out that the child should live and gives up her claim to him. Solomon gives the child to that woman, who revealed her motherhood in her desire to save the child's life.

Read 1 Kings 3:16–28.

This story, probably the best-known one about Solomon, appears in folklore all over the world. Whether history or legend, the story offers a wonderful example of judicial wisdom that shows understanding of the human heart.

Solomon's Oppressive System

Solomon, ignoring tribal boundaries, divides the land into twelve new districts and appoints an officer for each region. Then he forms an elite group of administrators and introduces forced labor and taxation to provide supplies for the palace and for government officials.

Read 1 Kings 4:1–7.

Peasants have long been exploited by corrupt governments, by wealthy landowners, and by foreign investors. Solomon's glory was built on income raised by oppressing his people in the same way. Farmers and shepherds had to provide palace supplies from their own crops and herds and take time from their work to hunt wild game for officials. The prophet Samuel had warned about these things long before, when the people first clamored for a king. With the reign of Solomon, the injustice came to pass.

Solomon's Wisdom

Solomon's reputation grows until "all the kings of the earth" know of his wisdom (1 Kings 4:34). He utters three thousand proverbs, writes one thousand and five—that is, numberless—songs, and discusses plants, beasts, birds, reptiles, and fishes.

Read 1 Kings 4:29–34 (or 5:9–14 in NAB or NJB).

The scriptural writers probably exaggerated the number of proverbs and songs that Solomon wrote, but no doubt he was the source of many wise words and a key figure in the intellectual wisdom movement of that time. Entire books of the Bible—in the category of Wisdom books—were later attributed to him, although this does not mean he actually wrote them.

We have to wonder, though, how deep the wisdom of Solomon actually was. True, his reign was a glorious time for Israel in terms of splendor and power and reputation among other nations. But how wise was he in the ways of God? In the end Solomon's reign is a disaster for Israel, a time marked by extravagance in the royal house, harsh oppression of the people, and even idolatry by the king himself.

The Temple as God's House

Rich and powerful, Solomon is now ready to build the **Temple** in Jerusalem. He asks a Phoenician king to send not only materials but also architects. Because Israel has never built a temple, a Canaanite model must be used. Solomon conscripts thirty thousand workers from his own people in addition to foreign labor. He also builds a fabulous royal palace complex and entire cities for his supplies, chariots, and horses.

God agrees to be present in the Temple, adding that if Solomon observes the Law and carries it out, Israel will not be forsaken. In a long prayer, Solomon himself wonders if his great accomplishment is futile: Can any building contain God?

When the Temple is dedicated, God repeats the promise made to Solomon and adds a warning: If Solomon and his descendants forsake the Covenant, the Temple will become a heap of ruins. These words must have pierced the hearts of the exiles in Babylon as they listened and remembered their own story of failure.

Read 1 Kings 5:1–6 (or 5:15–20 in NAB or NJB); 6:11–13; 8:27–30; 9:1–11.

The Bible devotes several pages to the construction, furnishings, and dedication of the Temple at Jerusalem. Indeed, Solomon is probably best known the world over for building his Temple. Financed by taxes, the building was a marvel of cedar beams, bronze pillars, ivory-paneled doors, golden vessels, and carved stonework. Its magnificence rivaled the monuments of Egypt.

The Temple had three chambers, as did the Canaanite temples. The people were relegated to the outer court, the priests and nobles to the inner court. The high priest entered the sanctuary, called the holy of holies, only once a year.

Solomon not only designed the Temple on Canaanite models but also adopted temple practices from his neighbors. In some ways Solomon's Temple became a symbol of wealth at the price of justice, and arrogance at the price of faith. Yet the Temple was always regarded as sacred because it was seen as the place where God chose to dwell with the people.

Israel's Temple becomes a source of pride and joy and a subject for many psalms like this one:

How lovely is your dwelling place,
    O LORD of hosts.
My soul longs, indeed it faints
    for the courts of the LORD;
my heart and my flesh sing for joy
    to the living God.

Even the sparrow finds a home,
    and the swallow a nest for herself,
    where she may lay her young,
at your altars, O LORD of hosts,
    my King and my God.
Happy are those who live in your house,
    ever singing your praise.

(Psalm 84:1–4)

Yet the building of the Temple marks the beginning of Israel's downfall. With the growing splendor of Solomon's reign will come oppression such as the people have never known before.

The Queen of Sheba

Solomon is visited by the queen of Sheba, seeking to discover if he is as wise as reputed. The queen asks Solomon some subtle questions—probably traditional riddles, a number of which survive in collections of tales about Solomon. Observing his wisdom and his wealth, the queen is breathless.
    Read 1 Kings 10:1–10.

The Sins of Solomon

As Solomon adds to his wealth and his harem, his love for God diminishes. He tolerates shrines where his pagan wives offer sacrifice, and he even joins in worshiping their gods. Finally, unable to distinguish right from wrong, Solomon prefers strange gods to the one God. Then God speaks: Solomon's line will lose the throne and all the tribes but Judah.
    Read 1 Kings 11:1–13.
    By now Solomon's failure is a foregone conclusion.

Trouble Brewing as Solomon's Reign Ends

After forty years of harsh rule, the discontent of Solomon's people lures his enemies back from exile to harass him. One of these, **Jeroboam,** is chief of the labor force fortifying the Jerusalem walls. Disenchanted, Jeroboam leaves Jerusalem to go north and meets a prophet, who tears his cloak into twelve pieces, one for each tribe. He gives ten of them to Jeroboam and tells him God promises him the throne of Israel in the north if he will follow the ways of God. One tribe, the prophet says, will go to a son of Solomon, so that David's line might continue in Jerusalem.

Solomon orders Jeroboam killed, but he escapes to Egypt to await Solomon's death. When at last Solomon dies, the golden age of Israel comes to an end.

Read 1 Kings 11:26–36,40–43.

In forty years Solomon has led Israel from a union of tribes under David, loyal to the Covenant, to subjection and near slavery, not to mention to the impending breakup of the kingdom. Although Israel is oppressed by taxes and forced labor, idolatry is the worst of the burdens it has inherited from its golden ruler. The nation, whose identity rests on its fidelity to God, has been led to the worship of false gods.

Nationhood Revisited

Why did Israel become a nation? There were good reasons, of course. The people wanted unity and strong leadership in the face of threats like the Philistines. Nationhood, too, would make long-term stability and continuity more possible for the Israelites.

Yet with nationhood came many evils—power struggles and betrayals, greed and oppression in the lust for wealth and honor, and the turning away from God, who had made the Israelites a people in the first place.

Imagine the exiles in Babylon wondering, How did we end up in this disaster of exile? With the help of the Deuteronomists, they began to get answers to that troubling question. They saw how they had grown to become a great nation and how that nation had begun to go wrong. It was one thing to sin and repent, as David had done. It was quite another to harden one's heart against God, as Solomon had. So the people recognized that the Covenant had been broken not by God but by kings like Solomon and most of the ones after him.

Questions for Reflection and Discussion

1. Does the Israelites' desire for a king have any parallels in our culture?

2. Read 1 Samuel 2:1–10 and Luke 1:46–55. Mary's Magnificat is said to have been modeled after Hannah's hymn of praise when she gives Samuel to God. What attitudes have you taken on from someone who has been a part of your tradition or heritage?

3. Samuel is described as both a judge and a priest, implying that in Israel, politics and religion were inseparable. Given the recent histories of countries who have tried to combine government and religion into theocracies, what would you judge to be the advantages and disadvantages of theocracy?

4. Is it possible for God to rule over us today even though we have elected officials in our local and national government? What does God's rule mean in a democracy or republic?

5. What does it mean for a nation to be a "light to all the others"? Do you think our country is like this?

6. "The key to their success will be fidelity to God." Comment on this notion as it applies to your life, to someone you know, or to a group of people.

7. Who has taught you the positive meaning and use of power? What did they teach you?

8. Politics at its worst can involve using or oppressing people. What does it look like at its best?

9. Considering your own flaws and weaknesses, do you believe it is possible that God can work through you in spite of these? Have you ever experienced that? What happened?

10. Who or what do you look to for wisdom?

11. Being portable, the ark held the Covenant of a people on a journey. The Temple, on the other hand, was set in stone, representing security and stability. Reflect on how both the ark and the Temple can signify God's presence with us.

7

Crying Out the Word of God

Why, O LORD, do you stand far off?
    Why do you hide yourself in times of trouble?
In arrogance the wicked persecute the poor—
    let them be caught in the schemes they have
        devised.

For the wicked boast of the desires of their heart,
    those greedy for gain curse and renounce the LORD.
In the pride of their countenance the wicked say,
        "God will not seek it out";
    all their thoughts are, "There is no God."

Their ways prosper at all times;
    your judgments are on high, out of their sight;
    as for their foes, they scoff at them.
They think in their heart, "We shall not be moved;
    throughout all generations we shall not meet
        adversity."

. . . .

Rise up, O LORD; O God, lift up your hand;
    do not forget the oppressed.
Why do the wicked renounce God,
    and say in their hearts, "You will not call us to
        account"?

But you do see! Indeed you note trouble and grief,
    that you may take it into your hands;
the helpless commit themselves to you;
    you have been the helper of the orphan.

. . . .

O LORD, you will hear the desire of the meek;
>   you will strengthen their heart, you will incline your
>   ear
to do justice for the orphan and the oppressed,
>   so that those from earth may strike terror no more.

(Psalm 10)

The First and Second Books of Kings, put in final form by the Deuteronomists during the exile, show how things went wrong for Israel, and why God's people ended up defeated and captive in Babylon some three centuries after Solomon.

The Books of Kings tell the story of the breakup of the kingdom of Israel into **two kingdoms** of north and south, **Israel** and **Judah,** and the abandonment of the Covenant by the people, led by their mostly wicked kings. During this time major empires, like the Egyptian, the Assyrian, the Babylonian, and the Persian, were rising and falling as

World Happenings
Between 900 and 600 B.C.E.

Africa
As the Saharan region in North Africa dries up, the inhabitants shift from using horses to camels as mounts and beasts of burden. In this same region, the Phoenicians found the city of Carthage and establish a trading empire in the western part of the Near East.

America
Earlier worship of jaguars as fierce and powerful totems develops into widely successful jaguar cults. Among the Olmecs of Mexico and the Chavin of Peru, these beasts are worshiped at great ceremonial centers.

they fought for as much of the known world as they could control, including the regions of Israel and Judah.

The northern and southern kingdoms had to pay tribute to these foreign powers to keep themselves from being overrun and enslaved. Or at times they agreed to submit to the sovereignty of one empire in exchange for being protected against another. As if that were not enough chaos to handle, at various times Israel and Judah actually were at war with each other.

During the slide toward disaster, first of Israel, then of Judah, prophets came forward. Called by God, they warned the people that they had strayed from true worship and had forgotten their role of witness to the Lord before the nations. Because the prophets were faithful to this call, they became the conscience of Israel (both Israel and Judah), risking their life to condemn the moral laxity of kings and the decadence of their people. Their harsh criticism of greed and idolatry endeared them to only a few followers.

China
Under the Chou dynasty, an aristocracy rules fiefdoms and presides over the practice of ancestor worship.

Europe
The Iron Age arrives and with it come the Celts, who use iron tools and weapons to hew and hack their way through central Europe.

India
Hindu priests become the most powerful caste within the social order. Wandering sages, disenchanted with religious rituals, practice yoga and meditation as a means of discovering wisdom.

The Near East
The Assyrian Empire reaches the height of its glory, then disappears when its capital, Nineveh, is destroyed in 612 B.C.E.

But the prophets' ringing accusations and pleas for fidelity and goodness have become a literature ranked among the noblest writings of the ancient world and among the most useful for the modern world.

We have already met two of the **former, or nonwriting, prophets:** Samuel, who rejected Saul's flawed kingship and anointed David as king; and Nathan, who denounced David's adultery. In the Books of Kings we meet two more of the nonwriting prophets, **Elijah** and **Elisha.** Appealing tales about them, a combination of history and legend, were probably collected and passed along by their disciples.

We will also meet for the first time some of the **latter,** or **writing, prophets,** whose messages are passed on to us in separate books of the Bible, which are named for them. Among the writing prophets are **Amos,** a herdsman; **Hosea,** a betrayed husband; the great **Isaiah** of Jerusalem, a confidant and counselor of kings; and **Micah,** a devotee of the poor.

The prophets addressed impassioned pleas to the kings of the north and the south to turn from idol worship and injustice and return to Israel's true God. Most of the kings refused to listen and, together with their people, continued to be self-serving. Inevitably this led both kingdoms to exile.

Two Kingdoms: Israel and Judah

Following the death of Solomon, the people of the south accept his son **Rehoboam** as their king. But the northern tribes set forth a condition for accepting him as king: Rehoboam must not oppress them as his father did. The elders of the court agree, and advise the young king to be a servant to his people, not a slave driver. But Rehoboam instead heeds the counsel of his young comrades, who call for more brutality, and the northern tribes reject him. Thus all Israel is divided into two kingdoms—Israel in the north, Judah in the south—and the unifying work of David is destroyed in the space of two generations. Rehoboam carries on David's royal line, or the house of David, in the south.

When the rebel Jeroboam is declared king in the north, he immediately breaks the Law of God and enshrines two golden calves, one at Dan and the other at Bethel. Then Jeroboam raises up non-Levite priests to offer sacrifices in the north, hoping to keep his people from going south to Jerusalem to worship, where they might rekindle their loyalty to the house of David. His strategy fails, as his dynasty only briefly outlives him.

Read 1 Kings 12:1–20,25–33; 13:33–34.

The Israelite tribes, as Jeroboam could have anticipated, soon turned to worshiping the golden calf itself, a terrible betrayal of their relationship with God. Jeroboam's rationalized deed only brought disaster. Many actions of Israel's unfaithful kings that we now view as wicked probably seemed only smart to the kings at the time.

The Wicked Kings of the North

The history of the northern kings of Israel reads like a police blotter: A string of violent deaths follows the reign of Jeroboam, as the assassination of a king and his whole family becomes a common way for a rival to assume the throne. The sixth king, **Omri**, builds a splendid capital city, **Samaria**, but he, like his predecessors, does "evil in the sight of the LORD" (1 Kings 16:25)—but more so. He is succeeded by his son **Ahab**, the worst of them all. Ahab marries the Phoenician princess **Jezebel**, a fiendishly wicked woman, and they become the villains in the stories about the prophets Elijah and Elisha.

Read 1 Kings 16:23–33.

The marriage of King Ahab to the pagan Jezebel is recorded with horror by the Deuteronomists, who knew that Jezebel went on to insist that Baal, not the Lord, be worshiped in Israel. Why did Ahab marry her? Such marriages between royalty of two nations—in this case Israel and Phoenicia—were common ways of building protective alliances against hostile empires. In Ahab's case his marriage gained for Israel the military strength of Phoenicia, but that came at a big price—putting Baal in God's place.

The Prophets Elijah and Elisha in the North

How could the people of Israel become what God had called them to be when each king was worse than the last? Who could speak of God to them?

The answer to these questions was the prophets Elijah and Elisha, nonwriting prophets of the northern kingdom. Among the Israelites, they alone had no interest in power, money, or any approval but God's. They saw, heard, and spoke nothing but God.

Prophesying is often seen as a kind of crystal ball gazing that foresees the future, but the prophets of Israel based their pronouncements on the will of God. When the kings became obsessed with power and wealth and led their people into idolatry, God called upon certain individuals to warn Israel of the consequences, and those individuals were the prophets.

The purpose of the stories in the Books of Kings about Elijah and Elisha—especially when told to the exiles in Babylon—was to show that when God spoke through the prophets, God expected Israel to listen. Elijah and Elisha were historical figures who, without a doubt, tangled with Ahab and Jezebel. Their period was the reigns of the kings of Israel from Ahab to Joash—from about 874 to 796 B.C.E.

Elijah Nourished by a Starving Widow

The stories about Elijah open with God's sending Elijah to tell King Ahab that he will be punished by a terrible drought, because apparently Queen Jezebel has ordered the slaughter of all the prophets of Israel. Elijah is next sent to hide by a stream, where ravens will feed him. When the stream goes dry, he is sent to the village of Zarephath in Sidon (Phoenicia), where a widow will care for him. Upon his arrival Elijah sees the woman and asks her for water and a crust of bread. But she has only enough flour and oil, she says, to make a barley cake for herself and her son before they die of starvation. Elijah promises God's help if she will divide the cake with him. The widow does, and afterward, until the drought is over, her jar of flour and jug of oil are never empty.

Read 1 Kings 17:1–16.

The obedience of Elijah is contrasted with the disobedience of the king. The prophet goes on a dangerous errand, entrusts his survival to ravens, and asks a starving woman for her last bit of bread. The woman, a pagan like Jezebel, hears the word of God and also obeys. It is a simple tale about saying yes to God and trusting that God will provide whatever is needed.

Jesus told his own people in Nazareth that the pagan widow of Zarephath had more faith and heard the prophets more clearly than they did. They confirmed this by immediately trying to push him off a cliff.

Read Luke 4:20–30.

Victory over the Prophets of Baal

Elijah remains with the widow of Zarephath until God sends him back to the court of Ahab. When Ahab blames Elijah for the drought, Elijah challenges the prophets of Baal to a contest to see whose god can produce rain. The prophets (priests in some versions) call to Baal in vain. Elijah taunts them to call louder—perhaps Baal is meditating, napping, or on a journey. The prophets slash themselves in an ecstatic frenzy—but no rain.

Then Elijah builds an altar to the Lord, digs a trench around it, arranges wood for a fire, kills a bull for sacrifice, and has the people—who have been shilly-shallying between Baal and God—drench it with water. He calls for a show of God's power, and fire (perhaps lightning) comes down to consume the bull, the wood, and the stones, even lap up the water. The unfaithful people fall to the ground and worship the God of Israel. Then Elijah has the prophets of Baal killed.

Read 1 Kings 18:17–40.

In this story Elijah accuses the people of halfheartedness in their faith: They must make up their mind. Biblical faith calls for commitment, not standing on the sidelines being careful.

Read Luke 11:23.

God in the Breeze

Angry at Elijah's victory over the prophets of Baal, Jezebel threatens his life. So Elijah flees to the desert, where an angel tells him to journey on to Horeb (Mount Sinai). There he takes shelter in a cave, and when God asks why he has come, Elijah, filled with self-pity, pours out his woe. There is no point in going on, he mourns; all Israel but he, Elijah, has abandoned God.

God bids Elijah to stand outside the cave to experience the presence of God. First Elijah hears a powerful wind, then he feels an earthquake, then he sees a fire, but God is not in them. At last a gentle breeze ("a sound of sheer silence" [1 Kings 19:12] or "a tiny whispering sound" [NAB]) speaks to Elijah of the presence of God, and Elijah hides his face in shame at his own disbelief and in gratitude for the patience of God. God sends Elijah back to work, reminding him that he is not the only one who cares, that seven thousand Israelites have remained faithful.

Read 1 Kings 19:1–18.

Elijah, feeling that he has failed, needs the strength of God's presence. God's strength comes to him not in a showy display but in the simplest way. God is like that for us. We may not find God's power in obvious successes or triumphs but in the quiet movement of God in our everyday life.

Condemning Ahab's Greed for a Vineyard

In another Elijah story, King Ahab wants a vineyard belonging to a man named Naboth, but Naboth refuses him because it is his ancestral land. When Ahab sulks to Jezebel about this refusal, she arranges for Naboth to be killed. She gets false witnesses to testify that Naboth cursed God and the king and thus deserves death by stoning. So Naboth is killed, and because the property of a condemned person reverts to the king, Ahab gets his vineyard.

God sends Elijah to curse Ahab. Elijah tells the king that as dogs licked the blood of Naboth, they will lick Ahab's blood and devour Jezebel. Elijah also predicts that

Ahab's line will disappear. All these things eventually do come to pass.

Read 1 Kings 21:1–29; 22:29–38.

Why did God allow the villainy of Ahab and Jezebel? The people of Israel recognized that all are free to choose either good or evil. Unfortunately, when someone chooses evil, it often destroys the innocent. The answer to "I can't believe in a God who would let this happen" is "God didn't; *people* did."

Off in a Chariot of Fire

Elijah, aware that his life is over, goes to the Jordan River with Elisha, a man who had earlier become his devoted follower. There he parts the water with his cloak, and the two cross over. In their last moments together, Elisha asks for a double portion of Elijah's spirit. Suddenly a flaming chariot with fiery horses comes between the two, and Elijah disappears in a whirlwind. Elisha watches, crying out. He tears his own cloak in half, strikes the Jordan's water with Elijah's cloak, and returns across the riverbed. For three days a community of prophets of the region search for Elijah but fail to find him.

Read 2 Kings 2:1–17.

Did the fiery chariot really appear and take Elijah to heaven? The storytellers had Elisha alone witness this event. The fiery chariot image may have been chosen to describe the fiery Elijah, who spoke out so fearlessly before the most powerful of the land—Ahab, Jezebel, the priests of Baal, and the entire court.

Eventually this tale gave rise to the belief that Elijah would return to announce the coming of the Messiah. This tradition was the basis for references to Elijah in the Gospel stories of Jesus and John the Baptist. In Luke, the priest Zechariah announces that John the Baptist has "'the spirit and power of Elijah'" (1:17). In the Gospel of John, John the Baptist is asked if he is Elijah. Later, Elijah appears at the Transfiguration of Jesus.

Read Luke 1:13,17; John 1:19–21; Luke 9:28–33.

Elisha's Miracles

From that time on, Elisha carries on the mission of his mentor, Elijah. His story is an unbroken succession of wonders. Elisha purifies Jericho's water supply, which has been causing deaths and miscarriages. He helps a widow avoid selling her children to pay her debts. He blesses a childless couple, and they beget a son. Later he raises this child from the dead in a manner that strangely suggests artificial respiration. He purifies poisoned stew and multiplies loaves of bread to make enough for a hundred people.

Elisha becomes known, even among foreigners, for his healing powers. In one incident Elisha cures Naaman, a commander in the Syrian army, of leprosy. He does this by having a servant tell Naaman to wash seven times in the Jordan River. Naaman balks at doing this because it seems so simple, but when he gives in and bathes in the river, he is cured. A grateful and humbler Naaman returns to Elisha, believing in Elisha's God. He offers Elisha gifts, but the prophet refuses them. Then Naaman asks for earth from Israel to take home so that every day he can stand and pray to God on Israel's soil.

Even in death Elisha has a healing touch. One story tells of how, after Elisha's burial, a dead man's body is thrown into Elisha's grave, and when it touches the prophet's bones, it springs to life.

Read 2 Kings 2:19–22; 4:1–44; 5:1–19; 13:20–21.

All four Gospels have accounts of Jesus miraculously multiplying loaves of bread for the hungry crowd, as well as Jesus healing many who came to him in trust. The multiplication of loaves by both Elisha and Jesus were signs of God's loving concern for people, as were the healings they did of the sick and the leprous.

We have seen in the Books of Kings the marvelous stories of the nonwriting prophets Elijah and Elisha, of the northern kingdom. Next, we turn to the writing prophets of the north, Amos and Hosea.

Amos and Hosea in the North

If, at first glance, the prophets all seem alike, it is for a good reason: They were concerned about the same things. They called Israel and Judah to remember the God who saved them, who made a Covenant with them, who wanted them to return to it and be a blessing to the nations. The prophets' language and symbolic actions said long ago what still needs saying today. However, in other ways the prophets were not alike. Their personalities, backgrounds, ways of speech, and actions were very different.

Amos: A Cry Against Riches Gained by Injustice

The time is about 750 B.C.E., and Jeroboam II is king in prosperous Israel. Amos, a shepherd from Judah, goes north to preach against the sinful kingdom of Israel. Amos is harsh, blunt, and angry—a prophet who is said to roar like a lion.

Amos first appears at Bethel in the north where, after the breakup of David's kingdom, Jeroboam I set up a golden calf. Amos's rustic garments are a sharp contrast to the worshipers' rich attire, but the worshipers recognize the voice of a prophet when he speaks. He condemns their unjust, exploitative actions toward the poor and the weak, and tells them God will punish them for this.

In Samaria, the capital of the kingdom, Amos condemns the rich women of Samaria, comparing them to fat cattle. He describes them lying on their couches and ivory beds and calling to their husbands, "Bring us drinks." They eat lamb and veal from the flocks, drink wine from bowls, and anoint their skin with perfumed oil—all at the expense of the poor. Amos warns that it will not last; the day will come when, like dead animals, they will be dragged away with hooks through their noses and deposited on the refuse heap outside the city.

Read Amos 1:1–2; 2:6–8; 3:1–2,9–11,15; 4:1–3.

Amos is not some disgruntled yokel who resents the rich. He is angered by Israel's disregard for God's Law, so designed to protect the people—both the poor from going hungry and the rich from becoming greedy. The Law was given to Israel when it was called to be God's nation, but now Israel has become like other nations: wealth is in the hands of a few, justice has been corrupted, and poor people are oppressed.

In an eloquent passage said to have been the favorite of Dr. Martin Luther King Jr., Amos says that the Lord hates and abominates processions, sacrifices, and hymn singing that do not come from sincere hearts. God wants hearts from which justice rolls down "like water, / and righteousness like an ever-flowing stream" (Amos 5:24).

Read Amos 5:21–24.

Through Amos's prophesying, God condemns not formal worship but empty worship, in which rituals of praise and sacrifice to God are not backed up with just actions toward others. False worship continues to be a problem in modern times. Before the civil rights laws and desegregation, widespread discrimination existed in many Christian churches in the United States—with African Americans unwelcome in white churches. Various forms of discrimination still exist in some churches.

Amos's Visions of Israel's Final Fate

Amos has visions of Israel's final fate, insights that come to him while he works. Watching locusts eating the crops, Amos sees that Israel is helpless to survive the fate it has brought upon itself. Seeing fire ravage the land during the dry season, he sees Israel being destroyed by the people's sin. Amos sees God measuring a crooked wall, about to collapse, with a plumb line, and he sees that Israel is also about to collapse. Referring to Israel as Jacob, Amos pleads for Israel to God. At first God relents, but finally says that Israel has chosen evil; God will leave it to its own destruction.

Amos crosses the line too many times with the powers that be in Israel, and he is ordered by the high priest at Bethel to go back to Judah. He goes, but not without telling off the high priest.

Read Amos 7:1–17; 8:4–12; 9:8–15.

Hosea: God as a Betrayed Husband

A line of corrupt kings makes the last years of Israel (786 to 721 B.C.E.) a sordid tale. During this period, toward the end of Jeroboam II's reign, the prophet Hosea from the northern kingdom appears. Hosea is involved in a terrible marriage. **Gomer,** the wife he loves, has deserted Hosea for other lovers—as Israel has deserted God for the Canaanite god Baal. Hosea, out of his own experience of betrayal, finds the words for his oracles to unfaithful Israel.

When Hosea speaks of himself and Gomer, he is telling Israel a parable of its own betrayal of God. If we keep this in mind, we will understand him clearly. The first three chapters of the Book of Hosea deliver his message. The remaining eleven chapters are fragments of oracles condemning Israel's sin.

As the book opens, God commands Hosea to take an unfaithful wife. That is, he is to take a wife who later will be discovered to be unfaithful. Looking back, Hosea sees his call to marry Gomer as prophetic. Without his own heartbreak, he could never have understood the magnitude of Israel's betrayal of God.

Hosea and Gomer have three children, to whom Hosea is told to give strange names. In telling his story to the Israelites, Hosea knows these names are symbolic of how God regards the children of the Covenant with Israel. The names stand for or mean literally "shameful butchery," "not pitied," and "not my people." By the time the third name is spoken, the people recognize what Hosea is saying—that God will break the Covenant. A more threatening image could not exist. No matter how it sinned, Israel has always presumed that God's Covenant with it would stave off punishment.

Read Hosea 1:1–9.

Be Exiled, but Come Back to Me

Chapter 2 of Hosea takes place in a divorce court, where Hosea testifies to Gomer's unfaithfulness and ingratitude. He is angry, and his plans for her punishment are harsh.

She has forgotten that he gave her everything she ever had—grain, wine, oil, silver, and gold. He will take these things away. She has even credited her lovers with the gifts Hosea gave her. He will punish her until at last she is abandoned and forlorn and returns to him.

As Hosea's story proceeds and he speaks of his longing to forgive Gomer and be reunited with her, he fantasizes of days to come. Strangely, his voice seems to be replaced by the Lord's, as though God is speaking now without the pretext of the parable. God speaks hopefully of the future with Israel:

> Therefore, I will now allure her,
>> and bring her into the wilderness,
>> and speak tenderly to her.
> From there I will give her her vineyards,
>> and make the Valley of Achor a door of hope.
> There she shall respond as in the days of her youth,
>> as at the time when she came out of the land
>> of Egypt.
>
> (Hosea 2:14–15)

God and Israel will remarry. In a canticle of joy, God promises to make up for every deprivation Israel has suffered. Every good gift will be restored, and their children (the Israelites) will be renamed.

God tells Hosea to seek out Gomer and pay a bride-price for her again—or a ransom should she be a slave or in the hire of Baal's priests as a temple prostitute. Then, after she has been through a period of waiting and faithfulness, he is to take her back.

Read Hosea 2:2–23 (or 2:4–25 in NAB or NJB); 3:1–5.

Hosea is the first book to feature the relationship between God and Israel as a marriage and to use the language and images of marriage in describing it. To God, "infidelity" in Israel's behavior means betrayal of justice, compassion, integrity, or true worship; or as Hosea says, Israel "played the harlot" (2:7, NAB).

According to the custom of the times, Gomer could be sentenced to death for her infidelity. Instead, Hosea wants to punish his wife for a while but then take her back tenderly. Similarly, Hosea is saying that God will not wipe out the Israelites even though they deserve it. God will let Israel go through a time of exile and abandonment, and this experience will eventually bring Israel back into its loving relationship with the Lord.

Assyria Defeats and Scatters Israel

Even with the warnings of prophets like Amos and Hosea, chaos and infidelity to God abound in Israel. Palace revolutions, assassinations of kings, and worship of Baal continue to weaken the nation. Israel turns more and more to making deals with foreign powers for security in a hostile world rather than trusting in God. But the overwhelming might of the **Assyrians**—the fiercest, most brutal empire of the ancient Near East—makes it impossible for Israel to be secure. Finally, after a long siege of Israel's capital, Samaria, the Assyrians take the city; the northern kingdom of Israel is finished. The date, as we estimate it today, is 721 B.C.E.

Assyria deports thousands of Israelites, particularly their leaders, forcing them to live in exile in the Assyrian Empire. The Assyrians put their own people in charge of the land that once was Israel, and they bring in foreign colonists, who will intermarry with the locals. In the Second Book of Kings, the scriptural text describing the dismantling of the northern tribes ends tersely: "The LORD was very angry with Israel and removed them out of his sight; none was left but the tribe of Judah alone" (17:18).

Read 2 Kings 17:5–24.

Scripture scholars tell us that some of the Israelites fled south to Judah, where they knew they would have common religious roots. They hoped that despite past periods of war between Israel and Judah, the southern kingdom would accept them as their fellow Chosen People of God. Some of the fleeing northerners brought their traditional stories and writings with them to Judah. Many of these stories found their way into the Scriptures as they were edited centuries later during the Babylonian exile.

The Samaritans

Later in the history of Judaism and in the Gospels of the New Testament, we run into people called **Samaritans**, who were intensely disliked by the Jews. They were the descendants of those Israelites who remained in the north after Samaria's collapse (generally the common folk, not the leaders) and intermarried with the foreign colonists brought in by Assyria. So, centuries later, they were like distant lost cousins to the people of Judah. The Samaritans' religion, while it had traces of the old Israelite worship, was seen by Jews of the south as polluted with paganism. So they had no time or regard for anything or anyone Samaritan.

The Assyrians

Sometime after 2000 B.C.E., history began to hear from the Assyrians, a Semitic group that took its name from its major city, Assur. The story of Assyria tells about alternating periods of domination and decline and about the struggle for leadership of the region against the rulers of Babylon, about two hundred miles southeast of Assur. Assyria was located in the area now belonging to northern Iraq.

The Babylonians are best remembered as culture lovers, and the Assyrians have a reputation as warmongers. The Assyrians often tried to negotiate disputes with their neighbors, but more frequently their kings adopted tactics of terror that made them feared and despised throughout the Near East.

The height of Assyrian domination came in the seventh century B.C.E. In the reign of Ashurbanipal (668 to 627 B.C.E.), the Assyrians ruled the largest empire in the world—including all of Iraq, Syria, Lebanon, and Jordan; much of Egypt; and some of Turkey.

Historians compare the Assyrians to the Romans. Like these later empire builders, the Assyrians became efficient administrators and war tacticians. They were one of the first nations to train a professional army and to deploy it in formal lines of battle. Just as the Romans borrowed much of their culture from the Greeks, the Assyrians embraced the Babylonians' literature and their religious, economic, and legal concepts. The Assyrians' lasting achievement was Ashurbanipal's library in his capital city, Nineveh. It contained twenty thousand tablets on such topics as history, astronomy, and mathematics.

At its peak the Assyrian Empire was overextended, undefendable, and doomed to collapse. In 612 B.C.E., fifteen years after Ashurbanipal's death, Nineveh fell to the Babylonians.

Isaiah in the South

The greatest of the writing prophets was Isaiah, although the Book of Isaiah was composed by more than one "Isaiah." But before looking at the First Isaiah's message, let's back up two centuries to see what events led up to his prophesying in Judah to the south while Israel in the north was heading for its own disaster.

The Southern Kingdom of Judah

Each kingdom—Judah and Israel—had its own kings after Solomon's death in about 922 B.C.E. But the kings of Judah had one major difference from those of the northern kingdom. Whereas Israel's kings came from a variety of families, Judah's kings all the way down to the Babylonian exile were of the house, or family line, of David. So the kings of Judah felt rather proud of that, and secure in the knowledge that their line would continue unbroken.

After David's son Solomon died, his son Rehoboam ascended to the throne and made a point of being harsh and cruel to the northerners. The breakup of the united nation of Israel into two kingdoms followed shortly after that. Besides being a harsh ruler, Rehoboam started things off on a bad foot for Judah by being unfaithful to God.

After Rehoboam the record of the southern kings was mixed but mostly bad. There were a few reformers, like Hezekiah and Josiah. But for the most part, Judah's kings were as bad as the kings of the north. They allowed worship of Baal; in some cases they even made room for it in the Temple. Besides that, they were as murderous and treacherous as Israel's kings, with royal assassinations being common.

By the 740s B.C.E., Judah had become idolatrous, prosperous, and greedy. At this time Isaiah had a vision in the Temple at Jerusalem in which he answered God's call to become a prophet to his nation that was in such trouble. The Book of Isaiah is named for this man, the greatest of Judah's prophets.

The Book of Isaiah is the longest and most influential of the prophetic books, covering from two hundred to two hundred and fifty years and written by a number of authors. It is usually recognized as falling into three parts, the work of three principal authors:

- **First Isaiah,** or **Isaiah of Jerusalem,** who pleaded with Judah's kings and people before the Babylonian exile— chapters 1 to 39
- **Second Isaiah,** who spoke during and at the end of the exile—chapters 40 to 55
- **Third Isaiah,** who was with the people when they returned to Judah from exile—chapters 56 to 66

The entire collection is named after Isaiah of Jerusalem because he was the first and most important contributor. The other "Isaiahs" seem to fall into the category of disciples who shared his vision and passionate desire to bring Israel back to God.

The Book of Isaiah is a story of infidelity, suffering, repentance, and consolation for the people—and of threats, condemnations, promises, and comfort by the prophets. This story is told not so much in events as in oracles and poetry. Isaiah contains some of the most beautiful language in the Bible, spoken by people who were geniuses and saints.

First Isaiah, Isaiah of Jerusalem

Isaiah son of Amoz was probably a lad in Judah when the prophet Amos (no relation) preached in Israel. Isaiah lived in Jerusalem during the reigns of four kings of Judah, including the abominable Ahaz and his surprisingly faithful son Hezekiah. Isaiah was married and the father of at least two sons, and he was familiar with the court and a counselor to kings. His Hebrew, the best in the prophetic writings, suggests a high-placed, well-educated—perhaps even priestly—family background.

When the young Isaiah has a vision of God in the Temple at Jerusalem (about 742 B.C.E.), Judah is in serious peril because of its injustice to the poor and its practice of idolatry. Israel, to the north, has not yet been exiled, but the Assyrian Empire looms ominously over both the northern and southern kingdoms.

The threat of Assyrian invasion sets the scene for the forty years of First Isaiah's career. Israel and Judah, fearful of Assyria, are in danger of invasion, and Israel joins a coalition of neighboring states to stave off the empire. But Judah refuses to participate in that alliance and instead tries to solve the problem by becoming a vassal of Assyria and paying tribute—all the while dreading the day when its "landlord" might want more.

"Sinful Nation"

The Book of Isaiah does not start in chronological order with the vision and call of Isaiah in the Temple. Rather, the first five chapters get right to the hard message of Isaiah: a savage condemnation of Judah and Jerusalem for infidelity and corruption. These chapters are broken briefly by a hope-filled passage about a day of reconciliation.

The prophet decries the greed and injustice of Jerusalem's leaders and warns that God will punish them if they do not change. He calls Judah to trust in God, not to plot ways to avoid invasion.

The Lord is a forgiving God, no matter how grave the sin. Isaiah assures the people that God promises forgiveness if Judah and Jerusalem will turn from injustice and idolatry. God can make sin that is as red as scarlet to be as white as snow, sin like bloodstained garments to be as white as new wool. A change of heart can show Judah and Jerusalem new ways to solve the dilemma with Assyria. Repentance and prayer can open them to the wisdom of God, who knows how things work.

God will protect the people of Judah—but if they ignore the Lord, no treaty or alliance will be able to save them. Yet Judah and Jerusalem turn a deaf ear to Isaiah's warnings.

Read Isaiah 1:1–4,18–20,24–31.

Characteristic of Isaiah's message is his insistence on the majesty and glory of God. He calls God the one to whom all nations and creatures owe existence and, therefore, obedience and honor. Seeing Judah and Jerusalem ignore God's majesty and goodness is the cause of his rage.

To illustrate this point, in Isaiah 1:2–3 the fidelity of the ox and the donkey is contrasted with the infidelity of the people. Even the dumb ox and the stubborn donkey, Isaiah says, recognize their master—but Judah does not. This passage is probably the source of the ox and the donkey in the Christmas manger scene; the Gospels do not mention them.

A Punishment of Judah's Own Making

Isaiah describes the coming fall of Judah and Jerusalem and the people's deportation, first to Assyria and later to Babylon. Hero, warrior, judge, prophet, elder, captain, nobleman, counselor—all will be taken. Only the poor and the weak will be left in the land. Judah and Jerusalem "have brought evil on themselves," says God (Isaiah 3:9). Their leaders have devoured God's "vineyard" (v. 14), wresting loot from the poor, grinding down the helpless. Their punishment is their own doing. They, not God, are responsible for it.

Isaiah's language concerning the "daughters of Zion" (v. 17), or the rich women of Jerusalem, makes Amos's berating of the women of Samaria sound mild.

Read Isaiah 3:1–24.

The Vineyard Song: A Brokenhearted Lover

The Vineyard Song is like a country music ballad telling of a brokenhearted lover lamenting betrayal by a faithless sweetheart. It starts with Isaiah telling the story of a friend, but soon that text changes to the first person, and the betrayed lover is revealed to be God, the unfaithful lover to be Judah.

Read Isaiah 5:1–7.

"Here Am I: Send Me!"

After five chapters that give the broad picture of how things were in Judah, Isaiah begins to focus on specific events and the people taking part in them: Isaiah's vision in the Temple, his status as a counselor to kings, and his efforts to make them listen to God.

In the Temple, probably on a feast day, Isaiah has a shattering experience of the All-holy One. He sees God enthroned, surrounded by chanting angels, with the divine presence filling the Temple. Overwhelmed by his own sinfulness, Isaiah fears that he will die because he has seen God. But an angel descends and with tongs picks a live coal from the altar and cleanses Isaiah's lips to cleanse him of his sinfulness. When a voice cries out, "'Whom shall I send?'" Isaiah answers, "'Here am I; send me.'" (Isaiah 6:8).

In answer God gives Isaiah a strange errand. He is to make the hearts of the people sluggish—dull their ears and close their eyes to the message of God. In other words, when Isaiah speaks the truth to hearts that are already hard, they will become all the more hardened—not a happy prospect for the young man. Isaiah asks how long this will continue and is told that it will be until exile.

Read Isaiah 6:1–13.

The angels' hymn in Isaiah 6:3 is sung daily in the contemporary Jewish morning service and is known to Catholic Christians as the Sanctus (meaning "holy") of the Mass. Seraphim with wings covering themselves have become a traditional symbol in religious art.

A Child Will Be Born: "God Is with Us"

God tells Isaiah to find Judah's young king **Ahaz** outside of Jerusalem, where he is preparing for a siege by Syria (Aram) and Israel (Ephraim), who are in league against him. Isaiah tells Ahaz that faith in God, not elaborate preparations, will overcome these enemies. The prophet bids Ahaz to ask God for a sign. But with a great show of false humility, the young king refuses to ask. He has already abandoned God, having sacrificed his son by fire and having worshiped false gods on the "high places."

Isaiah angrily replies that Ahaz will get a sign, like it or not: a virgin ("young woman" in Hebrew) will bear a son named **Immanuel,** meaning "God is with us."

Another of Isaiah's prophecies of a blessed child to come tells of titles the child will have that belong only to the greatest of all kings, one who will rule forever.

In another passage Isaiah prophesies that from the "stump of Jesse" (that is, the roots of David's father, Jesse) will come a child who will lead the people to a time of peace never before experienced, symbolized by the contented friendship of traditional enemies from the animal world—like the wolf and the lamb, the calf and the lion (Isaiah 11:1,6).

Read Isaiah 7:1–14; 9:2–7 (or 9:1–6 in NAB or NJB); 11:1–9.

The Future King

Isaiah's oracle about the birth of Immanuel has been interpreted in various ways but not, at the time, as a passage about a coming messiah. In the days of Isaiah of Jerusalem, belief in a messiah had not yet developed, so the prophecy seemed to refer to the future birth of a perfect Davidic prince who would rule Judah in an age of peace and justice—thus "God is with us."

Christians have always believed that Isaiah's longing for the ideal king, through whom God would be revealed fully, was accomplished in the **Incarnation** of Jesus. Jesus was the **Messiah,** the one to whom Isaiah's prophecies pointed. The words of Isaiah about the birth of a savior child are understood as describing Jesus, and they are familiar to Christians from the liturgy of Christmas:

> For a child has been born for us,
>   a son given to us;
> authority rests upon his shoulders;

and he is named
   Wonderful Counselor, Mighty God,
      Everlasting Father, Prince of Peace.

(Isaiah 9:6)

Read Matthew 1:22–23.

Jerusalem Is Saved from Assyria

In the Second Book of Kings (chapter 16), Assyria comes at Ahaz's invitation and seizes Judah's enemies, Israel and Syria. So Judah is rescued though not by God's power but by a worldly empire. Ahaz must become a vassal of the Assyrian king in return for protection. To curry favor with his new "master," Ahaz eventually replaces God's altar in the Temple with one to an Assyrian god.

Fortunately, Ahaz's son **Hezekiah** is faithful to God. As king of Judah, he destroys the pagan shrines that his father had erected, and he insists that sacrifices be made only in the Jerusalem Temple. Naturally Isaiah is pleased with this turn of events. But meanwhile the northern kingdom of Israel is conquered by Assyria and its leading citizens are deported into exile (about 721 B.C.E.).

When Hezekiah flirts with the idea of revolting against Assyria, Isaiah must warn him away from this. To revolt against such a monstrous empire would be foolish. As a symbol of how Judah will be stripped bare if it revolts, Isaiah walks around Jerusalem in nothing but a loincloth.

A few years later (about 701 B.C.E.), the Assyrians have captured some of Judah's northern towns. Pressing in on Jerusalem, the Assyrian army is camped outside it, prepared to invade the capital. Even though Hezekiah has previously sent gold from the Temple as tribute to Assyria, this is not enough to keep Jerusalem from being crushed. Hezekiah turns to Isaiah in this dark moment, praying to the Lord for help, and Isaiah assures the king that the city will indeed be saved.

What happens next seems miraculous to the people of Jerusalem. During the night that the Assyrian army is poised to storm the capital, the "angel of the LORD" (2 Kings 19:35) strikes the soldiers down in their camp. Thousands of Assyrians are found dead in the morning. So the survivors, under their king, must retreat to their home capital, Nineveh.

Read 2 Kings 18:1–12; 19:14–20,32–36.

The Judahites, grateful to be spared in the nick of time in such an amazing fashion, see their good fortune as a sign of God's favor on Judah. It is one more assurance of God's Covenant with David—that his royal line of Judah's kings will last forever.

As the next chapter shows, this sense of divine protection will backfire on a later generation of Judahites. They will become complacent, refusing to acknowledge that Jerusalem can ever fall to its enemies and turning a deaf ear to prophets who warn them otherwise. "With God on our side," they will reason, "how can we ever be defeated? We can always count on God to work a miracle at the last minute, just like the night the Assyrian army was stricken by an angel of the Lord when they were about to storm Jerusalem."

Sincere trust, according to the Scriptures, goes much deeper than that.

First Isaiah Concludes:
Both Disaster *and* Hope Ahead

Isaiah of Jerusalem, as we might expect, is never lulled into complacency. He knows that in the future Judah will not be safe from suffering and even disaster if its kings and people disobey God. His words point to the day when Jerusalem (called Ariel or "altar hearth" in this passage) will be overcome by its enemies because the people's hearts are far from God. When they worship they are only going through the motions; their "wise" leaders are really foolish.

Isaiah, however, sees beyond the coming disastrous defeat (which will be, more than a century later, the Babylonian exile). On the other side of defeat, says Isaiah, is hope—hope for new life to bloom for Jerusalem out of the desert of exile.

Isaiah of Jerusalem leaves as his heritage a passion for God and an unquenchable hope that Israel will one day reclaim its role as a light to the nations. The Isaiahs who follow him continue his work—begging Israel to be Israel.

Read Isaiah 29:1–4,13–16; 35:1–10.

Micah: Sympathy from the Bottom of Society

In about the same time period as Isaiah of Jerusalem, there lived Micah, a man of humble origins from the countryside twenty or so miles from Jerusalem. Like Isaiah he was inspired to speak God's truth no matter how unpopular it made him. Unlike Isaiah, who was well educated, Micah's sympathy for the poor came from his own experience near the bottom rung of society's ladder—probably as a farmworker. His language is blunt and uncompromising, and his passionate condemnation of those who oppress the poor reveals an intimate knowledge of the sufferings of poverty.

The Book of Micah is short, only seven chapters, but it contains passages that have become universally known, such as the prophecy of a time of peace when the nations "shall beat their swords into plowshares" (4:3) and the eloquent description of what God requires of us: "to do justice, and to love kindness, / and to walk humbly with your God" (6:8).

Micah mourns the crimes of both Israel and Judah. Calling them both Jacob, he describes their sins, the ruin in store for them, and how he goes about lamenting them.

The rich, says Micah, lie in bed at night concocting schemes for depriving the poor. He vividly accuses the nation's rulers of exploiting the people, saying it is like the rulers are tearing the skin off the people and eating it, chopping up their bones like meat for a kettle of stew. But God will punish Jerusalem because of the wicked, unjust deeds of the people.

Read Micah 1:1–9; 2:1–4; 3:1–4,9–12.

Beat Swords into Plowshares

Micah calls for Israel to repent and return to God, and believes that it can happen. He writes hopefully of a time when the nations will walk in the way of the Lord, a time of justice and peace. Creating one of the world's most well-loved images of peacemaking from his own farming background, Micah imagines the day when the nations "shall beat their swords into plowshares, / and their spears into pruning hooks," and no one will train for war (Micah 4:3).

Read Micah 4:1–3.

Isaiah 2:2–4 contains an almost identical passage, and Micah perhaps was Isaiah's source.

Since the 1960s, a movement of peace activists in the United States has called itself the **Plowshares.** It has taken Micah's prophecy to heart, living it out in protests against war and the instruments of war. Plowshares' actions have been controversial. For instance, groups of Plowshares have entered production plants and hammered on the nose cones that carry nuclear warheads to symbolically "beat them into plowshares"—instruments of peace, not war. Even so, Micah would probably have understood these Plowshares' actions.

A Great Shepherd from Bethlehem

Micah foresees a day when a descendant of David's line—from little Bethlehem, the hometown of David—will rise up and lead Israel to the reign of peace and justice. He will shepherd his flock in the strength of the Lord, and "he shall be great / to the ends of the earth; / and he shall be the one of peace" (Micah 5:4–5).

Read Micah 5:2–5 (or 5:1–4 in NAB or NJB).

Christians have seen great significance in this passage from Micah, for it points not only to the family of David for the origins of a messiah-king but also to Bethlehem as the place from which the Messiah will come. Two of the Gospels—Matthew and Luke—situate the birth of Jesus in the town of Bethlehem.

What God Requires

In a beautiful, simple statement, Micah puts in perspective what God wants from the people, who are typically so prone to be misled by their own projections of what will impress God. No elaborate sacrificial offerings and rituals are required, Micah says, as he tries to point out the emptiness of showy displays. What God requires is the sincerity of the human heart, shown in justice, kindness, and humility.

Read Micah 6:6–8.

Is Anybody Listening?

Prophets like Elijah and Elisha, Amos and Hosea, and Isaiah and Micah certainly did their job of announcing God's point of view to the rich and powerful of Israel and Judah. They must have wondered, Is anybody listening? For the most part, no matter what the prophets said or did, both kingdoms continued on their downward trek of injustice and idolatry toward the pit of exile.

We might wonder, too, if the prophets had any impact. (Isaiah of Jerusalem did get a hearing from King Hezekiah, but he seems to have been an exception.) Was their risky, bold truth-telling all in vain?

The Deuteronomists, editing the history of the kingdoms in the Books of Kings, saw the whole thing from the perspective of the exile. For them, the answer to Is anybody listening? was, "Yes. *We* are. We who are in exile see clearly what you prophets were talking about. We have learned from you. Your message has taken root in us, and we will pass it on to future generations."

The words of the prophets continue to be passed on. Some of the great movements of this past century have found their inspiration from the prophets: the civil rights movement, the peace movement, the movements for national and global economic justice. Is anybody listening? Yes, some are. But in every age, humankind is challenged to listen again.

Questions for Reflection and Discussion

1. The Israelites turned to false gods, and we have a steady tendency to do the same. But, why do people turn to these kinds of false gods?

2. "We may not find God's power in big, obvious successes or triumphs but in the quiet movement of God in our everyday life." Does this ring true to your experience?

3. What experience from your life shows either the destructive effects of evil or the nature of good, which is fruitful and multiplies?

4. We use the word *miracle* to mean many things. What do you mean by *miracle?* Are there extraordinary miracles and ordinary miracles?

5. Who are the people in your life who keep calling you back to goodness? Who are your prophets?

6. If Hosea were to name his children to symbolize corruption in our time or in our country, what names do you think he might choose?

7. What are some prophetic messages of our time, that is, messages that challenge us—beyond what is comfortable—to be faithful?

8. Read Matthew 21:33–41. Jesus frequently quoted from the Book of Isaiah. Compare the symbols and message of the parable of the vineyard with those of the Vineyard Song.

9. Ponder the following questions:
   - Is the knowledge of God's willingness to forgive an encouragement to laxity and sin? Or does it inspire deeper love and gratitude?
   - What about the opinion that "a little fear never did anyone any harm"—meaning that the fear of hell and damnation is an inducement to avoid sin? Is it?

10. Some Scripture scholars consider Micah 6:8 to be the most powerful passage in his book. How is Micah 6:8 a complete statement of what God requires of Christians?

8

Prophets of Warning, Consolation, and Hope

O LORD, you have enticed me,
    and I was enticed;
you have overpowered me,
    and you have prevailed.
I have become a laughingstock all day long;
    everyone mocks me.
For whenever I speak, I must cry out,
    I must shout, "Violence and destruction!"
For the word of the LORD has become for me
    a reproach and derision all day long.
If I say, "I will not mention him,
    or speak any more in his name,"
then within me there is something like a burning fire
    shut up in my bones;
I am weary with holding it in,
    and I cannot.

(Jeremiah 20:7–9)

The Deuteronomists, who composed the biblical history, knew that all the injustice, infidelity, and idolatry of the two kingdoms, Israel and Judah, was to end in crushing defeat for them. First, Israel was defeated by the Assyrians. Then, as this chapter tells, Judah, under its own delusion that Jerusalem could never fall, was overrun by the Babylonians. Its Temple was destroyed, and its citizens captured and exiled to faraway Babylon. From the vantage point of the exile, the Deuteronomists pointed out the path the Chosen People had taken to their own destruction. The concluding five chapters of the Second Book of Kings complete the Deuteronomists' history, with accounts of the last of Judah's kings, the defeat of Judah and Jerusalem, and the exile itself.

The main focus for us is on the prophets. They confronted and warned the kings before the exile, and then turned around and consoled the people and offered them hope once they were defeated and captive in Babylon. The prophets' role was, as modern prophet Dorothy Day said, to both "comfort the afflicted and afflict the comfortable."

The story of the exile in this chapter takes us through the Second Book of Kings and covers these prophetic books:

- The Books of **Zephaniah, Nahum,** and **Habakkuk** speak briefly of a coming time when God's justice will finally be done.
- The Book of **Jeremiah** recounts that prophet's call, his futile struggle to make the kings listen to God's message, his persecution, the fall of Judah and Jerusalem, and the exile. It offers the hope of a new Covenant for Israel, written on the people's hearts, after the exile has purified them.
- The Book of **Lamentations** is a group of five poems expressing Judah's grief over the loss of Jerusalem.
- The Book of **Baruch,** although set in Babylon during the exile, was actually written centuries later when many Jews lived dispersed around the Greek Empire far from home and needed encouragement for the hope of return someday.
- The Book of **Ezekiel** tells of that prophet's symbolic actions, his acted-out messages from God before the exile about the impending disaster. During the exile Ezekiel offers a vision of hope and renewal to the people.
- Second Isaiah is filled with hope and expectation of the return to Jerusalem and a coming reign of peace. It also describes a mysterious servant of the Lord who suffers for the sake of the people.

Judah's Slippery Slope

The reforms initiated by Hezekiah, the good king who heeded Isaiah's advice, do not last long. His wicked son, **Manasseh**, next rules as king of Judah. Hopelessly dominated by the Assyrian Empire, Manasseh bows to their gods. He abandons God, puts pagan shrines in the Temple, offers his son as a sacrifice, and drenches Jerusalem in blood. The son who succeeds him is assassinated, but his grandson Josiah grows up to be king and one of Judah's great reformers.

A High Point on the Way Downhill

During King Josiah's repair of the Temple in about 622 B.C.E., a copy of the Book of the Law is found. (This was probably part of what later would be known as the Book of Deuteronomy.) When the king hears it read and then consults the prophetess Huldah to help explain it, he is appalled that Judah has abandoned the Law of God so shamelessly.

So Josiah leads the people in a renewal of the Covenant and a celebration of the Passover, and then commences his reforms. First he destroys pagan altars and executes pagan priests and temple prostitutes. Then, driving north, he reclaims territory lost to Judah for a hundred years—and Israel, it seems, will be its old self again. Assyria, now past its zenith, is fighting for its life far away.

The zealous reform helps slow down Judah's slide to ruin, but unfortunately it does not reverse it. Although external changes occur, most people's hearts are not affected enough to turn things around. Josiah is killed in a battle with Egypt's pharaoh in 609 B.C.E. The externals of his reform are undone as his son **Jehoiakim**, yet another terrible king, takes the throne of Judah as a puppet of Egypt.

Read 2 Kings 21:1–6,16; 22:1–20; 23:15,19–25.

Josiah's zeal for the Covenant, however, has left a deep and lasting impression on some of his followers. Sometime before the exile, a movement that calls the people back to the Covenant springs up. Its leaders—known by us as the

Deuteronomists—begin assembling Israel's ancient texts of its history. During and after the exile, they rework and edit these texts to compose the account we have been calling the Deuteronomic history. Without the Deuteronomists we probably would not have the Bible.

Other individuals during and after Josiah's lifetime call Judah to repentance and hope. Inspired in part by his reform, some of these individuals also inspire the Deuteronomists. These are the prophets of the years before the exile: Zephaniah, Nahum, Habakkuk, and, above all, Jeremiah. Of all the prophets, Jeremiah is the one whose spirit is most apparent in the work of the Deuteronomists.

Zephaniah: The Remnant

For almost a century after First Isaiah, there is no prophetic voice in Judah. Then Zephaniah speaks in about 630 B.C.E., during the early reign of Josiah, a few years before Jeremiah.

Zephaniah's three short chapters tell of "the day of the LORD" (2:3), a time of judgment not only for Judah's enemies but for the unfaithful of Judah and Jerusalem as well. On that day the guilty will be judged for their deeds, not for their religious affiliation.

Zephaniah introduces an idea only briefly touched on by Isaiah and Hosea: The unfortunate and impoverished, the "humble of the land," will become God's **remnant**, a new kind of "chosen people" from whom God will build the new Israel.

Read Zephaniah 2:3; 3:11–13.

Zephaniah's words would have sounded like heresy to the upper-class citizens of the time. The poor were considered sinners. Their poverty made it impossible for them to keep the laws about washing, contributing money, and offering sacrifices—because they could not buy animal offerings. If reduced to begging, people were outcasts; if ill, they were considered unclean. To the respectable Temple-going citizens, the poor were beyond the reach of God.

Words that exalted the lowly were as shocking to the self-satisfied citizens of Jesus' time as they were to the people in the days of Zephaniah—and as they are to some people today.

Read Luke 6:20–26.

Nahum: Nineveh Will Fall!

Nahum, a little-known prophet, prophesied during Josiah's reign. He spoke several years before Nineveh, the capital of Assyria, fell to the Babylonians in 612 B.C.E.

As the Book of Nahum's book opens, Josiah's reform is in full swing. Nahum is jubilant because it looks like Assyria, Judah's fiercest enemy, will soon be destroyed by Babylon. Assyria has bathed the Near East in blood for three hundred years, devising unspeakable butchery for its captives. Nahum—rejoicing that God will use Babylon as the instrument to punish Assyria—gloats over his vision of its vanquished soldiers, their shields scarlet with blood, and Assyria's queen and her ladies moaning with grief.

Encouraged by Josiah's ongoing reform, Nahum assumes that all will be well in Judah. Nahum does not call Judah to repentance but to hope, because it looks like Judah is getting back on track with the reform and Assyria is soon to be crushed by Babylon. Little does Nahum dream that Judah will become corrupt again and that God will use the same Babylon as an instrument for Judah's purification.

Read Nahum 2:1–9 (or 2:3–10 in NAB or NJB).

Habakkuk: Why, God, Why?

Habakkuk was probably a prophet in the Jerusalem Temple during the reign of Josiah's son, the detestable Jehoiakim—609 to 598 B.C.E. Habakkuk had a marvelous way with words and wrote his short book at God's bidding after a vision in the Temple. Its third chapter is actually a psalm, probably adapted from Temple worship.

In chapter 1, Habakkuk complains to God that he has prayed endlessly that Judah, corrupted under Jehoiakim, be punished for its injustice and violence. But his prayer has not been heard. Now he wants to know why. When God replies that his prayer *has* been heard and Judah will indeed be punished—by the Chaldeans (Babylonians)—Habakkuk is appalled. An exchange between Habakkuk and God finally leaves the prophet praising God and humbled by his own ignorance of divine ways.

Read Habakkuk 1:1–17; 2:1–20; 3:16–19.

Habakkuk's book is the first to introduce the question Why? Why, if God is present, does God seem not to be? Why, when God says that prayer will be answered, does it seem not to be? Why does God not stop human evil? Habakkuk's questioning was a bold step forward in the people's understanding of God: It is all right to challenge and question God.

Jeremiah: Persecuted for God's Sake

Jeremiah, who is one of the great tragic figures of the Bible, preached to the complacent, falsely secure Judahites in the years before the exile, and after Jerusalem was destroyed. Jeremiah communicated God's message not only through his words and oracles but also through his own life of suffering and struggle. His message of warning and of the suffering to come was an unwelcome one.

The role of a prophet is never easy, and that was especially true for Jeremiah. He did not relish the idea of confronting people with truths they did not want to hear. He longed for the security of a normal life, with friends and family who loved him. But instead he did not marry—which was unthinkable for young Jewish men in those days. He was despised and persecuted by the people he was trying to save, and he struggled with God and poured out his anguish over his miserable fate. In spite of repeated failures at reaching the people, he loved and served God all his life—even as he was dragged off to Egypt to an unrecorded death. He lived from about 650 to 570 B.C.E.

The Book of Jeremiah is a combination of prose, poetry, and biographical material combined by its editors (probably the Deuteronomists) in themes rather than in chronological order. This means that the writings treating similar themes are found together, even if they describe events that occurred at different times.

Jeremiah pointed out the inevitable doom to come for Judah and Jerusalem if they did not turn around, but his message did not stop there. From within his own broken heart, he was able to find seeds of hope that would later grow in the hearts of his people—hope that after their period of suffering, God would bring forth something new in them, a new Covenant.

A Reluctant Prophet

Jeremiah was born of a priestly family in a village just north of Jerusalem. We are not told where he is when God calls him at about age twenty, during Josiah's reign. But the calling is an interior experience, profound and frightening. Jeremiah is not eager to respond to the call. When he cries out, "I am too young!" God tells him not to fear: God will put the right words into Jeremiah's mouth. And Jeremiah gives in to God.

Jeremiah has two visions: He sees a branch of an almond tree—also called a watching tree—symbolizing that God is watching to see if Judah and Jerusalem will change. The prophet also sees a boiling cauldron tipped on a hearth in the north, meaning that God will summon kingdoms from the north to be poured out over Judah if it does not change. These warnings, says God, will outrage people and create enemies, so Jeremiah must stand fast.

Read Jeremiah 1:1–19.

Notice that to tell the bad news to Judah, God chooses a young man who feels terribly inadequate to the task. Being hated by others is not Jeremiah's idea of a good time. He is not nervy. But God thinks Jeremiah *is* up to the task. Perhaps God even prefers that the message come through a tenderhearted young man, rather than from someone who relishes a fight.

Jerusalem, Your Time Is Coming!

After King Josiah is killed in a battle with Egypt, the Egyptians choose Josiah's son Jehoiakim to be king of Judah. Jehoiakim then sides with Egypt in its struggle against the king of Babylon, **Nebuchadrezzar II**, for control of the region around the eastern Mediterranean. Jeremiah despises Jehoiakim's politicking, and is convinced that God will use Babylon to punish Israel for its unrepentant heart.

Through Jeremiah, God warns that Judah and Jerusalem will get the punishment their crimes deserve. When God bids Jeremiah to search the city for an honest person, he can find none. The people have filled their houses with loot taken from the poor and have grown rich and fat—all the while winking at evil. Their time is coming.

Read Jeremiah 4:18; 5:1–5,26–29.

To ignore God's instructions for how things work is to ask for the consequences. Jeremiah's prophecies were not predictions of what was bound to happen but of what *could* happen if the people and nations continued to be hard-hearted. Alas, they were not willing to change.

Why did the Judahites feel so confident in ignoring Jeremiah's message? They had convinced themselves that God would never allow Jerusalem to be overcome. After all, the holy Temple was there, the place of God's dwelling. They remembered the incident (see 2 Kings 19:32–36) a century earlier, during Hezekiah's reign, when Jerusalem was under siege by the Assyrian army, but a mysterious "angel of the LORD" (2 Kings 19:35) had killed the Assyrians just as they were about to break through the walls of the city. This apparent miracle, and the pledge that God would be with David's royal line forever, they saw as proof that they were safe. God would never permit Jerusalem or the house of David to be destroyed.

The Temple: No Guarantee of Safety

God tells Jeremiah to preach in the Temple, and Jeremiah warns his listeners that even the Temple does not assure God's presence. Unless they stop oppressing aliens, shedding innocent blood, and worshiping idols, unless they treat their neighbors with justice and show mercy to widows and orphans, they will be lost. How can they steal, murder, commit adultery and perjury, worship strange gods—and still believe they are safe?

Outraged, the priests and court prophets start a riot and call for Jeremiah's death. Fortunately, Jeremiah is whisked away while the ruckus is being quelled, and he escapes alive.
Read Jeremiah 7:1–15.

Ridiculing Idols

Through the prophet Jeremiah, God ridicules the idols the people of Jerusalem honor—gods fastened with nails lest they totter, carried because they cannot walk, and able to do neither good nor evil. By contrast, the one God is true, living, eternal, the maker of the earth, the stretcher of the sky, the mover of the waters. God's inheritance is Jacob, God's tribe is Israel, and the Lord of Moses is God's name; *there is no other God.*
Read Jeremiah 10:1–16.

Up until about the time of the exile, the Israelites generally believed the Lord was the only God who mattered, superior to all others, but not the *only* God. Here the prophet denies that other gods exist at all; those "gods" are powerless pieces of carved wood.

Jeremiah's Suffering and Inner Torment

After Jeremiah demonstrates for some of Jerusalem's leaders that God will smash the city like a piece of pottery, he is accused of blasphemy. A court prophet has him beaten and put in stocks overnight.

Jeremiah feels tricked by God into this life of prophecy and persecution. He cries out that God has duped him; he will never mention God's name again. But he cannot hold in his prophetic message; it becomes like a fire burning in his heart. People whisper against him and try to entrap him, but when Jeremiah realizes that his enemies have failed, he shouts jubilantly, "The Lord is with me" (Jeremiah 20:11).

Just as quickly his mood plummets, and he utters his most horrific cry of despair and curses the day he was born.
Read Jeremiah 19:1–6,10–11; 20:1–18.

Jeremiah wants to be faithful to his calling, but God never makes it easy for him. He is ravaged with inner torment, feeling abandoned and even tricked by God. In spite of his suffering, though, Jeremiah knows in his bones he must continue to speak the truth. Glimmers of light and hope come to him in his darkness, but then his terrible agony returns.

We can imagine that Jesus, six centuries later, must have felt close to Jeremiah. And for the early Christians, Jesus' sufferings reminded them of Jeremiah. Like Jeremiah, Jesus was sent to teach God's ways, but was despised, plotted against, and entrapped by his enemies. Jesus, too, felt abandoned, crying out to God from the cross the opening words of a Jewish psalm, "'Why have you forsaken me?'" (Mark 15:34).

The First Exile: Do Not Resist Babylon!

The jockeying for power by the major empires continues. Babylon, under King Nebuchadrezzar, now controls the region. King Jehoiakim foolishly withholds tribute from the Babylonian monarch, so Babylon attacks Jerusalem (but does not destroy it). Jehoiakim is killed, and his son, the young King **Jehoiachin**, is sent off to exile in Babylon with his court and many professionals, craftsmen, and soldiers. This event in 597 B.C.E. is the first exile for Judah; a larger one will follow a decade later.

What is Jeremiah's response to the Babylonian attack and the exile? Basically his message is, "Do not resist Babylon. Go willingly into exile, and make the most of this sad situation. It will be a time for something new to happen in you."

In a letter to the exiles in Babylon, Jeremiah tells them to settle down there, build houses, plant gardens, and find spouses for their children. They must increase in number and promote the good of the city, for one day God will bring them home. Exile is not for annihilation, as they have dreaded, but for purification, so they can return to the role God chose for them long ago—God's witness before the nations.

In Jerusalem another son of Jehoiakim, **Zedekiah,** becomes king. He is weak, a man curious to hear from Jeremiah but afraid to follow his advice. He stupidly takes part in a revolt against Babylon. When Babylon besieges Jerusalem in retaliation, Zedekiah clings to the false hope that God will rescue Jerusalem once more, just as happened under Hezekiah a century earlier. The court prophets have encouraged the king in his illusions. But Jeremiah knows better and says that Jerusalem must go willingly into exile or it will be destroyed.

Although the king and his prophets would like to believe that Jeremiah does not speak for God, they are deeply threatened by him. His words have the ring of truth.

Read Jeremiah 29:1–14; 27:12–15.

Jeremiah will be accused of treason—of deserting to the Babylonians and demoralizing the army with his call for surrender. He will be beaten and imprisoned, and court nobles will throw him into a muddy, deep cistern to die (fortunately he will be saved by the secret intervention of an Ethiopian courtier). Such harsh treatment is not surprising for a man who says that surrender to the enemy is better than fighting for king and country. But God wants Judah to repent, and the purification of exile is the only means left, as Isaiah said long before and Jeremiah understands.

A New Covenant

The times are indeed bleak for Jeremiah. Yet in such a dark moment, God speaks to him of a great hope—the future return of the people from exile. Moreover, the people will not simply return home to their same old ways, their same broken relationship with God. No, they will be made anew as God's beloved! At that time God will make a **new Covenant** with the people, writing the Law on their hearts instead of on stone tablets; God will forgive their evil and remember their sin no more.

Read Jeremiah 31:31–34.

The new Covenant prophesied by Jeremiah will be a turning point for Israel. The Law, the basis of the Sinai Covenant, would no longer be merely a matter of external practices and norms imposed from outside the person. In this new Covenant, the Law would be written on each person's heart. Each individual would know God and what God wants from deep within. This would be the fruit of their long period of suffering in exile.

Jeremiah's own sorrow and suffering—we can think of it as an exile from his own people—has brought him to a deep and intimate relationship with God. He has struggled mightily within his soul to come to an acceptance of his own suffering, and to find security in God alone. Now he is telling Israel that it must do the same. Out of Israel's acceptance of its exile will come hope—hope for an entirely new, living relationship with God.

The Second Exile: Jerusalem Destroyed

In 587 B.C.E. time finally runs out for Jerusalem. The Babylonians return, breach the city's walls, and torch its buildings; the Temple is destroyed, and many of the people are deported to Babylon. King Zedekiah is captured, forced to see his sons slain, and then blinded and hauled off in chains to Babylon.

Jeremiah stays behind with the Judahites still in Jerusalem, and tells them they will be safe if they remain in the ruined city and give in to Babylonian rule. Once again the people refuse to listen to Jeremiah. They flee to Egypt, seeking comfort and security, taking Jeremiah and his scribe, Baruch, with them. Few of them will ever return to Jerusalem.

With that, Jeremiah disappears. No one knows what happens to him. One tradition holds that he is murdered in Egypt by his fellow Judahites, which is possible but not recorded anywhere. Baruch, however, returns to Jerusalem.

Read Jeremiah 39:1–14; 42:1–12; 43:1–7.

Contemporaries of Jeremiah saw him as a complete failure. His people never paid attention to his warnings; he was despised by almost everyone, and he was dragged off to die in a land he never wanted to be in.

Later, though, Jeremiah's failure was remembered by the exiles and succeeding generations of Jews—including Jesus and his followers. They saw the "failure" of Jeremiah's life, like the sorrow and humiliation of the exile, as a seed of hope and transformation. Israel's heart was broken so that God could at last enter it. Indeed the exile turned out to be the time when Judaism as a religion came to birth. Its Scriptures, its monotheism, its Law-centeredness, its prayer and worship, and many of the practices we know today were fruits of that period.

The experience of Jeremiah and the exile was that failure and suffering do not have to crush us. Our own hearts can be made anew through sorrow, and we can find new life once again.

The next two books of the Old Testament, Lamentations and Baruch, are connected with Jeremiah in tradition.

Lamentations: Judah Grieves

The Book of Lamentations is a collection of five hymns of grief composed shortly after the fall of Jerusalem. Although not written by Jeremiah, these dirges have been attributed to him because the writer sounds like Jeremiah. Each chapter is a separate poem, perhaps each by a separate author.

The first, second, and fourth chapters are funeral laments for the lost Jerusalem. The third chapter tells of the author's suffering and of the hope that one day God will bring it to an end. The fifth chapter is the voice of a people admitting their guilt, expressing their hope, and praying for restoration. The Book of Lamentations seems to have helped Judah by giving it a way to grieve—recalling its agony, lamenting, and asking for healing.

Read Lamentations 1:1–7,10,18–19; 2:11–13.

Baruch: Keep the Faith!

The Book of Baruch, though attributed to Jeremiah's faithful scribe, Baruch, was written by several authors centuries after the exile. Its setting is the exile, but it was actually meant to nurture the faith of the later Jews of the Dispersion (those living away from Jerusalem) and to encourage them to return home someday. The scribe Baruch probably did inspire the Jews during the exile, reminding them of Jeremiah's witness, and the authors of the Book of Baruch hoped they too would touch the hearts of their fellow Jews far from home.

Chapter 6 of Baruch is a letter attributed to Jeremiah but actually written much later, like the rest of the book. The letter is a powerful and amusing ridicule of the idols that surround the Jews in these far-off lands. These idols have tongues smoothed by woodworkers and covered with gold and silver, but they cannot speak. They are decked out in garments, wrapped in purple, but are not safe from moths or corruption. Lamps are lighted for them, but they cannot see. If they fall to the ground, they must be picked up. They need dusting; their faces are black from the smoke of candles, and from when the bats and the swallows light on them.

The point is this: Do not be fooled, you faraway sons and daughters of the one God; there is no other God but the Lord!

Read Baruch 6:1–22 (Baruch, chapter 6, is called the Letter of Jeremiah in some versions of the Bible).

Ezekiel: From Hearts of Stone to Hearts of Flesh

Like Jeremiah, Ezekiel prophesied in Jerusalem in the years before the exile. And as Jeremiah did, he confronted the hard hearts of the people, shaking them out of their complacency and letting them know that the time of God's patience with them was just about up.

After Jerusalem fell, Ezekiel was one of those deported to Babylon. He is best known for his prophesying there, where he inspired hope in the discouraged exiles that all was not over for Israel: God had forgiven Israel and would create it anew, giving it a new heart and a new spirit.

Unlike the other prophets, Ezekiel's gifts were not writing and poetry but drama, symbol making, and storytelling. This fiery prophet certainly had dramatic flair, so much so that he often seemed out of his mind to people, or possessed by a demon. But Ezekiel was possessed by God, driven to communicate God's messages in vivid, unsettling ways.

An Awesome Call

Ezekiel's life of prophecy begins with being called through a strange vision. He sees a bright light in a chariot drawn by four winged creatures, each with four faces—those of a lion, an ox, an eagle, and a man. On a throne above the creatures is a being of light resembling a man, which appears to be a likeness of the glory of the Lord.

A voice instructs Ezekiel to tell the people of the Lord's displeasure with them, and it bids him to eat a scroll on which God has written words of lamentation and mourning and woe. When he does eat the scroll, the taste is as sweet as honey. God tells Ezekiel that he must speak the message of woe to the people.

Ezekiel is warned that the people will be stubborn and hard-hearted, but he must not be afraid of them; he must stand his ground. And he must communicate to them through actions, not simply words. God tells him to be silent until bidden to speak. Ezekiel is no longer his own man; he is God's.

Read Ezekiel 1:4–14,26–28; 2:2–10; 3:1–11.

What could be sweet about a scroll containing words of woe? Perhaps the sweetness is a symbol of how good it is to know the truth, even when the truth seems bitter, because ultimately the truth frees us. "Sweet as honey" also seems to convey how good it is to know what God is calling us to do—even when the thing we are called to do is very hard—because God will be with us through it all.

Prophetic Actions and Storytelling

With one bizarre wordless performance after another, Ezekiel tries to convince the people of Jerusalem that their rescue is *not* at hand, Jerusalem will *not* be saved, and exile will last a long time. But up until Jerusalem is captured, they continue to believe that because Jerusalem has the holy Temple, God will come charging in to save them.

Following are some examples that show the amazing lengths this prophet goes to in his efforts to get through to the people:

- Ezekiel makes a model of Jerusalem on an unbaked clay brick, using sticks and stones around it to signify a siege with battering rams, towers, and ramps. He wedges a large iron griddle into the ground behind the "city," and he lies down and gazes at it for over a year. This symbolizes God watching Nebuchadrezzar's siege of Jerusalem but doing nothing about it. *Read Ezekiel 4:1–8.*

- Ezekiel cuts off his hair and beard, burns one-third of it within his model city, strews a third around the city and strikes it with a sword, and tosses the final third in the wind. A few hairs he keeps in the hem of his garment, but even some of these will be burned. This striking dramatization signifies that Jerusalem will be cut down, with some people dying of pestilence, some being slain, and some being exiled. Only a few will return. *Read Ezekiel 5:1–3,11–12.*

- Ezekiel packs his baggage, leaves his house, and goes through an elaborate acting out of escaping from the city. Later he explains that his actions represented King Zedekiah in disguise escaping the city. But the king will be caught, blinded, and taken to Babylon, where he will die. Ezekiel stands in front of the people and trembles as he eats bread and water—as they will do when they are captives. *Read Ezekiel 12:1–16.*

- Ezekiel tells the whole history of Israel through an allegory—a symbolic story. It is a love story reminiscent of the prophet Hosea's, in which Jerusalem proves to be God's vain and faithless spouse. Only when Jerusalem has shamed herself entirely—taking countless lovers, paying for their services, destroying her beauty, and behaving worse than her sisters Sodom and Samaria—only then will God forgive her and renew their marriage. *Read Ezekiel 16:1–63.*

- Ezekiel's wife, the delight of his eyes, dies, and he is told by God not to show his grief. His silence embodies a message to the people. Ezekiel tells them that the delight of *their* eyes—the Temple, Jerusalem, and all its people—will also be taken from them. Ezekiel's failure to mourn outwardly for the loss of his dear wife symbolizes the people's not mourning their lost relationship with God. *Read Ezekiel 24:15–27.*

Even through the tragedy of his wife's death that he is not allowed to mourn, Ezekiel tries to communicate the truth to the people of Jerusalem. But they continue in their hard-heartedness.

Denial does not serve the people well. Jerusalem does fall and is utterly destroyed. All that Ezekiel, like Jeremiah, has prophesied comes about. Unlike Jeremiah, however, when the city is captured, Ezekiel does not stay behind with those who remain there. He accompanies the exiles on their long journey through the desert to Babylon.

"A New Heart . . . and a New Spirit" Within

Once the disaster Ezekiel prophesied has become reality, his role with the people changes. He now becomes a counselor, a teacher, an inspirer to the disheartened exiles. No longer do they need to hear of God's anger but of God's tender mercy. By living through their sorrowful time of exile, their hearts will be softened and made anew.

In a passage that echoes the new Covenant prophesied by Jeremiah, Ezekiel hears God speak through him these great words of hope to the people: "A new heart I will give you, and a new spirit I will put within you; and I will remove from your body the heart of stone and give you a heart of flesh" (Ezekiel 36:26). God will bring the exiles back to their land, where what has become desolate will flourish again and where the ruined towns will be full of people once more.

Read Ezekiel 36:22–36.

The Vision of the Dry Bones

Despite Ezekiel's hopeful words, the exiles still feel not only discouraged but lifeless. Their life as a people seems over; they are dead. "'"Our bones are dried up,"'" they moan (Ezekiel 37:11). Ezekiel has a vision of a valley filled with dry bones. And when God asks him, "'Can these bones live?'" (37:3), Ezekiel replies that only God knows. With this, he is told to say, "'O dry bones, hear the word of the LORD'" (37:4). As he speaks there is a rattling sound, the bones come together, sinew and flesh covering them, but the bodies have no life. Ezekiel is told to call forth breath, or spirit, for the bones; he does, and suddenly standing before him is a vast array of living people. This is the whole house of Israel, whose grave of exile God will open, to lead them back to their land and to give them a new spirit, and there they will turn to God once more.

Read Ezekiel 37:1–14.

Probably the most familiar of the Ezekiel stories, his vision of the dry bones is about a kind of spiritual resurrection—the raising up of a nation that has lost hope. Israel has tried to manipulate its own fate and has failed lamentably; now it is God, whom they have ignored, betrayed, and rejected, who alone can save them—and will.

Christians have seen in Ezekiel's vision of the dry bones come to life an image of Jesus' Resurrection and the new life his rising brings to those united with Christ. The passage is one of those read at the Catholic Easter Vigil service on Holy Saturday.

The Vision of a New Jerusalem

The last chapters of Ezekiel are a vision of the return to Jerusalem, the rebuilding of the Temple, and the return of the glory of God. The Lord orders Ezekiel to tell the priests and the people how to worship; celebrate feast days; and observe the laws of ritual, the rules for nobles, and the laws for division of land. Then Ezekiel announces that the name of the city shall henceforth be "'The LORD is There'"

(48:35). But Ezekiel does not live to see Jerusalem again—except in his vision. He dies in exile.

Read Ezekiel 43:1–9; 48:35.

After years of his message of repentance being ignored, Ezekiel became the herald of Israel's hope, at long last its teacher and counselor. One can imagine that when the exiles, filled with remorse, finally asked him, "Why did it happen?" he reminded them not only of their infidelities but, far more eagerly, of their God, a saving God.

The Babylon of the Exiles

The city of Babylon dates from before 2000 B.C.E. but did not achieve fame in the ancient world until the reign of King Hammurabi (1792 to 1750 B.C.E.). Hammurabi is famous for his code of laws. For the next twelve hundred years or so, the rulers of Babylon withstood the sieges and sackings of, and were sometimes governed by, many other nations, such as the Assyrians.

Babylon had inherited from its predecessors a rich cultural and religious tradition going back to 4000 B.C.E. The Babylonians themselves produced extensive literature, including the famous *Gilgamesh Epic*. Cities under Babylonian rule were governed by law, with courts and police, contractual business arrangements, and the guarantee of private property. Among their other accomplishments, the Babylonians designed the Hanging Gardens, famous as one of the Seven Wonders of the Ancient World. Because Babylon heard and often acted upon the will of its people, some scholars refer to it as a primitive democracy.

In 612 B.C.E. the Chaldeans (who had taken over Babylon from the Assyrians) demolished the Assyrian capital, Nineveh. Twenty-five years later the Chaldean king Nebuchadrezzar II was the one who destroyed Jerusalem and carried the citizens of Judah into exile in Babylon.

Although the Jews came to Babylon as captives, they were not slaves. In fact, during the exile there, they played an important part in the empire's economy and became farmers, bankers, merchants, artisans, contractors, and landowners. Some Jews felt enough at home to take Babylonian names. Although Babylonians permitted some freedom in economic life, Jews were not allowed to build a temple or practice their religious rituals in any public way. The Babylonians' temples were the only ones in town. Jews who could not stomach worship of the strange Babylonian gods, such as Marduk, tried to preserve their religious identity and heritage as best they could.

So the Jews carefully preserved the words of the prophets and the sacred writings of the Torah. Much of the Jewish Bible came into its final form in this period. The people gathered together as families or in community to read the Scriptures, pray, and chant their hymns and psalms.

The exile proved to be a time of great creativity for Israel, as the religion focused more on the word of God and the community, and less on the place of worship, the Temple. It was then, too, that male circumcision, kosher dietary practices, and the Sabbath as a day of rest became so significant. These customs reminded the Jews of *who they were* as God's Chosen People.

The religious renewal drew many in the Jewish community closer together. But Babylon with its sophisticated ways no doubt was alluring to many Jews, especially the younger ones. As the decades in Babylon went on and Jerusalem seemed farther and farther away, people must have wondered whether the Lord had forgotten them or was simply a weak God. There must have been arguments between parents and children, sisters and brothers, grandparents and grandchildren, even neighbors, over following the old ways and being faithful to the one and only God. Some may have been tempted to throw their allegiance to the chief Babylonian god, Marduk, who, they thought, must be more powerful than the God of the Israelites.

So Jews in Babylon in 550 B.C.E. varied in their faithfulness to God. Some compromised to the extent that they blended in with the Babylonians. Even among faithful Jews, many were content to stay in Babylon with their established homes and businesses. They could express their religious identity through their customs, their Law, and their worship centered on the Scriptures and prayer; they did not require the Temple in order to be faithful to God.

In the centuries that followed the exile, many Jews remained in Babylon and were true to Judaism. They trained exceptional scholars in the Mosaic Law, and in the sixth century B.C.E., produced the Babylonian Talmud—the most influential Jewish writing other than the Jewish Bible.

Second Isaiah:
Toward a Joyous Return

Isaiah of Jerusalem prophesied more than a century before the exile. Scholars call him First Isaiah because he was the inspiration for the later "Isaiahs," whose writings follow his in the Book of Isaiah. First Isaiah comprises chapters 1 to 39.

In Babylon toward the end of the exile, around 550 B.C.E., lived a prophet (or prophets) whom scholars call Second Isaiah, author of chapters 40 to 55 of the Book of Isaiah. Second Isaiah had a challenge—to raise the hopes of the people for the day when they would make a joyous return to Jerusalem. That day would come soon—in 538 B.C.E., when Cyrus, king of Persia, overcame the Babylonians and set the exiles free. By that time almost all the original exiles had died. Their offspring would need to be passionately inspired to make the difficult journey across the desert back to Judah and the ruins of Jerusalem, beginning life over again. In fact, only a fraction of the Jews in Babylon did return.

The chapters of Second Isaiah are full of joyous expectation of the return to Jerusalem; of the Promised One, the Messiah; and of the day when all nations will gather to worship God in justice and peace. Appropriately, these writings are called the Book of Consolation. Included also are four songs of a mysterious servant of God, one whose mission is to bring salvation to all peoples through his own suffering.

Cyrus the Anointed: Liberator

Second Isaiah foresees the day when God will summon **Cyrus the Persian** to overthrow Babylon and to allow Israel to return home. Exile will end with a new Exodus!

Cyrus is called God's "anointed," and God calls him by name. Cyrus does not know the one God, being ruler of a foreign empire with its own gods. But that does not stop God from choosing him to be the instrument of his blessings. God is ruler and creator of *all* the earth—that means

The Jews of the Dispersion

Beginning with the eighth century B.C.E., many Jews left Israel, victims of the Assyrians, the Babylonians, and the Persians. Jewish refugees and deportees settled in cities around the Near East and became artisans and merchants.

Some Jewish communities were large, prosperous, and long-lived, like the group remaining in Babylon after the exile, which survived into the Middle Ages. The largest of all the Jewish communities was in the Egyptian city of Alexandria, a cultural and literary hub of the Near Eastern world. In the last centuries before Christ, its Jewish population grew to nearly one million.

In Alexandria, in the third century B.C.E., Jewish scholars began work on the *Septuagint,* the Greek translation of the Old Testament and today the oldest complete version in existence.

Within the Alexandrian community, as elsewhere, many Jews chose to abandon the Law and adopt the local lifestyle. Others kept the Sabbath and the dietary laws, continued to regard Jerusalem as their spiritual capital, contributed to the upkeep of the Temple, and made pilgrimage there.

At the same time, Jewish communities built synagogues, where worship, education, and traditional celebrations could take place. The synagogue, a prominent part of life for Jews, also played a vital role in the origins of Christianity. In the Gospels we find Jesus attending synagogue services and teaching there.

foreign nations and kings! "I am the LORD, and there is no other" (Isaiah 45:5). God joyously bids nature to let justice descend from the heavens like rain, and salvation bud forth from the earth.

Read Isaiah 45:1–8.

Unlike other conquerors Cyrus does not resort to rape, genocide, or the deportation of populations. He allows conquered peoples to return home, asking only that when they worship their gods, they pray for him as well. God calls Cyrus "the anointed" out of respect for his kingship.

But the Jews of the Dispersion often paid a heavy price for their unusual customs. Mob attacks on Jews—called *pogroms* in modern times—were reported in the records of Alexandria and Rome.

As the gods of the ancient world lost their attraction, people hungered for a more spiritual and moral religion, and many were attracted to Judaism. In the time of Jesus, millions of Jews lived throughout the entire Roman Empire. The growth of a large Jewish population in Roman times suggests that Jews earnestly pursued their mission to reveal the one God to the world and that they actively sought—and received—converts.

Potential believers could not always make a full commitment to Judaism, however—perhaps because of the stigma of circumcision or the fear of persecution. Such seekers became an eager audience for the early Christian missionaries, who did not demand compliance with the Jewish regulations. Saint Paul gained many converts with his teaching that salvation depended on faith in Jesus Christ, not on obedience to the Law.

As the ancient prophets saw it, the infidelity of the Jews caused the Dispersion, but in time the Dispersion proved the durability of their faith. Judaism survived the destruction of both nation and Temple in 70 C.E. and, lived out in settings far from home, became one of the most creative and moral forces in history.

In this passage we see not only a picture of a liberating Cyrus but, even more important, the image of a "universal" God. This is the God of *all* the nations, who can accomplish the divine purposes through anyone, of any nation, of any religion.

Comfort My People

In Second Isaiah, God offers comfort and shows the exiles that the way home will be made ready for them:

"Comfort, O comfort my people"

. . . .

A voice cries out:
"In the wilderness prepare the way of the LORD.

. . . .

Every valley shall be lifted up,
    and every mountain and hill be made low."

(40:1–4)

God will come to lead Israel home—like a shepherd who leads his flock and carries his lambs in his arms. For anyone who is afraid or discouraged, God offers strength:

Those who wait for the LORD shall renew their strength,
    they shall mount up with wings like eagles,
they shall run and not be weary,
    they shall walk and not faint.

(40:31)

Read Isaiah 40:1–11,27–31.

In the Gospels, John the Baptist is spoken of as using the passage from Second Isaiah about one who prepares the way of the Lord. This Gospel reading and many other hope-filled passages from Second Isaiah are part of the Christian liturgies for Advent, the season of anticipating the coming of Jesus Christ.

Read Luke 3:2–6.

The Songs of the Suffering Servant

In Second Isaiah appears the mysterious **suffering servant**, an innocent man who suffers greatly—not as punishment for his own sins but in order to save the people from theirs. In the songs of the suffering servant, his identity is not clear. Often he seems to be Israel, sometimes the prophet, sometimes a composite portrait of Israel's great men, an ideal of what Israel is called to be. Christians have always seen a prophetic image of Christ in the suffering servant.

In the first song, God speaks of a chosen one, one set above others. He has been given God's spirit, and his mission is to bring justice to the nations. He will not raise his voice in noisy authority but will speak with gentleness and act tenderly toward the "bruised reed"—hopeless Israel.

In the next song, the speaker is the prophet. He likens himself to a sharp-edged sword, a polished arrow that God had hidden in a quiver. He was called from his mother's womb to restore Israel as a light to the nations—so that the salvation of the Lord can reach to the ends of the earth.

In the third song, the servant is subject to insults and derision; he is beaten, his beard plucked, his face spat upon. Patiently he endures this abuse, certain that God will uphold him. His tormentors will wear out, he says, like moth-eaten clothing.

In the fourth song, the suffering servant seems to be Israel, who, before finally being exalted, is first spurned and avoided and so disfigured as to seem inhuman. The people think that he is being punished for his sins, but in reality he is suffering for the nation's wrongdoing. Like a lamb led to slaughter, he is taken away, "cut off from the land of the living" (Isaiah 53:8), and buried in a criminal's grave, although he has done no wrong. But because he has "poured out himself to death" (53:12) and was counted among the wicked, he will win pardon for the sins of many.

Read Isaiah 42:1–4; 49:1–6; 50:4–9; 52:13–15; 53:1–12.

In the songs of the suffering servant, Second Isaiah introduces a new concept, a different way for Israel to be a light to the nations. Israel's light will shine not through being a glorious nation, as many Israelites in former times believed. No, Israel will bring salvation to the whole world through the willingness to suffer for the sake of others.

The songs of the suffering servant (Isaiah 52:13–15; 53:1–12) are used today in the Good Friday liturgy, the memorial of Christ's death on the cross. Christians interpret the suffering, death, and triumph of the servant as a prophetic image of Jesus.

The Tenderness of God

To the complaint that God has forgotten Jerusalem, God responds, through Second Isaiah, with one of the most beautiful passages in the Scriptures. Even a mother might forget her infant or be without tenderness for the child of her womb, but God will never forget Israel.

In another passage God becomes a woman in labor, gasping and panting as she struggles to bring forth Israel as a reborn nation.

Read Isaiah 49:14–15; 42:13–14.

Come to the Feast!

A joyful poem in Second Isaiah invites the people to a great feast: All those who thirst, come to the water! Come and enjoy the rich food of God's life. It's free, and it's the kind of food and drink that satisfies—not the kind that leaves you empty and parched.

Second Isaiah closes in a hymn of joy, with God promising peace, mountains that break into song, trees that clap their hands, cypresses instead of thornbushes, myrtle instead of nettles. No wonder the returning exiles leave Babylon with high and hope-filled hearts!

Read Isaiah 55:1–13.

The Fruits of Exile

The prophets Jeremiah, Ezekiel, and Second Isaiah guided Israel through its time of purification in exile, calling the people to a deeper relationship with God. Judaism as a religion, with its unswerving belief in the one and only God, its Law and distinctive practices, and its rootedness in the written word of God, was born in exile. Jeremiah and Ezekiel saw the new Covenant that was coming for Israel.

And Isaiah and Jeremiah pointed to the transforming and saving power of suffering, rather than its being simply a punishment for sin. That insight into suffering would be crucial to the Jews throughout their history of oppression and persecution up to the present, and to Christians in their belief in the saving power of Jesus' suffering and death, leading to resurrected life.

At the end of the exile, relatively few Jews would return to Jerusalem to begin again. Those who did saw themselves as the "faithful remnant" prophesied by Zephaniah and others. However, that did not make the Jews of the Dispersion unfaithful. For them as well as for the returning exiles, the fruit of the exile was new life. With the center of the Jews' faith in their Scriptures and their distinctive practices, Judaism was no longer tied to one particular land, Israel, and one place of worship, the Temple. It became a portable religion, which later spread throughout the Greek and Roman Empires. Its portability enabled Jews to be faithful wherever they were, truly a "light to the nations."

Questions for Reflection and Discussion

1. God did not will bad things to happen to the Jews. Their loss of cohesion and religious identity divided them, making them weak. They had become corrupt. In exile they realized their dependence on God. They came back to a harmony with God and a goodness of life because of this purification. What "exile" or "purification" have you experienced that has brought you back to God's ways?

2. How might the challenges of being a prophet in Jeremiah's time differ from the challenges of being a prophet in our time?

3. Often our response to approaching pain or disaster is to try to avoid it at all cost. Jeremiah's message is different. He advises that we go with the pain and accept it as a time for changing and growing. Can you think of an

experience from your life or that of someone you know when embracing pain might have been more beneficial than fighting it?

4. We follow some laws or rules simply because that is what is expected of us and we know we might be punished for disobeying them. Think of a law or rule that is "written on your heart"—that is, one you follow because, in your heart, you know it is right and good.

5. Ezekiel says that the scroll describing God's mission for him tastes as sweet as honey. Have you had a similar experience of the sweetness of doing the good?

6. Ezekiel uses the image of dry bones to describe the Israelites, who have become lifeless and faithless. Think of something in your life that appears lifeless. How could you, with God's grace, bring life back?

9

Making a Home
After the Exile

God is our refuge and strength,
  a very present help in trouble.
Therefore we will not fear, though the earth should
      change,
  though the mountains shake in the heart of the sea;
though its waters roar and foam,
  though the mountains tremble with its tumult.

There is a river whose streams make glad the city of God,
  the holy habitation of the Most High.
God is in the midst of the city; it shall not be moved;
  God will help it when the morning dawns.
The nations are in an uproar, the kingdoms totter;
  he utters his voice, the earth melts.
The LORD of hosts is with us;
  the God of Jacob is our refuge.

Come, behold the works of the LORD;
  see what desolations he has brought on the earth.
He makes wars cease to the end of the earth;
  he breaks the bow, and shatters the spear;
  he burns the shields with fire.
"Be still, and know that I am God!
  I am exalted among the nations,
  I am exalted in the earth."
The LORD of hosts is with us;
  the God of Jacob is our refuge.

(Psalm 46)

The day of liberation finally came for the exiles in Babylon. As Second Isaiah had foreseen, Cyrus, the king of Persia, was the liberator, taking over Babylon and issuing an edict that freed the exiles to return home to Judah. This chapter tells what happened after the exiles returned to Jerusalem—the period known as the **restoration.**

In 538 B.C.E. a group of exiles made the long trip back to Judah, followed by later groups over the decades. Most of the exiles, however, remained in and around Babylon, where life was more certain. The ones who returned to Judah thought of themselves as "the remnant"—those few in number but strong in faith that Zephaniah and other prophets had foretold would be the basis of a new Israel.

This group of exiles came home quite literally. But even more important, they needed to come home in a spiritual sense by reinforcing and defending the major beliefs and practices of Judaism. The period after the exile was a time to build a strong spiritual center, a vital faith that Jews could carry with them into foreign lands—like Egypt, Greece, and other places around the Mediterranean Sea where Jews eventually did form communities. With a vital spiritual center, wherever they lived, the Jews would be "at home."

This meant setting boundaries—not the geographical kind like the borders of a country or city but the spiritual kind that define the limits of a person or group: "This is *who we are.* There are certain things we do, and certain things we don't and won't do. These are the lines we must not cross if we are to be faithful to who we are." For the Jews such boundaries were essential if they were to survive as a people in strange lands where they were treated as aliens if not as enemies. Their boundaries gave them a spiritual home that would endure despite the many attempts through the centuries to wipe out the Jewish people.

Because so much of Jewish practice developed during the period after the exile, scholars say that Judaism as the religion we know came to birth in those years. After the exile the term *Jew*—from *Judah*—came into common use, along with *Jewish* and *Judaism.*

In the two **Books of Chronicles,** the history of Israel was told again, up through the exile. Then the Books of

Ezra and **Nehemiah** continue with the story of the return from exile, the rebuilding of Jerusalem and the Temple, the people's recommitment to the Law, and the centering of their religion in the Bible. Woven throughout this chapter are the messages of prophets, who urge the people to faithfulness and hope: **Third Isaiah, Haggai, Zechariah, Malachi, Joel,** and **Obadiah.**

Finally, we will consider the Jewish people's struggle to maintain their identity and boundaries in the face of the power and allure of the Greek Empire, which conquered the region in 330 B.C.E. The two **Books of Maccabees** tell of a period of terrible persecution of the Jews by the Greeks that began about 175 B.C.E. and the Jews' brave resistance to oppression that lead to a time of limited independence for Judah. The **Book of Daniel,** written in the midst of cruelty and torture at the hands of the Greeks, offers inspiration and hope by drawing on stories of a courageous figure named Daniel, who faced oppression during the exile in Babylon. Both the Second Book of Maccabees and Daniel express belief in an afterlife and the hope of resurrection, concepts that emerged in Judaism in the two centuries before the birth of Jesus.

Chronicles: History as It Should Have Been

The two Books of Chronicles were written sometime after the rebuilding of the Temple, possibly in about 400 B.C.E. The books retell Israel's history in terms of its meaning in God's unfolding plan, rather than in factual, chronological events. They are a valuable prologue to the Books of Ezra and Nehemiah, named for two men whose leadership in Jerusalem was key to the development of modern Judaism.

Why are we told still another version of Israel's history, one that skips over large sections of it, puts the emphasis on David and Solomon—omitting all their sins—and still claims to be inspired Scripture?

The Books of Chronicles were the writer's effort to put things in focus. They reminded the Jews that they were called to be a priestly people and a holy nation, not an empire. The Chronicler was not concerned with Israel's scandals, wars, or wealth. Israel's political greatness was over, but that did not matter because by holding to the ideal set forth by David, Israel would keep on course to the greatness that was its destiny.

So the Chronicler made David and Solomon the key figures in his saga and retold their story the way it *should* have been. He recalled how David took Jerusalem, rebuilt it, made it the capital of the twelve tribes, and brought the ark of the Covenant there. David dreamed of a house for God, purchased land for it, drew plans, provided materials, wrote regulations for the Temple, trained choristers and musicians, and even wrote music for Israel's worship. Much of this information appears for the first time in Chronicles.

World Happenings
Between 600 and 1 B.C.E.

Major religious and philosophical movements arise in the period preceding Jesus' life—movements that shape our ideas about God and goodness today.

China
The teacher K'ung-Fu-tzu, better known as Confucius (551 to 479 B.C.E.), promotes social ethics, courtesy, and good government. His contemporary Lao-tzu writes the *Tao Te Ching*, which prescribes living in joy and harmony with nature. Their complementary systems—Confucianism and Taoism—guide Chinese culture and politics into modern times.

Greece
In the Athens of the fifth and fourth centuries B.C.E., democracy blooms, and thinkers such as Socrates, Plato, and Aristotle lay the foundations for Western philosophy, emphasizing a systematic search for wisdom.

The story of Solomon is told with emphasis on his wealth, his building and dedication of the Temple, and his wisdom—no mention of his idolatry. Only when the Chronicler got to the stories of the later kings who led Israel into infidelity, idolatry, and exile did he criticize and condemn. He ended with the decree of Cyrus, which at last freed Israel to return from exile to Jerusalem to start again.

The Deuteronomists, in the Books of Samuel, portrayed David as a great warrior-king and a repentant sinner. The Chronicler, however, presented David as a liturgist and leader in worship in order to inspire the Jerusalem community to return to a vibrant religious life.

Read 1 Chronicles 22:1–6,17–19; 28:9–21; 2 Chronicles 6:1–11.

India

The monk Vardhamâna (599 to 527 B.C.E.) establishes Jainism, a religion based on equality and nonviolence. (India's present-day dominant religion, Hinduism, eventually adopts nonviolence as part of its own teachings.) About the same time, the prince Siddhartha Gautama (563 to 483 B.C.E.) has a spiritual awakening and, as the Buddha, teaches the principles of meditation and moderation. Although it does not take firm root in India, Buddhism spreads throughout the rest of the Eastern world.

The Near East

The prophets of Israel and Judah preach monotheism and justice—religious and social ideas that become core beliefs in the great Western religions.

The reformer priest Ezra revives the Jewish community in Jerusalem, teaching the obligations and restrictions set down in the Torah. Later tradition acclaims Ezra to be a second Moses.

In the sixth century B.C.E., the reformer priest Zoroaster revolutionizes Persian religion with his teachings on free will and the afterlife.

The Return:
Discouragement and Struggle

The first six chapters of the Book of Ezra are about the return home from exile in 538 B.C.E. (The book was named for a priest and scribe, Ezra, who came from Babylon to lead a religious renewal in Jerusalem about a hundred years after the exiles returned to Judah. So Ezra himself does not appear in the book named for him until chapter 7.)

The book opens with the decree of Cyrus giving freedom to all the Jewish exiles in the Persian Empire who wish to return to Jerusalem. Cyrus suggests that the exiles remaining behind in Babylon contribute supplies to those who are returning and that all artifacts taken from Solomon's Temple be restored.

The exiles start out from Babylon full of hope and excitement, buoyed by Second Isaiah's prophecy of a new Jerusalem. But when they arrive in Jerusalem, they find nothing but a miserable little village perched on a pile of rubble—its wall and Temple in ruins—and ahead of them a future promising nothing but hardship. Judah is an impoverished land spanning a mere twenty-five miles from north to south. The poor residents of the land, descendants of the Jews that were left behind at the time of the exile to Babylon, resent the newcomers. To the north the Samarian Jews observe the returnees with suspicion. It hardly seems to the exiles like a great homecoming.

The exiles resettle in their ancestral towns and several months later gather in the city to offer sacrifice. Led by **Zerubbabel** (a grandson of King Jehoiachin and thus a descendant of David) and the high priest Joshua, they lay a foundation for a new Temple and commence work.

News of this enterprise travels to the north, and the Samaritans come down to help, saying that they too worship Israel's God. But to the exiles, who consider themselves the remnant (the *true* Israel), these hybrid Jews are not Jews at all, and their offer is rebuffed. The angry Samaritans return to the north and report the project to their Persian rulers as rebellion. Because Cyrus is dead and the present king is unfamiliar with the decree permitting the Jews to rebuild their Temple, the work is halted—for eighteen years.

Read Ezra 1:1–4; 4:1–24.

The Samaritans were Jews whose ancestry went back to the time of the northern kingdom of Israel, with its capital in Samaria. Recall that when the northern kingdom's elite were deported to Assyria in 722 B.C.E., foreign settlers were brought in to colonize the former Israel. The foreigners were ordered by the Assyrians to marry with the local Israelites and worship Israel's God as well as their own gods. The result was a weakening of tribal identity and religious fidelity. The Samaritans—the descendants of the Jews and foreign settlers of the north—were regarded as inferior by the Jews of the south, not "real" Jews, and this prejudice carried over into Jesus' time and beyond.

Third Isaiah:
Get Back on Track, Keep the Vision Alive!

The last eleven chapters of Isaiah (chapters 56 to 66) focus on the state of affairs in Jerusalem after the return of the exiles. The writings speak of the far-from-glorious state of affairs in the Jersualem community, painting a sad picture of the returnees' behavior as they struggle to get back on track again but fail at it.

The vision of a new Jerusalem painted by Second Isaiah during the exile obviously has not yet come true for the returning exiles. The prophet or prophets known as Third Isaiah, probably disciples of Second Isaiah writing around 540 to 510 B.C.E., respond to the grim reality of what the returnees face. Third Isaiah challenges the people to look deeper into the vision that inspired them, to see it as a promise for a day when they have grown into God's plan for the whole world. They are not there yet.

Third Isaiah sees things going downhill rapidly after the arrivals' shock at the ruin in Jerusalem, followed by the obstruction of their Temple project. Laxness and religious apathy settle over the community like a blight. The poor are reduced to hopelessness, the rich care only for themselves, the leaders are faithless, and infidelity and idol worship are rife.

When the rich ask why God ignores their fasting and prayer—and because they alone have enough food, they alone can fast—the answer is that God desires *true* fasting. True fasting is working for the release of the unjustly imprisoned, freeing the oppressed, sharing bread with the hungry, sheltering the homeless, and clothing the naked. For people who fast in this compassionate sense, God promises them great renewal: "Then your light shall break forth like the dawn, / and your healing shall spring up quickly" (Isaiah 58:8).

Read Isaiah 58:1–11.

Third Isaiah tries to stir the people to believe in their own possibilities. If they will learn the ways of justice, God's glory will be with them, they will shine forth a great light, and the nations of the world will gather around them. No more will Jerusalem be called forsaken; instead it will be the hope of the world. One will appear who is anointed to bring good news to the oppressed, to release captives, and to heal the brokenhearted. The new heavens and the new earth will come to pass, and all the world will worship the Lord.

Read Isaiah 60:1–7; 61:1–2; 66:18–23.

Centuries after Isaiah, in the Gospel of Luke, Jesus reads aloud the passage about the anointed one in his hometown synagogue, proclaiming that it is now fulfilled.

Read Luke 4:16–21.

The Book of Isaiah is a masterpiece of the Old Testament. First, Second, and Third Isaiah have different authors, moods, and historical settings, but together they weave a theme: God's love for Israel and tender care for Zion, or Jerusalem. Particularly in Second and Third Isaiah, we find the notion of **universalism**, the dream that God's love for Israel will make it a "light to the nations," ultimately bringing together all nations and peoples of the earth under God's Reign.

The Second Temple: A Focus for Faith

Despite Third Isaiah's attempts to keep the vision of Israel's destiny alive, many of the returning exiles are still disheartened and cannot seem to get back on track. After Jerusalem has languished in apathy for eighteen years, the prophets Haggai, Zechariah, and Malachi appear. They are appalled that God's people have forgotten their calling and realize that the Temple is crucial if the Jews are to keep their religious identity. They waken the people with powerful oracles.

Haggai: No House for God?

Haggai, a speaker with a concise, humorous style, would probably be a political organizer today. He sees the delay in rebuilding the Temple as not entirely the fault of the Samaritans. Poverty, and the powerlessness that goes with poverty, is widespread in Jerusalem, and the rich care only for getting richer—so who is surprised that the leaders are halfhearted and the people religiously lax? or that all agree on one thing only: there are more important things to do than rebuild a temple that has been in ruins for almost seventy years.

Without the Temple, however, the Jerusalem community will lose its faith. Haggai rails at the people for ceasing work on God's house when they have found time to build their own. His eloquence moves Zerubbabel (named governor of Judah by the Persians) and Joshua, the high priest, to action. The people join them, hasten to the site, and begin work!

Read Haggai 1:2–15.

Later in the same year (520 B.C.E.), God asks the people if they are discouraged with their efforts. In truth the new building they are constructing does not remotely compare with Solomon's great Temple. God tells them to take courage, "for I am with you" (Haggai 2:4). But their fervor is centered on the building project, not on the state of their lives or their worship, and they fail to understand.

Read Haggai 2:3–5.

God makes a strong point about the appearance of the Temple being built: The people of Jerusalem need the Temple in order to focus their faith on God's presence among them, worship together as a community, and renew their commitment to God's call. But the Temple's size and furnishings should be a minor concern.

Zechariah: The Messiah Will Come

Zechariah was a visionary concerned with the coming of the Messiah, a Davidic king who would rule in peace and justice, uniting all the nations in the worship of God. (Isaiah's universalist theme is also evident in Zechariah). The New Testament contains over seventy references to Zechariah, mainly in the Book of Revelation. The two halves of the Book of Zechariah are written by two different authors. One author is Zechariah, who spoke shortly after Haggai; the other is an anonymous prophet who wrote about two hundred years later. Scholars have named them First and Second Zechariah.

First Zechariah sees Zerubbabel, the heir to David's throne, as a messianic figure. He thinks that all God's promises to Israel will be fulfilled in Zerubbabel and all the nations will come together in the worship of God under him. (In actuality, however, Zerubbabel never is made king but only governor; the high priest Joshua has more authority. After the exile it is the high priests, not kings, who are the highest leaders of the Judah community. Zerubbabel and the royal line of David disappear from view.)

A beautiful description of messianic times ahead is given: Jerusalem will be a city where the elderly enjoy their leisure and where children play in safety. People will speak the truth, and days of fasting will be occasions for joy.
Read Zechariah 8:1–8.

Like the earlier chapters, Second Zechariah (chapters 9 to 14) has a messianic focus. Now, though, the expected Messiah is not a rich and powerful king but a peaceful Messiah of the poor. We know this from the images the prophet uses. Warrior-kings always ride horses; the messianic king of peace will ride a white donkey—a symbol of peace. The horse, the chariot, and the bow—all symbols of war—will be banned by the messianic king.

Chapter 11 provides an allegory of a shepherd: in it the people wander like sheep without a shepherd until the prophet becomes the true shepherd. In chapter 12 the prophet shows Jerusalem grieving for someone they have apparently murdered and, stricken with guilt, seeking forgiveness. It is easy to understand why the early Christians saw these images as referring to Christ.

Read Zechariah 9:9–10; 11:4–5,7; 12:10.

As a good Jew, Jesus was aware of Zechariah's prophecies about the Messiah and saw them as related to his own life and mission. On the Sunday before his death, he chose to enter Jerusalem as the peaceful king, riding on the back of a donkey, as Zechariah described. And the shepherd passages in Zechariah, together with those in Ezekiel, may have been the source of Jesus' perception of himself as the Good Shepherd.

Read Matthew 21:1–9; John 12:12–16; 10:7–15.

Malachi: Sacrilege, Despite the Temple

The prophet Malachi spoke sometime after the Temple rebuilding project was completed (515 B.C.E.), but before the coming of Nehemiah as governor of Judah (445 B.C.E.). Malachi's book reveals the dismal conditions in Jerusalem, even though the people now have a Temple in which to worship. Malachi is a pen name meaning "my messenger."

The Book of Malachi depicts faith at its lowest in Jerusalem. The sacrifices offered in the Temple can only be called sacrilegious—with blemished, lame, and blind animals offered instead of the perfect ones required by the Law. God, through the prophet Malachi, suggests that the priests try giving such gifts to the governor and see what he says. All over the world, says God, the Gentiles worship with pure offerings, but God's own people profane the altar and call worship a burden.

The people are as guilty as the priests. Returning from exile, they have divorced their Jewish wives and married rich pagan women in order to live more prosperously. They have not only broken vows to God and to their wives but deprived the community of its rightful children. Indeed, they now believe that "'all who do evil are good in the

sight of the LORD'" (Malachi 2:17), and claim that it is unjust of God not to agree.

Read Malachi 1:6–8,10–14; 2:7–8,13–17.

Malachi announces that God will send a messenger to
prepare the people for the coming of judgment. He will be
like a refiner's fire that burns the impurities out of gold or
like the fuller's lye with which the new wool is cleansed.
The people ask, "How shall we return to the LORD?" and
Malachi tells them to *tithe*—that is, donate a tenth of their
income. Evidently the storehouses in the Temple are empty because the offerings have been stolen. Shallow faith has
led the people to admire the successful as the blessed, to
approve even prosperous evildoers who hold God in contempt. But, says Malachi, God is keeping a record. Only repentance will save the people.

Read Malachi 3:1–10.

The people of Judah after the exile have put their hopes
once again in a building, the Temple, to ensure they have
God's favor. Yet the Temple is far from a guarantee of righteousness, as prophets like Jeremiah knew before the exile. If
worship in the Temple is not sincere, it is as good as worth-
less. Something more profound than building a second Temple is needed to bring about the community's renewal.

Renewal: Drawing the Community's Boundaries

Renewal of the Judah community came through the two
greatest leaders of Judah after the exile. Nehemiah was a
governor, and Ezra was a priest. Together, they gave the
people something they desperately needed at that time: a
sense of the boundaries of Judaism and therefore of the
people's own identity—who they were as Jews.

Nehemiah and Ezra labored in Jerusalem while Judah
was under the reign of the tolerant Persian Empire. Little
did they know that after them, terrible times would be
ahead for Judah. The territory would one day fall under the
harsh rule of the Greek Empire, then the Roman Empire.

Without the firm boundaries set by Ezra and Nehemiah, Judaism as a religion would have been washed away in the coming centuries of oppression.

Nehemiah: Rebuilding the Walls

Much of the Book of Nehemiah, written beginning in 445 B.C.E., was taken from Nehemiah's private journal and was meant for God alone. It reveals to us one of the most admirable people in Israel's history—a model public servant.

Nehemiah, a Jew, has a privileged position in the court of the Persian king in the empire's capital. His brother comes from Jerusalem and tells of the city's walls still in ruins, gates gutted, and people demoralized, and Nehemiah grieves and fasts for several days. With the sympathetic king's consent, Nehemiah travels to Jerusalem. There, on a moonlit night shortly after his arrival, with only a handful of companions, Nehemiah rides around the city's walls to inspect the ruins. The walls are so devastated that at times he has to dismount and walk his horse through the rubble.

In the following days, Nehemiah calls everyone in the city to rebuild the walls of Jerusalem. This will protect the city and also recover its former status in the eyes of neighboring peoples. Impressed with his words, the people of Jerusalem want to start work immediately. Neighboring governors accuse the Jews of rebellion and try to frustrate the work. But Nehemiah promises that God will help the people, and the task gets under way.

Read Nehemiah 1:1–4; 2:1–20.

The walls of Jerusalem are, quite literally, its boundaries. Nehemiah is less interested in physical boundaries than in the clear spiritual boundary lines that say, "This is Jewish; that is not." But the walls of the city symbolize the outlines of Judaism's identity. And they are a good place for Nehemiah to start. After all, secure walls will make the inhabitants of Jerusalem safe from foreign attack. In order to attract people to live in the city, Nehemiah has to provide them with a sense of security.

Involving the Whole Community

True to Nehemiah's leadership as a model public servant, he involves the whole community in the construction project. A long list of workers rebuild the walls and gates of the city. The high priest and his staff build the sheep gate, the gate closest to the Temple. The guilds of goldsmiths and perfumers build; fathers and sons build; and one man who has no sons builds with his daughters. The list recorded in the book is a tribute to Nehemiah's record keeping. It also shows how an inspired leader could get the people to roll up their sleeves and begin work lifting rock out of decades of debris to rebuild Jerusalem.

The enemies of the rebuilders try to attack them, but Nehemiah posts guards, arms whole families, and stations a trumpeter to blow an alarm. He writes in his journal that in readiness for an attack, neither he nor his attendants take off their clothes, even at night.

Read Nehemiah 3:1–2,12.

Insisting on Justice

Before the walls are completed, Nehemiah hears the common people cry out against the affluent people of Jerusalem. The common folk have had to pawn their fields, vineyards, homes, and even sons and daughters in order to buy grain to eat. Reduced to poverty, now some of their daughters are even being molested by wealthy kinsmen.

Nehemiah is outraged. He orders the wealthy to return everything to the people they have cheated and to repay any interest they have charged. Modeling the justice he wants to see in the community, he and his friends and family loan money and grain to the poor without charge. The wealthy people agree to do as he says, and Nehemiah makes them swear to it in the presence of the priests.

Read Nehemiah 5:1–13.

As governor of Judah, Nehemiah refuses to use an expense account, to benefit from taxes, or to take land for himself. During the rebuilding of the walls, he sets a table with food and wine for the workers, at his own expense.

But even a model public servant can have enemies. Two men, Sanballat and Tobiah, resent Nehemiah's power. They try to ambush him, they start a smear campaign, and they even try to lure him into the Temple and arrest him. Nehemiah avoids their schemes, and at last the walls are finished. He orders that the gates never be opened before the sun is hot and always be closed before sundown, and he has a guard stationed at all times.

The Jewish leaders take up residence in Jerusalem, and lots are cast among the people to decide who will live there; the rest of the Jews must reside in the other cities. The wall is finally dedicated with great ceremony, and after the religious rituals are celebrated, a gigantic feast is held for all.

Read Nehemiah 5:14–19; 6:1–15; 11:1–2; 12:27–31.

Honoring the Sabbath, Not Marrying Foreigners

Nehemiah journeys back and forth between the Persian court and Jerusalem several times. Returning to Jerusalem for the last time, he finds that his archenemy Tobiah is living in the Temple and that the tithes of grain, wine, and oil for the Temple attendants have been stolen or given away. He has Tobiah thrown out, the chambers purified, and the supplies restored. He calls back the Levites, who have gone home to grow food (they were responsible to care for the Temple). He appoints trustworthy administrators.

But even worse, the Jerusalem farmers and merchants are not keeping the Sabbath—they are conducting trade in the city—and the people are shopping on the Sabbath. Nehemiah reminds them that it was such contempt for the Law that led to Israel's downfall in the past and orders the city gates sealed before the Sabbath and opened only when it is over.

Next, Nehemiah condemns the Jews who have married foreign women and whose children cannot even speak Hebrew. He curses those Jews and has them beaten—so dangerous does he believe this mixing of blood to be for the future of Israel. He warns the other Jews not to give their children in marriage to these half-breeds—as they appear to him. He reminds the people of how Solomon married foreign wives and dissipated the blood of the Davidic line, causing the nation to be divided. He conducts a rite of cleansing so they might be free of all foreign contamination, and with a brief summary of the provisions he has made for the Temple, his book abruptly comes to a close.

Read Nehemiah 13:4–31.

Nehemiah's two final reforms pose tricky questions and may seem quite extreme to us. To understand his motives, we must put ourselves in his time.

Buying and selling on the Sabbath was forbidden by the third commandment. According to the Book of Exodus, the penalty for doing so in Moses' time was death (Exodus 35:1–2). In Nehemiah's time people were not, as many are today, required by their employers to work three shifts or rotate schedules—sometimes on the Sabbath. If they worked or traded on the Sabbath, it was for greed. The prophets loudly condemned the attitude that put money and profit before religious commitment, and Nehemiah was in their tradition, as was Jesus (see Matthew 6:24).

The second reform was to insist that Jews not marry foreigners. In Nehemiah's time intermarriage was the quickest way to weaken a people's religious commitment. That was why the Assyrians had demanded that the settlers in the old northern kingdom marry the local Israelites. Those conquerors wanted to weaken the Israelites' sense of who they were as a community and make them easier to control. And as Nehemiah knew, all the years in Babylon had led many Jews to wonder if the Babylonian god Marduk was not the equal of, or even superior to, Israel's God. The threat of divided loyalties was real and had hurt the people in the past. So the requirement that Jews marry only Jews made sense; they needed a clear identity with undivided hearts if they were to go forward as a united people.

Ezra: Recommitting to the Law

Ezra was a priest and scribe who lived in Babylon about a hundred years after the exile. He came to Jerusalem sometime in the period of Nehemiah, probably on a visit. The sequence of events is a bit unclear, but it seems Ezra then went back to Babylon, returning to Jerusalem after several decades.

Ezra loved the Torah. We can imagine that in Babylon, Ezra was an ardent student of the Torah, perhaps even helping to edit it into book form. Ezra understood that faithfulness to the Law of Moses, God's commandments at the heart of the Torah, was essential for Jews.

We first hear about Ezra in the Book of Nehemiah. But we know about his later work in Jerusalem from the Book of Ezra, where his personal journal is quoted in chapters 7 to 10.

Helping the People Remember Who They Are

Nehemiah, chapter 8, opens with the people gathered at the water gate. Ezra is reading aloud the Book of the Law, probably the Torah, to the men, the women, and all the children who can understand. When he concludes, they fall to their knees weeping. Both Ezra and Nehemiah bid them to rejoice, not weep, and they celebrate the event as a time of renewal.

The following week the people celebrate the feast of Booths—another name for Sukkoth. For seven days they live outdoors in booths made from tree branches. This is to recall their ancestors' years in the wilderness, when God provided for them whatever they needed before they entered Canaan. A number of days after the festival, dressed in sackcloth and covered with ashes, the people confess their sins. Ezra retells the history of Israel to the people and calls them to make a new pact with God. Once again they commit themselves to the Law and reject the sins of their past.

Read Nehemiah 8:1–18.

Firming Up the Boundaries

Ezra evidently goes back to Babylon, but years later (about 398 B.C.E.) he returns to Jerusalem to do what his heart is set on doing—teaching the Torah to the people of Judah. The Persian king gives him permission to go, and to take along any Jews who want to go. Ezra is given gold and silver to be used in Temple worship, and the king decides that no taxes will be imposed on anyone who works in the Temple. Obviously, the king wants Ezra to succeed in his mission to Jerusalem.

Once settled in Jerusalem, Ezra turns his attention to reports that in spite of Nehemiah's warnings, the Jews have continued to marry foreigners. Nehemiah set the boundary that Jews may marry only within Judaism in an effort to unify the people and keep them from abandoning their faith. But now that boundary has broken down.

Ezra tears his cloak, pulls out his hair and beard, and in a retelling of Israel's past infidelities, begs God to pardon its wickedness now. Weeping, the people offer to put aside their foreign spouses and children. Then after Ezra has prayed, he announces that they must do so at once. But it is the rainy season, and the people, shivering in the cold rain, beg for more time. They are given two months to complete the arrangements. The Book of Ezra ends with this forlorn statement: "All these had married foreign women, and they sent them away with their children" (10:44).

Read Ezra 7:1–27; 8:21–23,31–33; 9:1–15; 10:1–17,44.

Again, as with Nehemiah, we may wonder at the extreme nature of Ezra's rules about marriage. Whatever we may think of Ezra and Nehemiah as persons, history has shown that their policies were effective. At a time when the Jewish community was disintegrating, they set the hard boundaries that would ensure the survival of Judaism.

Ezra's greatest gift to Judaism was his preaching the Law, or Torah, the core of the Jewish Bible, which had been put into book form in Babylon. He thus provided a kind of constitution for the Jews—rooting their lives in a common faith and a common code of behavior. Judaism has survived because it is centered in the Bible. As people of the Book, they could continue faithfully even after the Temple was destroyed by the Romans in 70 C.E.

Some good, faithful Jews in the time of Ezra and Nehemiah no doubt took issue with the narrow-mindedness, legalism, and self-righteousness that resulted from their exclusivist policies. Scripture scholars speculate that two books of the Bible were attempts to critique those attitudes.

Recall that the Book of Ruth, probably written after the exile, is a story about a Canaanite woman in the time of the Judges who marries an Israelite and becomes the great-grandmother of King David. So, the author of Ruth seems to be saying, we would not have had our hero David without his ancestor, a foreign woman. God works in mysterious ways, so don't close off your heart.

Then, as we will see in the next chapter, the Book of Jonah is a satirical story of a prophet who bitterly resents it when Judah's old enemies, the Assyrians, repent of their sins and receive God's mercy. The author of the book intended to get across God's universal love for all peoples. But he also must have enjoyed poking fun at the mean-spiritedness of the fictitious prophet Jonah. He held up Jonah's image like a mirror to those Judahites who got carried away with their prejudices.

Joel: Locusts!

The Book of Joel is thought to have been written around 400 B.C.E.—close to the time that Ezra urged the people to recommit themselves to the Law. The book focuses on a plague of locusts that ravages the land. The plague symbolizes the coming catastrophe of God's judgment on the people for their continuing infidelity.

Joel paints the picture of the plague vividly. Everyone is weeping and wailing. Wheat, barley, fig trees, pomegranates, date palms, and apple trees have dried up. Barns have collapsed; cattle and sheep have perished. Joel bids the people to don sackcloth, proclaim a fast, and beg God to spare them. After the people have fasted and prayed, God promises plenty and peace again.

Read Joel 1:1–12; 2:12–18,28 (or 3:1 in NAB or NJB).

Joel contains some passages that may be familiar to you. One passage (2:12–18) is often heard in Catholic churches on Ash Wednesday, when the forty-day fast of Lent begins. Another passage (2:28, or 3:1 in NAB or NJB) is also well known:

> I will pour out my spirit on all flesh;
> your sons and your daughters shall prophesy,
> your old men shall dream dreams,
> and your young men shall see visions.

Saint Peter would quote these words from Joel in his sermon on the first Pentecost.
Read Acts 2:14–17.

Obadiah: Woe to Edom!

Obadiah, the shortest book in the Bible, is a one-chapter attack on Edom (a small state in what is now Jordan), possibly for its part in the Babylonians' sack of Jerusalem. Because Esau, the founder of Edom, and Jacob were brothers (recall their rivalry for Abraham's blessing in the Book of Genesis), Obadiah accuses Edom of fratricide—killing one's brother. Edom has been gloating over its brother's ruin, looting his goods, and selling his survivors.

Obadiah is sure that Edom will pay for its crimes, and that Israel deserves better times ahead—and will see them.
Read Obadiah 1:10–15,17,21.

Keeping the Faith Alive Under Fire

The last part of this chapter takes the story of Israel up to about one hundred years before the time of Jesus. The two Books of Maccabees and the Book of Daniel have as their context the period of Jewish resistance to Greek domination.

The identity of Judaism had become firmly established with Ezra and Nehemiah's reforms, which the Persians not only tolerated but supported. However, the era of tolerant Persian oversight ended when **Alexander the Great** conquered the Persian Empire in 330 B.C.E. Then for about two centuries, the **Greek Empire** dominated Judea (the Greco-Roman name for Judah), with periods of terrible persecution that severely tested the faith of the Jews.

The problem of Greek domination was not just that the Greek rulers were harsh and powerful, punishing the

Jews with torture and death for practicing their religion during certain time periods. Perhaps the subtler but greater problem was the allure of the sophisticated Greek lifestyle and bold new way of thinking. The Greek style included the belief that human reason is more important than religious faith, the emphasis on the individual over the community, and an appealing culture of philosophy, drama, literature, science, architecture, and athletic games.

During peaceful periods, when there was not open persecution, the Greek way of life must have seemed quite exciting to young Jews, who were accustomed to being considered strange in the Greek world because of their religion. With the Greek language becoming popular, many young people did not even learn Hebrew anymore. And within a few generations, Greek became the language of everyday life for most Jews. In fact, some of the later books of the Bible were originally written in Greek because so many Jews did not understand Hebrew. The boundaries set so firmly by Ezra and Nehemiah were under attack as the dominant Greek culture eroded traditional Jewish life.

Some Jews insisted on the old ways, allowing no concession to Greek thinking or customs. Another group believed that compromise was possible, that adaptation to things Greek—even abandonment of Jewish religious practices—was the realistic method of survival. These two groups grew further and further apart. Soon their conflict mushroomed into full-scale civil war between the pro-Greek Jews and the anti-Greek Jews.

The anti-Greek Jews' resistance to Greek domination grew until the Greek Seleucid dynasty that controlled Judea decided to crush the opposition. This situation is the historical context for the two Books of Maccabees and the Book of Daniel.

The Books of Maccabees: Taking On the Greek Empire

The two Books of Maccabees were written by two unknown authors around 100 B.C.E.—but they are set in the period of harsh Greek persecution that began in 175 B.C.E. First Maccabees is a history of the revolt of the Jews under the domination of Greek rulers. It tells of the struggle of Judas Maccabeus and his brothers to free the Jews from Greek control, confirms that God is with the people, exalts the Jews who remain faithful to God, and condemns the apostates, those who have renounced their faith.

Second Maccabees tells in detail of a cruel persecution of the Jews. It confirms belief in the resurrection of the dead, the intercession of the saints, and the offering of prayers for the dead.

Greek Oppression Heats Up

The First Book of Maccabees opens when the Seleucid king **Antiochus IV** comes to the throne in 175 B.C.E., calling himself Epiphanes, meaning "God made visible." His subjects soon change this name to Epimanes, meaning "madman."

In Jerusalem the pro-Greek Jews, led by a corrupt high priest, build a gymnasium where young men participate in athletic events naked—a practice that the traditional Jews condemn; those in the games hide their marks of circumcision so as not to be obviously Jewish. Then when Antiochus takes the treasures from the Temple to pay for his military adventures, animosity among the faithful Jews mounts. Two years later he sends a military force to Jerusalem to control the anti-Greek Jews. The soldiers burn houses, kill people, and build a citadel. The citadel is to house more military troops who will occupy Jerusalem; it is also to be a haven for protecting the apostate Jews.

When these measures fail to counter Jewish resistance, Antiochus orders that everyone in his realm must embrace his religion. Under penalty of death, the Jews must abandon their Law, destroy their scrolls, offer sacrifices to Greek gods, cease circumcision, and ignore their dietary rules. The Temple is defiled by the occupiers, the altar profaned with sacrifices of swine, and, most horrible of all to the Jews, an altar to the god Zeus is erected on the altar of holocausts. But many Jews stand firm in their resolve to be faithful.

Read 1 Maccabees 1:1–63.

Heroic Martyrdom for the Sake of the Young

At this time a Jewish elder named **Eleazar** has been arrested by the Greeks for his refusal to eat pork, a meat forbidden by Jewish Law as being unclean. In charge of his execution are young Jews who work for the Greek authorities. They have known Eleazar all their life and are deeply disturbed at the thought of his death. They propose to bring him meat that is not pork but looks like pork. He can eat it without breaking the Law yet dupe the king by seeming to eat pork. Eleazar replies to their scheme in effect, "If you think that to save my life for a few short years, I would scandalize all the young who are watching me, you are quite mistaken." And he dies, "leaving in his death an example of nobility and a memorial of courage, not only to the young but to the great body of his nation" (2 Maccabees 6:31).

Read 2 Maccabees 6:18–31.

A Mother and Her Seven Sons: We Shall Live Again

The Second Book of Maccabees tells about the same period of persecution under Antiochus IV as in the First Book of Maccabees. A remarkable incident testifies to the courage and magnificent faith of the Jerusalem Jews.

A mother and her seven sons are arrested for refusing to eat pork. When torture fails to persuade them, the mother is forced to watch all her sons, from the eldest to the youngest, endure unspeakable torments and be put to death, after which the mother is also slain.

As several of the sons go to their horrible deaths, they and their mother proclaim their belief that they will live again with God and one another. "'One cannot but choose to die at the hands of mortals and to cherish the hope God gives of being raised again by him. But for you there will be no resurrection to life!'" one brother, near death, declares to his torturers (2 Maccabees 7:14). And the last brother to be killed says, "'For our brothers after enduring a brief suffering have drunk of ever-flowing life, under God's covenant'"

(7:36). The account remarks, simply and eloquently, "So he died in his integrity, putting his whole trust in the Lord" (7:40).

Read 2 Maccabees: 7:1–42.

The story of the martyrdom of the mother and her seven sons is a powerful testimony to the belief in **resurrection** —that God will raise the just to new life with God and one another after death. This belief was just emerging within Judaism in the late centuries before Christ. Belief in resurrection also appears in the Book of Daniel.

The Maccabees: A Revolt That Succeeds

The remainder of the First Book of Maccabees tells how a Jewish family led by one brother named **Judas**, also called **Maccabeus** ("the hammerer"), takes on the mighty Greek Empire (a revolt that began in 166 B.C.E.) and manages to achieve a measure of independence for little Judea. Along the way the rebels also kill pro-Greek Jews. In the Maccabees' mind, violent resistance is the only way left to keep the Jewish faith alive under such an oppressive empire.

By 164 B.C.E. the Jews take back control of the Jerusalem Temple, which has been defiled by the Greeks. The region continues to be under Seleucid rule. But for certain periods, interspersed with wars and persecutions, Judea is allowed to govern itself—until the Roman Empire takes over Judea in 63 B.C.E.

The Origins of Hanukkah

The Jewish **feast of Hanukkah** has its origins in the celebration that followed the rededication of the Temple after the Greeks had defiled it. Here is how it came about:

The Maccabees find the Temple forlorn and abandoned—its altar desecrated, the gates burned, and weeds growing in the courts. First they mourn; then they get to work. They purify the sanctuary and the courts, remove the profaned altar and build a new one, make new sacred vessels, light a new lamp, hang curtains, and place fresh loaves on the altar of holocausts. A year from the day of its defilement, the Temple is consecrated again. The people celebrate for eight days, and Judas decrees that these days be celebrated on the anniversary every year. This is the event celebrated by our Jewish brothers and sisters on their feast of Hanukkah.

Read 1 Maccabees 4:36–59.

On the celebration of Hanukkah, Jews tell a much-loved legend not found in the Bible:

When the priests, led by Judas Maccabeus, were about to light the menorah, the seven-branched candelabra, they were alarmed to find that the specially prepared oil was gone. Jugs of this oil were always kept sealed by the high priests, but only one small jar was left—barely enough oil for one night. But to their delight, the oil miraculously lasted for eight full days while the people celebrated and prepared more oil.

Hanukkah, which takes place in early December, is also called the Festival of Lights and is celebrated for eight days with prayer and praise. In Jewish homes tiny candles or oil lamps are lighted on a candelabra, one each day, and gifts are given to the children.

Daniel: Stories and Visions for the Faint of Heart

"Resist Greek oppression with all your heart! Do not give in to the Greeks and do not compromise the faith!" This was the message the Jewish people needed to hear during the era when the Greek Empire threatened to wipe out their religion. The spiritual boundaries of Judaism, drawn so firmly by Ezra and Nehemiah three centuries earlier, had to be defended, or Judaism would cease to exist and Israel would never become a light to the nations.

The Maccabees offered a strategy of resistance—a military campaign for Jewish independence. But the anonymous author of the Book of Daniel offered a different response—a spiritual and theological approach that contrasted sharply with the violent strategy of the Maccabees.

Writing during the time of the Greek persecution, the author of Daniel tried to inspire the Jews to nonviolent resistance, with a radical trust in God's power to make everything come out right in the end. Both approaches aimed at preserving the boundaries of Judaism and remaining faithful to God. But the Maccabees focused on human power and might to set things right, while the author of Daniel held out God's love and justice as the ultimate power that saves.

Although the stories and visions in the Book of Daniel are set in Babylon in the time of the exile, they really address the situation of the Jews under Greek rule. But to keep from being killed himself by the Greeks, the author had to avoid any direct references to the Greek oppressors in his writing. So the book is filled with code names and plenty of analogies to the plight of the Jews living under Greek rule, which they, but not the Greeks, would have readily understood. It was a clever way to resist—inspiring frightened people with hope-filled stories and visions from another time and place. It was not unlike what the black slaves of the U.S. South did, as they fired up their dreams of freedom by telling the old stories of Moses and the escape of the Israelites from slavery in Egypt, all through God's power.

In the Fiery Furnace and the Lion's Den

Chapters 1 to 6 of Daniel tell stories about a young man named **Daniel** and his friends who, in the time of the exile in Babylon, refuse to give in to their rulers' demands that they worship idols. Most familiar are the stories of the three young men in the fiery furnace and the story of Daniel in the lion's den. In these wonderfully told stories, we see that the refusal to give up the faith leads to fierce persecution. But in the end, God's power saves the resisters from harm.

Read Daniel, chapters 3 and 6. (The NAB and NJB versions include the entire text of chapter 3; the NRSV puts the verses of a prayer and a song of praise into the apocryphal or deuterocanonical Scriptures.)

What was the author of the Book of Daniel trying to say to young Jews under Greek persecution? The author and the Jews of his time knew that Jews who resisted the Greeks were being killed on a regular basis. They would have been aware of persons like Eleazar and the mother and her seven sons, martyrs for Judaism who suffered brutal torture before dying.

The storyteller of Daniel was trying to say: *"Ultimately, you will not be harmed. You may die in the physical sense but your spirit will not be crushed. God will be with you and save you for the kind of life that lasts forever."*

The Book of Daniel, like the Second Book of Maccabees, points to life after death, to resurrection, and to an unquenchable hope in God despite circumstances that seem overwhelming and defeating.

Visions of How It Will All Turn Out

With chapter 7 of Daniel, the book turns to Daniel's disturbing visions. In one dream four powerful beasts—representing four nations that are Israel's enemies—rise out of a boiling sea. But God condemns them and gives dominion to "one like a son of man" (7:13, NAB)—meaning one like a human being—whom all peoples and nations will one day serve as king in an everlasting reign.

Read Daniel 7:12–14.

In a later vision, an angel tells Daniel that great anguish will one day come to his people but that the just will be delivered from harm. Many "'who sleep in the dust of the earth shall awake, some to everlasting life, and some to shame and everlasting contempt'" (Daniel 12:2). Those who lead others to justice will shine like the stars for all eternity. These words affirm a belief in the afterlife and in resurrection similar to the belief we saw in the Second Book of Maccabees.

Jesus used the term *Son of Man* eighty-two times in the Gospels, sometimes clearly referring to himself. Christians have always seen the promise in the Book of Daniel of the coming reign of "one like a son of man" as fulfilled in Jesus Christ.

Read Matthew 26:59–64.

Apocalyptic Literature

Daniel's visions in chapters 7 to 12 are prime examples of **apocalyptic literature,** a form of writing widely used in Judaism from about 200 B.C.E. to 200 C.E. The Book of Revelation in the New Testament is also of this type. This kind of writing is characterized by strange symbolic images that represent events, places, and even particular people of the time in which it is written. Usually that is a period of crisis or persecution, such as the persecution of the Jews by the Greeks or of the early Christians by the Romans. Thus the author uses a pseudonym to disguise the writer's identity. The literature's symbols are code language for those "in the know," which keeps the true subject of the writing secret from the oppressors.

Apocalyptic writing was intended to give hope and inspiration to those oppressed by powerful forces. It affirms that in the great cosmic struggle between good and evil in the world, the power of good—that is, the power of God—will prevail in the end. For those who are in distress, apocalyptic literature offers a bold, rallying vision of God's ultimate triumph over injustice and suffering. It proclaims with deep conviction that in the end God is in charge, and God will win. The message for the audience, in so many words, is this: "Bear suffering patiently now and keep your faith in God, because one day God's victory will be ours!"

Apocalyptic literature has often been misunderstood to predict certain real events in the future. For example, some have claimed the Book of Revelation predicts a global catastrophe like nuclear war or the fall of particular world powers like the Soviet Union. Presently we are in the period surrounding the turn of the millennium, the year 2000. No doubt there will be a great flurry of claims that symbols from apocalyptic literature, particularly the Book of Revelation, are being played out in contemporary world events. However, such claims show an inadequate understanding of apocalyptic literature and are distractions from the powerful message that the writer intended.

Up to the Time of Jesus

The scriptural history of Israel comes to an end with the Maccabees accounts and the apocalyptic visions of Daniel, which emerged from the period of Greek persecution. As noted earlier in this chapter, in 63 B.C.E. the Romans conquered the Greeks and took over the region of Palestine, in which Judea was located. At the time of Jesus' birth (about 5 B.C.E.), the little territory was held tightly under the huge thumb of the **Roman Empire**, the most powerful and efficient of the ancient empires. Many Jews put their hopes in a messiah sent from God, "one like a son of man" (Daniel 7:13, NAB). They believed this messiah would save them, transforming them from a humiliated, subjugated people to a people whose destiny as a beacon of God's love and light to the world would finally be fulfilled.

Questions for Reflection and Discussion

1. Recollect some situations in your life in which it was helpful, even essential, to know who you were, what you stood for, and what your boundaries were.

2. What do you think it means to bring together all nations and peoples of the earth under God's Reign? Is it possible to unite all people?

3. The spirit behind tithing is that we give the first 10 percent of our income to charity and to our church, trusting that God will take care of our needs, no matter what financial struggles we might meet. The giving should happen before we buy anything or pay our bills, not from leftover money. Tithing is an act of justice and an act of faith. What is your opinion about tithing? Do you think you could do it?

4. Who would be some contemporary models of servant-leadership like Nehemiah?

5. In your experience have you witnessed any good examples of people accepting the new and yet remaining faithful to their heritage?

6. In the era of Greek rule, the threats to Jewish religious practice were obvious. What are some not so obvious threats to your religious practice today?

10

Wisdom and Wit

> But the souls of the righteous are in the hand of God,
> and no torment will ever touch them.
> In the eyes of the foolish they seemed to have died,
> and their departure was thought to be a disaster,
> and their going from us to be their destruction;
> but they are at peace.
> For though in the sight of others they were punished,
> their hope is full of immortality.
>
> (Wisdom 3:1–4)

During the centuries before the birth of Jesus, as noted in chapter 9, the people of Israel were under foreign domination. Judah fell under Babylonian control, followed by Persian, Greek, and finally Roman rule. In the Dispersion, Jews were scattered beyond Palestine to places far from home, where they settled as strangers in strange lands. Whether in Judea or far away, Jews were controlled by the major empires. So they had to respond to the challenges that foreign cultures and powers brought to every aspect of their life.

The Old Testament books considered in this chapter were composed at various times after the Babylonian exile, some quite late, when foreign influences were swirling around Judaism. First the chapter focuses on six **wisdom books: Proverbs, Job, Ecclesiastes, Sirach, Wisdom,** and the **Song of Songs.** Then it turns to the wonderful stories told in the Books of **Tobit, Judith, Esther,** and **Jonah.** The **Psalms,** also counted among the wisdom books, will be treated in chapter 11.

In different ways the authors of the books covered in this chapter tried to address questions such as these:

- What does it mean to be a wise person?
- What is the meaning and purpose of life? Where are we going?
- Why do good people suffer and bad people prosper? Why should we be good in a world that is unfair?
- How can we live good and faithful lives when surrounded by those who are hostile to our beliefs?

Life According to Proverbs, Job, and Ecclesiastes

Biblical wisdom literature grew out of a kind of writing that flourished in non-Jewish cultures of the ancient Near East, especially in Egypt. These earlier writings instructed administrators in royal courts on how to act. They contained maxims on the acquiring of virtues and, often, on the problem of good versus evil—although they were not religious texts.

Influenced by such literature, Jewish sages adapted this kind of wisdom writing to Israel's own faith, which saw God as the source of all wisdom. Israel's wisdom books speak to the individual about the wholeness and integrity of a good life, and about the personal disintegration caused by sin. The goal of the biblical teachers of wisdom was to inspire moral integrity.

Proverbs: What Is a Good Life?

The Book of Proverbs appeared sometime after the Babylonian exile, during the period of the second Temple. It consists of several collections of wisdom teachings, intended to instruct the young especially. Some sections of the book are probably from as early as Solomon's monarchy, when scribes in the royal court collected and wrote down wise sayings.

Proverbs, like other wisdom writings, is concerned with how to live a good life; it is full of down-to-earth, practical advice. Here is a sampling:

- *Parenting.* "Discipline your children while there is hope; / do not set your heart on their destruction" (19:18).
- *Communications.* "A soft answer turns away wrath, / but a harsh word stirs up anger" (15:1).
- *Attitudes.* "Pride goes before destruction, / and a haughty spirit before a fall" (16:18).
- *Manners at court.* "A gift opens doors; / it gives access to the great" (18:16).
- *Work.* "In all toil there is profit, / but mere talk leads only to poverty" (14:23).
- *Conducting business.* "The integrity of the upright guides them, / but the crookedness of the treacherous destroys them" (11:3).
- *Reputation.* "A good name is to be chosen rather than great riches, / and favor is better than silver or gold" (22:1).
- *Leadership.* "If a ruler listens to falsehood, / all his officials will be wicked" (29:12).
- *Gossip.* "A perverse person spreads strife, / and a whisperer separates close friends" (16:28).
- *Learning.* "A fool takes no pleasure in understanding, / but only in expressing personal opinion" (18:2).
- *Relationships with neighbors.* "A generous person will be enriched, / and one who gives water will get water" (11:25).

You may have noticed in these examples a literary device that is typical of wisdom sayings. The same wise truth is stated in two ways, for instance, "Misfortune pursues sinners, / but prosperity rewards the righteous" (13:21). We might imagine young Jews of biblical times memorizing these sayings in school, with the teacher calling out the first half of the proverb, and the students responding with the second half.

According to Proverbs, success and prosperity, rightly gained, are the reward for a virtuous life. Honor, dignity, and a good name are a person's memorial—there is no hint of an afterlife. The importance of living prudently, honestly, generously, and diligently can be seen in a famous passage about the "ideal wife," which ends the Book of Proverbs.

Read Proverbs 31:10–31.

Where is God in all this wisdom? Most of the sayings do not mention God. However, the perspective of the Jewish sages was that true wisdom is from God, no matter where we find it—in the advice of family and friends, in common sense, in nature, even in other cultures with their appealing wisdom sayings. The sages saw the world as full of God's wisdom. Strikingly, in chapters 8 and 9 wisdom is portrayed as a woman who came forth from God in the beginning before the world was created. She was with God as the "master worker" while the heavens and the earth were made; thus wisdom fills the whole world. So it is not surprising that the sages looked to everyday experience of the world to find wisdom.

Read Proverbs 8:1–11,22–31.

Proverbs' image of God's wisdom as a woman adds a feminine voice and quality to the traditional Jewish image of God as masculine. This feminine image of wisdom has been called Lady Sophia, after the Greek word for wisdom.

Job: Why Do the Good Suffer?

While the wisdom writers of the Book of Proverbs taught that a virtuous life brings success and prosperity, an unknown Jewish sage after the Babylonian exile was questioning that mentality. "Wait a minute," he must have reasoned, "it's not necessarily the case that good people have wealth, health, and the admiration of their family and community. What about the good people who have a miserable life of poverty, sickness, and rejection? And what about the wicked people who have plenty of money and a grand, comfortable life? How do you explain that?" Most Jews of the time, including this sage, did not believe in an afterlife where good would be rewarded and evil punished. They thought that rewards and punishments had to be given out in this life, or never at all.

Many people today, even those who believe in the afterlife, struggle with the same kind of questions: Why does a mother of three young children die? Why do people starve in a famine while others have so much food they don't know what to do with it? Why were six million Jews killed by the Nazis during World War II? The dilemma of why the good suffer and the wicked prosper in this life presents us with the ancient **problem of evil**. We first saw this issue raised in Israel's consciousness by the prophet Habakkuk, who asked, "Why?"

The author of the Book of Job struggled with that dilemma and wrote a poetic story considered one of the world's great literary treasures. In it a virtuous and prosperous man named Job loses everything—wealth, family, health. He bears his suffering patiently, trusting in, not questioning God.

Read Job 1:1–22; 2:1–13.

The figure of Satan—the adversarial spirit—in the story is a heavenly prosecutor allowed to work in the human world, whose job is to test the genuineness of human virtue.

In his suffering Job finally calls out, "Why?" and curses the day he was born. His friends insist that Job's sin must be the reason for his misfortune, that if he prays to God and repents, all will be well again. But Job disagrees, arguing with them in a series of disputes.

Read the following passages from Job:
- *3:1–3,11–26 (Job's cries)*
- *4:7–9 (the words of Job's friend Eliphaz)*
- *6:8–10,24–25 (Job's reply to Eliphaz)*
- *8:3–7 (the words of Job's friend Bildad)*
- *11:1–6 (the words of Job's friend Zophar)*
- *13:1–5,15–16 (Job's reply to Zophar)*
- *27:3–6 (Job's words to Bildad)*
- *33:1–6,8–13 (the words of a young man named Elihu)*

At last, after all the arguing has brought no satisfying answers, God, who has been silent all along, speaks out of a whirlwind to Job:

> "Where were you when I laid the foundation of the earth?
>   Tell me, if you have understanding.
> Who determined its measurements—surely you know!"
> (Job 38:4–5)

In a long discourse, God reminds Job that God, not Job, is the Creator of the universe who sustains everything in existence. Job, awed and humbled, admits that the mystery of life is too great for him to understand. God's wisdom is far beyond his own. At last Job believes this truth and accepts what has happened.

Read Job 38:1–30; 39:19–30; 42:1–6.

The "Answer"

The Book of Job does not give a definite answer to the question of why good people suffer. But it clearly dismisses the easy answers of Job's smug friends—that suffering is a punishment from God and prosperity is a sign of God's approval. Rather than answers, the story leaves Job with a sense of humility in the face of mystery: some things are simply beyond the grasp of the human mind, and all we can do is bow before the mystery of God.

The message of the Book of Job is that we may never rationally understand the existence of evil in the world. But we can trust that even in the darkest moments, God is in charge, loving and caring for us through it all.

Ecclesiastes: Is Life Lived in Vain?

Another sage reflected on the meaning of life during the time Jews were under Greek rule, about 250 B.C.E. Like the author of Job, he questioned the common notion that virtue leads to good fortune, and wickedness to misfortune. "It's not so simple! Life is a lot more complex than that," he seemed to say. His response was the Book of Ecclesiastes, a Greek word for the name Qoheleth, which is Hebrew for "teacher." (His pupils thought of him as *the* teacher.)

The book is known for what appears to be a pessimistic outlook on life. Where Habakkuk and Job asked God, "Why?" Qoheleth's response to life's inconsistencies was, "Who's surprised?" On the other hand, he may have been the kind of man who liked to startle his students with unexpected questions and provocative comments—just to make them think. For example:

- In his book Qoheleth says that nothing makes a difference—people are born, die, and are forgotten—and there is nothing new under the sun: "Vanity of vanities! All is vanity!" (1:2). (Here *vanity* means "vaporizing quickly" or "meaningless.")

- Then he reverses this dour comment with his famous poem (3:1–8): "For everything there is a season, and a time for every matter under heaven. . . ."
- At the poem's conclusion, he seems to say that all things, including reward for the righteous and punishment for the wicked, will be accomplished in God's time (3:17), though we cannot expect to understand God's ways.

Qoheleth worried about injustice and wickedness and about their victims, who were doomed, he believed, to a dead end in earthly life. As for eternity, he knew nothing of a heaven hereafter. But in the end he came to the conclusion that life was a mystery he could not solve. The sensible thing, he says in his book, is to accept it from the hand of God and enjoy it as well as one can.

Read Ecclesiastes 1:1–11; 2:18–26; 3:1–22.

Wisdom, Sirach, and the Song of Songs: Life with God

The author of the Book of Wisdom (often called the Wisdom of Solomon) was a scholarly Jew who lived in Alexandria, Egypt, sometime after 100 B.C.E. Like the wisdom teachers who wrote Job and Ecclesiastes, this sage struggled with the problem of evil, and with the meaning and purpose of life. He refused to accept the conventional wisdom that God rewards goodness and punishes sin in this life. After all, not long before his era, virtuous Jews had been tortured and put to death for refusing to give up their faith. Something more than the conventional wisdom of Proverbs was needed for people to accept such undeserved suffering.

The answer for this sage was that rewards and punishments will not necessarily come in this life. Beyond this life lies the soul's destiny. What are we made for? Death is not the end of us. Our destiny is life forever with God.

Read Wisdom 1:12–16; 2:21–24; 3:1–7.

At the final judgment, the wicked will see that their wealth and success are not rewardable in the arithmetic of eternal life. They will remember their mockery of the just ones and see that all the while they themselves were the fools.

Read Wisdom 5:3–10,15–16.

The author of Wisdom joins the other late Jewish biblical writers who asserted the existence of the soul's life after the physical body's death. Recall that the Second Book of Maccabees and the Book of Daniel, written in the context of Greek persecution, proclaimed this same truth of everlasting life.

This concept of the soul as capable of life separate from the body indicates the author's exposure to Greek thought. Generally the Jews saw the person as a whole, inseparable being. When physical life ended, there was no way for a person to live on except in people's memories. But the Greeks introduced the concepts of body and soul to Judaism. With this innovation in thought, the Jewish sages could see the possibility of life beyond death. Up to this time, any Jewish conception of life after death had more to do with the rare event of restoring people to *earthly* life—as in the miracle by Elisha (2 Kings 4:32–37).

Sirach: Wisdom in the Teachings of Israel

A man named Jesus ben Sirach ran a school for scriptural study and Jewish wisdom in Alexandria, Egypt (then under the Greek Empire), and wrote between 200 and 175 B.C.E. He wanted to instruct his fellow Jews who were confused by the philosophical questions of the Greeks. He wrote that all wisdom comes from God—not from Greek thought!

The Book of Sirach depicts wisdom as a woman who was with God at Creation—like the image described in the Book of Proverbs. Unlike most Jewish wisdom literature, though, Sirach is deeply concerned with the history of Israel, its heroes, and its institutions. According to Sirach, wisdom's home is in Israel. Wisdom is found specifically in the teachings of Israel as given by God, and keeping the Commandments is the way to wisdom. (The book's alternate name is Ecclesiasticus, which means "church book," but that title should not be confused with Ecclesiastes.)

The advice given in the Book of Sirach is as full of wisdom for us as it was for the ancients.

Read Sirach 1:19–23; 2:1–6; 3:1–4; 4:1–5,8–10; 5:9–14 (or 5:11–17 in NAB); 6:8–12,14–17; 11:1–3,7–9; 24:1–8.

Chapter 24 of Sirach is one of the greatest writings about wisdom in the Bible. Sirach says that wisdom came forth from the mouth of God to make her dwelling place with Jacob's people. He is reminding the Jews that God's wisdom dwells with us. Wisdom may test us with difficulties, but times of difficulty can be seed times, times for growing strong.

The Song of Songs: Human and Divine Love

The Song of Songs is one of the wisdom books, but it differs from the others in theme and concern. Rather than a book of teachings about wisdom, it is a collection of love poems written by unknown authors sometime after the Babylonian exile, about 450 B.C.E. It is a dialog between a bridegroom and a bride, who speak of their love and longing for each other, with now-and-again asides from their friends. (At one time the book was attributed to King Solomon, so in some Bible versions, it is called the Song of Solomon.)

Why is the Song of Songs a book of the Bible, when it does not even mention God? The ancient Jews and Christians who decided to include it in their respective Bibles recognized that God designed human love as a powerful and holy bond. In itself, human love is good and a gift from God.

Early interpreters of the book saw the work as a religious allegory. For both Jews and Christians, the bride and groom's mutual love was an image of God's love for and passionate devotion to Israel. For Christians, it was also a figure of Christ's love for his "bride," the church, and also for the soul of an individual believer.

In the Song of Songs, the bride describes herself as dark, like the tents of Kedar that are woven from black goat's hair. She wistfully asks where her lover pastures his sheep. It is the kind of yearning all lovers know.

Read Song of Songs 1:5–7.

The bride compares herself to a flower of the field, unlike the exotic blooms that grow in the gardens of the rich. But the groom says that compared to the other women, she is a lily among thistles!

Read Song of Songs 2:1–6.

A walled garden has long been a symbol of virginity. The groom sings with joy of the maiden who has kept herself for their bridal union.

Read Song of Songs 4:12–16. (In chapter 4, verse 12, the term *sister* is one of endearment, not kinship.)

The bride longs to be as close to the groom as the name seal that he wears on a cord about his neck, resting on his heart. She would be one with him—as he and his name are one. In this passage we hear the well-known tribute to the power of love:

> Set me as a seal upon your heart,
>   as a seal upon your arm;
> for love is strong as death,
>   passion fierce as the grave.

(Song of Songs 8:6)

Read Song of Songs 8:6–7.

Love can overcome death. This is the wisdom offered us by the Song of Songs.

Stories of Encouragement

We saw in the stories of Jacob, Rebekah, David, Saul, Jonathan, and the rest the history of Israel's calling to be God's people. The later stories that are covered in the remainder of this chapter were tales told during the centuries after the Babylonian exile; they were meant to inspire courage and faith in times of trial. The stories reminded the people over and over that goodness and faithfulness will triumph in the end. The Books of Tobit, Judith, and Esther are listed among the historical books of the Bible; Jonah is listed as a prophetic book. However, all these books are treated here as storybooks because modern Scripture scholars have determined that they are not accounts of historical events. As storybooks, however, they are inspired by God, conveying God's truth just as the historical accounts of the Bible do.

Tobit: The Faithful Jew

The Book of Tobit was written by an unknown author in about 200 B.C.E., to encourage faithful Jews to be righteous and patient during the difficult period of Greek oppression. The story is set around five hundred years earlier, in the Assyrian capital of Nineveh after the fall of the northern kingdom of Israel.

The story is of a good, faithful Jew, Tobit, and his family. Tobit's love for his fellow Israelites extends to burying their corpses in time of Assyrian persecution—even at great risk to his own life.

Tobit, however, is discouraged and sad because he has become blind with cataracts. In a faraway city, a young woman, Sarah, also grieves her misfortune. Every man she marries (there have been seven) has died on their wedding night, killed by a jealous demon. Tobit and Sarah, mournful about their respective situations, pray to God to end their life—at the same moment, but separated by many miles.

God, however, is caring for both of them in their sorrow, weaving their lives together through the intervention of an angel—Raphael—who appears as a man named Azariah. The angel accompanies Tobit's son Tobias (called Tobiah in some versions) on a long journey to retrieve some money owed to Tobit. Along the way the angel matches up Tobias with Sarah. She is related to Tobit's family and known as the woman whose husbands mysteriously die on their wedding night. Under Raphael's (Azariah's) guidance, Tobias trusts that all will be well. Tobias and Sarah are married, and sure enough, the husband-killing demon is banished that night with the help of the wise angel. Tobias and Sarah pray together for their marriage before they go to bed.

Soon, they all return home to Tobit and his wife, Anna. Tobit's blindness is miraculously cured, again with the help of the angel, Raphael, who reveals himself as God's messenger and then disappears. And the story ends happily, with the faithful goodness of Tobit and the trust of his son Tobias being rewarded.

Read Tobit, chapters 1 to 12.

The Book of Tobit reminds us that in the end faithful goodness and trust in God are rewarded with blessings. The simple goodness of Tobit and his family moves people today, and it must have deeply inspired Jews living under Greek domination.

The writer of Tobit was familiar with the folk literature of his time, and the Book of Tobit shows traces of several ancient stories—among them one called "The Grateful Dead." This folktale tells how a young man buries a corpse in perilous circumstances and later obtains a bride with the help of a companion and protector, who is ultimately revealed as the spirit of the deceased.

Judith: Courage and Piety

The author of the Book of Judith was probably a Palestinian Jew who wrote sometime after 150 B.C.E. The story is set in the Persian period after the Babylonian exile, and the first sentence of the book contains a blooper. Nebuchadrezzar, the author says, is the king of Assyria—when everyone knows that he was king of Babylon. It is so obviously wrong that we know that the author is teaching a lesson—not a history—in the manner of folk and hero legends. Judith may not have been a historical person, but she was a model of faith and courage, and that was what the Jews of that time needed.

The story tells of how a young Israelite woman saves her people from destruction at the hands of Holofernes, Nebuchadrezzar's cruel general.

The Israelite town of Bethulia is strategically located near the mountain passes where the Assyrians could enter and overrun Israel. If Bethulia falls, all of Israel will be crushed. Holofernes has control of Bethulia's water supply, so he decides that rather than attack the town, risking his troops, he can simply let Bethulia run out of water and wait for the people to die of thirst.

Weeks later, the townspeople, who have tried to ration their water but are panicking, are on the brink of surrender to Holofernes. Here the heroine Judith enters—a young widow who is pious, disciplined, intelligent, and fearless.

She insists the people must not surrender or else all Israel will fall, Jerusalem and the Temple will be destroyed, and the people will be enslaved.

Judith has a plan: She will get inside Holofernes' camp, and with God to make her strong, she will crush the enemy.

That is just what Judith does. She makes herself dazzlingly beautiful and, with her maid, charms her way into the enemy's camp, telling the Assyrian soldiers that she and her maid are running away from Bethulia before it falls, and that she has information for Holofernes about the mountain passes to use when he attacks.

Holofernes is astonished by Judith's beauty and is easily deceived by her clever plan. Judith tells him that to help him, she must leave the camp each night to pray to her God. In prayer, she says, God will tell her when it is the right time for Holofernes to attack. She and her maid must also carry their own food in a sack because of their kosher food requirements (*kosher* means "fit" or "proper" in Hebrew, and kosher food is prepared according to Jewish dietary laws).

So Judith and her maid go through the ritual of leaving the camp to pray each night, carrying their sack of provisions. By the fourth night, Holofernes, beside himself with desire for the beautiful Judith, invites her to a banquet—after which he plans to seduce her. But the excited general gets drunk during the meal and falls asleep. Alone with him Judith prays for strength, then takes his sword, grabs him by the hair, and cuts off his head. She rolls the head into the sack of "provisions," and, as the Assyrian soldiers have come to expect each night, she and her maid leave the camp to "pray."

The two women go straight to the city gates of Bethulia where Judith shouts, "Our God is with us!" She pulls the head of Holofernes from her sack, and the townspeople rejoice. Judith thanks God that by the power of her beauty and without defilement to her, she has triumphed.

The next day the Israelites pretend to attack the Assyrian camp. When the Assyrians discover that Holofernes is dead and Judith is gone, they panic and flee. Israel is victorious!

Read Judith, chapters 1 to 16.

The author of Judith wanted to remind the people that in the past Israel had trusted in its own schemes, and had fallen. Judith, on the other hand, trusted in God and thus won the victory for her people.

We might wonder at the methods used by the beautiful, intelligent Judith: assassination, deception, enticement. How good was her behavior in the story? Not very, according to our standards. But we have to recall the brutality of ancient times, and how Judith's deeds would have seemed tame to Jews in comparison with the butchery of the Assyrian, Babylonian, and Greek conquering armies.

The author of Judith was not so interested in applying a moral measuring stick to Judith's methods. Rather he was trying to emphasize that she trusted completely in God as she used her considerable wits and charm; God worked through her particular talents and gifts. The story also must have enormously entertained its early audiences, who were most often living in oppressive situations. It resembles the story of the judge Deborah, who slew an enemy general and thus saved Israel (see chapter 5).

Esther: A Timid but Heroic Queen

We do not know when the Book of Esther was written, but we do know that it had two purposes: to praise the goodness of God, who saved the Jews from annihilation, and to explain the origin of the feast called Purim. The festival celebrates the triumph of the lovely Queen Esther (a fictional character who is Jewish) over the villain Haman, who plotted to slay all the Jews in Persia. The time of the story is the reign of the Persian king Artaxerxes—called Ahasuerus in some versions—around 485 to 464 B.C.E. The place is Susa, a Persian city where many Jews of the Dispersion settled.

King Artaxerxes orders his queen to step down from the throne after an incident when he feels humiliated by her. To replace her he searches the kingdom for the most beautiful, pleasing woman in the land. Esther, a Jew, is encouraged by her cousin Mordecai to come forward and "try out" for the role of queen—without revealing that she is Jewish. Her loveliness and simplicity immediately win the king's heart.

As queen, Esther gains knowledge of a plot by the prime minister, Haman, to slaughter all the Jews in the land. Haman has a grudge against Mordecai, who refuses to bow to him, and he wants to punish not only Mordecai but all his people. Haman convinces the king that the Jews are treasonous people, and the king then goes along with Haman's plan.

At Mordecai's urging Esther agrees to plead for the Jewish people before the king. But she is terrified to go to court without the king's summons; such an improper act could risk her death. She decides to risk it for the sake of her people.

Esther, shaking with fear, appears before the king, and when he welcomes her, she faints. Finally, she invites the king and Haman to be her guests at dinner. After the meal Esther is too timid to tell the king what is on her mind. Instead, she asks that the two men return the next evening, when she will explain her purpose.

That night the king learns that Mordecai once uncovered a plot in the court to kill him, but has never been rewarded for this good deed. The king determines to honor Mordecai—unaware that Haman hates the man.

When Haman appears, having built a gallows on which to hang Mordecai, the king asks him what he should do to honor a certain man. Thinking that he himself is the man, Haman dreams up an elaborate procession. The king is pleased and says in effect, "Splendid—now go do it for Mordecai."

The next evening, when Esther is once again with the king and Haman, she tells the king that one of his nobles wants to murder the queen (herself) and all her people. Outraged, the king asks who, and Esther points to Haman. Wicked Haman now grovels before Esther, the king is wild with anger at him, and in the end it is Haman, not Mordecai, who hangs on the gallows.

Read Esther, chapters 1 to 7.

The Jewish feast of Purim honors the courage of the gentle and beautiful Esther, who overcame her fears to save her people. It gets its name from the lot—the *pur*—that Haman drew to determine the date of the slaughter of the Jews.

Jonah: A Parable of Mercy

The Book of Jonah, only four chapters long, uses some humorous satire to make its serious point—that God's mercy extends to all, not just to the "insiders." The book is fiction, including its main character. Its author is unknown, and its setting is the Assyrian Empire around 750 B.C.E.—

Modern Branches of Judaism

Judaism today has three main branches—**Orthodox, Reform, and Conservative.** They all share the belief in the one God and in the moral truths revealed by God in the Torah. However, they differ in the extent to which they observe the traditional ritual and dietary laws. Even within each branch, there is variety in terms of practice. In the United States, with more Jews than any other country, Conservative Jews are the largest branch, followed by Reform Jews, and then Orthodox Jews.

Orthodox Judaism, the oldest group, calls itself "Torah-true Judaism" because of its strict observance of the Law of Moses, including rules around worship, the Sabbath, diet, family rituals, and festivals. It was Orthodox Jews who first came to the Americas from eastern Europe.

Reform Judaism arose in the nineteenth century from the desire to adapt to modern society. It held to the high moral ethic of the Law, but it dispensed its members from most of the ritual and dietary laws. This liberal branch found many adherents in the United States, where Jewish people enjoyed greater freedom and acceptance than elsewhere, and wanted to fit into society rather than stand out as peculiar because of their customs. In the last several decades, however, Reform Judaism has returned to some of the ritual and dietary traditions. Reform Jews call their houses of worship "temples" rather than "synagogues," and they now ordain women rabbis. They are known as firm supporters of many justice causes.

Conservative Judaism formed later in the nineteenth century as a reaction against Reform Judaism, which, it was thought, had abandoned too much of the Law. It lies between the strict Orthodox and the liberal Reform branches. Its members keep although Jonah was written in the fifth century B.C.E. Jonah the prophet is depicted satirically; he is obviously not in the great tradition of the prophets Isaiah, Jeremiah, and Ezekiel. Rather, he is portrayed as a self-serving fellow who sulks when God turns out to be more merciful to sinners than he expected or wanted.

the ritual traditions of Judaism but adapt them or allow departures from them in keeping with modern needs. Women are beginning to become rabbis in the Conservative branch.

Within and beyond the three main branches of Judaism are other smaller groups and movements. **Reconstructionism,** a twentieth-century cultural and spiritual movement that branched off from Conservatism, aimed to revitalize Judaism and ensure the creative survival of the Jewish people. The movement, which has its own synagogues, fosters the art, music, language, literature, and customs of Jewish civilization.

A group that arose within Orthodox Judaism is known as the **Hasidim** (which means "pietism"). It was part of a mystical movement that developed in reaction to scholarly approaches to Judaism. Rather than intense study of the Scriptures, Hasidic Jews concentrate on simple, heartfelt faith, prayer, and personal devotion. A large concentration of Hasidic Jews is located in Brooklyn, New York, where they are recognized by their traditional appearance and practices.

Zionism came about in the late 1800s, and today has members within all major branches of Judaism. Named for Zion, the Jewish poetic term for Jerusalem and the Holy Land, the movement sought to return dispersed Jews to their ancient homeland in Palestine and to once again build their own nation there. Since the state of Israel was established in 1948, Zionism has focused on support for that nation in the midst of conflicts with its Arab neighbors and with the Palestinians of the land.

The population of Jews worldwide has climbed steadily since the end of World War II, when it was about 11 million. Today about 13.5 million Jews live around the world, with most living in three major centers—the United States, Israel, and Russia, in that order.

God tells Jonah to go to Nineveh, the capital of Assyria, and warn its people that their wickedness is known and is about to be punished. To Jonah the Ninevites are filthy pagans, and he wants nothing to do with them. So instead of doing as God instructs, he flees on a ship bound for a distant land. Out on the sea, a terrible storm comes up, and the ship's crew blames Jonah for their disaster and casts him overboard.

Jonah is swallowed by a fish, in whose belly he remains for three days and three nights until the fish belches him up on shore. Having gotten Jonah's attention by the ordeal in the sea, God sends Jonah to Nineveh a second time. This time he goes and delivers the message of the coming doom. After only one day of Jonah's preaching, the people repent, fast, and call loudly to God for mercy for their past wickedness. Upon hearing Nineveh repent, God decides not to destroy the city after all.

Even though God is pleased, Jonah is not. He throws God's mercy back in God's face. This was the reason he refused to go to Nineveh in the first place: he knew that God would be too kindhearted to the people.

God makes it clear to Jonah that this grumpy prophet has no good reason to be angry. If Jonah is so concerned about himself, shouldn't God be concerned about and show mercy to the city of Nineveh and its 120,000 people, "'who do not know their right hand from their left'" (Jonah 4:11)? And the book ends; we never hear Jonah's answer.

Read Jonah, chapters 1 to 4.

Recall that in the period when Jonah was written, Ezra and Nehemiah had worked to purify Judaism of foreign elements and build the boundaries of Jewish identity. Some Jews then took this to mean that Israel *alone* could be worthy of God's mercy. The Book of Jonah was probably written to argue against that narrow-minded spirit.

Through his brief satire on a fictitious prophet, the author wanted to remind his audience that God called Israel to be a light to the rest of the world, not to assume that others were beyond the reach of God's love and the hope of salvation. The Book of Jonah reminds us that no one—no religion, culture, nation, or subgroup—is beyond God's reach. We are all "insiders" when it comes to God's love and mercy.

Wisdom and Virtue for Then and Now

Judaism before Jesus was engaged in a kind of ongoing conversation—within itself, with God, and with the cultures in which it was immersed. Consider the variety of outlooks in the wisdom books, each helping to build up a rich tradition of insights on the meaning and purpose of life. That these outlooks vary and differ gives us a sense of the depth of God's wisdom, which cannot be penetrated by any single point of view.

Even the Books of Tobit, Judith, Esther, and Jonah are a kind of response, in story form, to the issues facing Judaism in those late centuries. But they speak just as powerfully to Christians today who are trying to live faithful lives while immersed in a society that is often in tension with Judeo-Christian values. The virtues that these stories encourage—generosity, faithfulness, trust, steadfastness, piety, heroic courage, humility, simplicity, and mercy—are all desperately needed in our day. The God who is worshiped by Christians and Jews today inspired those stories, and the ancient conversations that produced them, as gifts for all eras and times.

Questions for Reflection and Discussion

1. Reflect on some of the wisdom that you have learned from your elders, colleagues, children, and others.

2. Who are some wisdom figures in your life?

3. What do you think of God's "answer" to Job? What would be your own response to God?

4. What is your reaction to Qoheleth's attitude toward life? Do you agree or disagree with him? Why?

5. In Tobit we see the model of a faithful Jew in ancient Israel. What would characterize a faithful Christian today?

6. What do you think could have been Jonah's answer to God's question at the end of the Book of Jonah?

11

The Psalms, Pouring Out Heart and Soul to God

O Lord, you have searched me and known me.
You know when I sit down and when I rise up;
    you discern my thoughts from far away.
You search out my path and my lying down,
    and are acquainted with all my ways.
Even before a word is on my tongue,
    O Lord, you know it completely.

. . . .

For it was you who formed my inward parts;
    you knit me together in my mother's womb.
I praise you, for I am fearfully and wonderfully made.
    Wonderful are your works;
that I know very well.

(Psalm 139:1–4,13–14)

The Psalms and other prayers of the Old Testament can be connected with the life and history of the people of Israel. Many psalms refer to specific events and persons from biblical history. This chapter focuses on what the Psalms can teach us about how to pray—whether we are praying with the beautiful poetry of the Psalms or with our own words, using our own experiences.

Songs of the Heart

To begin, let's consider one particular prayer, Psalm 116. Try to imagine an experience or event that could have prompted this prayer in the heart of the person who originally wrote it.

> I love the LORD, because he has heard
>   my voice and my supplications.
> Because he inclined his ear to me,
>   therefore I will call on him as long as I live.
> The snares of death encompassed me;
>   the pangs of Sheol laid hold on me;
>   I suffered distress and anguish.
> Then I called on the name of the LORD:
>   "O LORD, I pray, save my life!"
>
> Gracious is the LORD, and righteous;
>   our God is merciful.
> The LORD protects the simple;
>   when I was brought low, he saved me.
> Return, O my soul, to your rest,
>   for the LORD has dealt bountifully with you.
>
> For you have delivered my soul from death,
>   my eyes from tears,
>   my feet from stumbling.
> I walk before the LORD
>   in the land of the living.
> I kept my faith, even when I said,
>   "I am greatly afflicted";
> I said in my consternation,
>   "Everyone is a liar."
>
> What shall I return to the LORD
>   for all his bounty to me?
> I will lift up the cup of salvation
>   and call on the name of the LORD,
> I will pay my vows to the LORD
>   in the presence of all his people.
> Precious in the sight of the LORD
>   is the death of his faithful ones.

O LORD, I am your servant;
    I am your servant, the child of your serving girl.
    You have loosed my bonds.
I will offer to you a thanksgiving sacrifice
    and call on the name of the LORD.
I will pay my vows to the LORD
    in the presence of all his people,
in the courts of the house of the LORD,
    in your midst, O Jerusalem.
Praise the LORD!

We do not know what experience originally prompted the heartfelt words of Psalm 116, but we can imagine. Perhaps the psalmist was deathly ill, and then got better. Maybe she or he was the victim of vicious gossip or false accusations. Perhaps the accusers were so cruel to the person that it felt like being near death—and then her or his reputation was restored when the truth came out. Or the psalmist might have been attacked and beaten on the road, or nearly killed in a fierce battle, and survived to tell the story.

Whatever the experience was behind the prayer, the psalmist wanted to give thanks to God for the marvelous rescue. In this case that meant going to the Temple in Jerusalem, where the Lord was believed to dwell, and offering a sacrificial animal in thanksgiving.

Although we do not know exactly what situations prompted the authors of the Psalms to write them, the strong feelings these prayers express could apply to situations in any place or time. In every era since biblical times, people have found that the Psalms say what is in their heart, and so they have been central to Jewish and Christian prayer and worship. Today, thousands of years after they were composed, we can identify our own life circumstances with the Psalms.

Lament, Thanks, and Praise

Many scholars categorize the Psalms by the sentiments they express. The Book of Psalms has three major types of prayers:

- **psalms of lament**, which express grief and complaint to God for some suffering, and beg for God's help
- **psalms of thanks**, which express gratitude for God's good deeds
- **psalms of praise**, which celebrate the majesty and wonder of God

We have already seen prayers like the psalms of lament in the Book of Lamentations, considered in chapter 8 of this book. Recall that those were laments over the destruction of Jerusalem by the Babylonians at the time of the exile.

It is not always clearcut which category a psalm is in, because many psalms express more than one sentiment. A psalm, for instance, might have features of both lament and praise, or praise and thanks. But most psalms focus predominantly on one sentiment or another—like Psalm 116 above, which is one of thanks.

Read Psalms 86 (lament), 30 (thanks), 104 (praise).

Developed over Centuries

Scholars believe that the Psalms were composed throughout several centuries, from about 1000 to 300 B.C.E. Half of them are attributed to King David, but it is likely that he wrote only a few psalms, if any at all. They were written in his spirit, though, and a number of them have a "tag line" at the beginning that identifies a particular situation in David's life. For example, Psalm 63, attributed to David, is preceded by the tag line, "A Psalm of David, when he was in the Wilderness of Judah" (that is, hiding out from the jealous King Saul). But the psalm is not about David's experience alone; it is the prayer of anyone who longs for God. In its first verse, for example, Psalm 63 uses the image of the desert wilderness to point to the inner thirst for God:

O God, you are my God, I seek you,
    my soul thirsts for you;
my flesh faints for you,
    as in a dry and weary land where there is no water.

Another example of a tag line related to David is the one for Psalm 51, a plea for God's mercy and forgiveness: "A psalm of David, when Nathan the prophet came to him after his affair with Bathsheba" (NAB). Recall that David had an affair with Bathsheba, and ordered that her husband be put at the front line in battle so he would be killed. David had sinned grievously and needed forgiveness. Psalm 51 expresses what anyone who regrets an awful deed can pour out to God. Following are its first two verses:

> Have mercy on me, O God,
>   according to your steadfast love;
> according to your abundant mercy
>   blot out my transgressions.
> Wash me thoroughly from my iniquity,
>   and cleanse me from my sin.

These tag lines remind us of the kinds of events in biblical history that could have prompted such prayers. But the Psalms most likely were composed decades or centuries later, not at the time of those particular events. The full collection of 150 psalms was put together from many shorter collections. The Book of Psalms as we now have it is divided into five smaller books.

Used in Worship

The Psalms can be used for personal, private prayer, but most were probably written with community worship in mind.

Today it is common to read or say the psalms in prayer. But the psalms are beautiful works of poetry originally set to music; they were composed to be sung in public worship. Some of the tag lines for the psalms even include musical instructions: "with stringed instruments" (Psalm 54); also "according to Lilies" (Psalm 69) and "according to The Deer of the Dawn" (Psalm 22)—both are melodies that would have been known by the ancient worshipers.

Some of the psalms are intended to be sung along with certain liturgical actions or services, for example, "for the memorial offering" (Psalm 38) and "A song for the Sabbath

Day" (Psalm 92). A whole group of psalms (120 to 134) are given the tag line "A Song of Ascents." These would have been sung as pilgrims to the holy city of Jerusalem ascended the hill in procession to worship in their revered Temple. For instance, here are the first two verses of Psalm 122:

> I was glad when they said to me,
>> "Let us go to the house of the LORD!"
> Our feet are standing
>> within your gates, O Jerusalem.

A psalm can express a whole community's sentiments about some experience they have shared—a victory, a defeat, or perhaps the renewal of spring as the land comes alive again. When it expresses a shared experience, singing the psalm together in worship bonds the people to one another and to God.

Some psalms point to specific events in the history of the people, for instance, Psalm 137, which recalls the exile in Babylon. Imagine how powerful it must have been for those who understood the choking grief of exile to sing this psalm together:

> By the rivers of Babylon—
>> there we sat down and there we wept
>> when we remembered Zion.
> On the willows there
>> we hung up our harps.
> For there our captors
>> asked us for songs,
> and our tormentors asked for mirth, saying,
>> "Sing us one of the songs of Zion!"
>
> How could we sing the LORD's song
>> in a foreign land?
> If I forget you, O Jerusalem,
>> let my right hand wither!
> Let my tongue cling to the roof of my mouth,
>> if I do not remember you,
> if I do not set Jerusalem
>> above my highest joy.

(Vv. 1–6)

In the Christian Liturgy

From early Christian times, followers of Jesus prayed the Psalms. Jesus himself had prayed them as a good Jew. In the local synagogues, where the earliest Christians worshiped (considering themselves still Jews), the Psalms were a part of the Jewish service of the word—as they are today. The service of the word consisted of readings from the Torah and the Prophets, with psalms sung in response to the readings.

In the liturgy of the word. Toward the end of the first century C.E., Christianity and Judaism split, and Christians were no longer allowed in the synagogues. But they continued to have their own service of the word modeled on the Jewish service, with readings and psalms. That service evolved into what Catholics call today the liturgy of the word, the first part of the Mass, which is another term for the Eucharist.

The liturgy of the word includes Bible readings, which are the word of God. The first reading is followed by the "responsorial psalm"—the people's response to the gift of God's word. So the Psalms play an important role in the Mass, as well as in most Christian worship services.

In the liturgy of the hours. The Psalms are also a major part of the liturgy of the hours, the official daily prayer of the Catholic church. Also called the Divine Office, the liturgy of the hours is designed to be prayed at specified times of the day, ideally by a community. In it, the Psalms are interspersed with biblical and other readings, hymns, and seasonal prayers. Over four weeks' time, almost the entire Psalter (Book of Psalms) is prayed during the liturgy of the hours. The Psalms, beloved to ancient and modern Jews, are the same prayers that have nourished and expressed the Catholic church's daily worship for centuries.

The Psalms as Poetry

Certain literary qualities of the Psalms make them ideally suited to prayer, whether they are used in a group or in solitude.

Easily Remembered and Chanted

The Psalms were written to be prayed from memory, not read. The beautiful sounds in the original Hebrew poetry helped people to remember them, but these sounds are lost in the translation to English. But even in English we can see other devices that would make the psalms easy to remember. Similar to the sayings in the Book of Proverbs, the Psalms include much repetition—expressing the same idea in more than one way. Psalm 51, also quoted earlier in this chapter, gives numerous examples of this:

> Create in me a clean heart, O God,
>> and put a new and right spirit within me.
> Do not cast me away from your presence,
>> and do not take your holy spirit from me.
>>> (Vv. 10–11)

The first part of each verse above is echoed by the second part of the verse. And sometimes, as in Psalm 20:8, the two parts of a verse express the same idea (in this case, "our victory") in two contrasting ways:

> They [the enemy] will collapse and fall,
>> but we shall rise and stand upright.

Structuring the Psalms with such repetition and contrast made them easier to remember. It also helped the person praying to dwell on the ideas and let them sink in, as one line added another layer of understanding to the previous one. This device also lent itself to chanting the verses of the Psalms back and forth between two groups during worship.

Concrete Language

Another literary feature of the Psalms that makes them beautiful poetry is their use of concrete, not abstract, language. To see the difference, compare these two styles of prayer:

1. O God, you are the all-powerful supreme being of the whole universe.

2. Bless the LORD, O my soul.
   O LORD my God, you are very great.

You are clothed with honor and majesty,
    wrapped in light as with a garment.
You stretch out the heavens like a tent,
    you set the beams of your chambers on the waters,
you make the clouds your chariot,
    you ride on the wings of the wind,
you make the winds your messengers,
    fire and flame your ministers.

(Psalm 104:1–4)

The first style uses abstract language to describe God's power, whereas the second, the psalm, uses concrete language—lengthier than the first but more appealing. The psalm verses are full of metaphors, vivid images that help us to sense the power of God, not simply to acknowledge the concept. The verses are full of action as well: God does not stand still but moves in the world; God is active and at work making things happen. These metaphors are not meant to be scientific understandings but poetic figures of speech that bring to life the abstract notion of an "all-powerful supreme being."

If a psalmist wished to tell of being saved by God, he or she would not say simply, "Salvation came from God," an accurate but unpoetic statement. Instead, the psalmist might pour out the seeable, hearable, touchable, feelable, even smellable words of Psalm 40, letting us know just what being saved felt like:

I waited patiently for the LORD;
    he inclined to me and heard my cry.
He drew me up from the desolate pit,
    out of the miry bog,
and set my feet upon a rock,
    making my steps secure.
He put a new song in my mouth,
    a song of praise to our God.
Many will see and fear,
    and put their trust in the LORD.

(Vv. 1–3)

The Psalms contain moving poetry, but they are much more than that. They are God's inspired gift to us, coming through the earthy humanity of the psalmists who wrote them. Through the Psalms God helps us pour out the deep longings, great sufferings, and ecstatic joys of the human heart and release them into God's loving care.

We will next turn to the major types of psalms—lament, thanks, and praise—to discover how they can heal and transform us.

Psalms of Lament: Crying Out in Suffering

Have you ever been so low that you felt completely overwhelmed, unable to keep going, desperate for relief from the burdensomeness of life? Such a state of mind and heart is a moment for a psalm of lament. Hear, for example, these verses from Psalm 69:

> Save me, O God, for the waters have come up to my neck.
> I sink in deep mire,
>   where there is no foothold;
> I have come into deep waters,
>   and the flood sweeps over me.
> I am weary with my crying;
>   my throat is parched.
> My eyes grow dim
>   with waiting for my God.
>
> More in number than the hairs of my head
>   are those who hate me without cause;
> many are those who would destroy me,
>   my enemies who accuse me falsely.
>
> (Vv. 1–4)
>
> But as for me, my prayer is to you, O LORD.
>   At an acceptable time, O God,
>   in the abundance of your steadfast love, answer me.
> With your faithful help rescue me
>   from sinking in the mire;
> let me be delivered from my enemies
>   and from the deep waters.

Do not let the flood sweep over me,
    or the deep swallow me up,
    or the Pit close its mouth over me.

.   .   .   .

You know the insults I receive,
    and my shame and dishonor;
    my foes are all known to you.
Insults have broken my heart,
    so that I am in despair.
I looked for pity, but there was none;
    and for comforters, but I found none.
They gave me poison for food,
    and for my thirst they gave me vinegar to drink.

(Vv. 13–21)

Let them be blotted out of the book of the living;
    let them not be enrolled among the righteous.
But I am lowly and in pain;
    let your salvation, O God, protect me.

I will praise the name of God with a song;
    I will magnify him with thanksgiving.

.   .   .   .

Let the oppressed see it and be glad;
    you who seek God, let your hearts revive.
For the LORD hears the needy,
    and does not despise his own that are in bonds.

(Vv. 28–33)

These excerpts show the elements found in most psalms of lament, though not necessarily in this order:
- an address to God
- a complaint or account of the misery suffered
- a plea for help
- an affirmation of trust in God
- a statement praising God

From Voicing the Pain to Being Transformed

A psalm of lament gives loud and emotional voice to a complaint or a series of them. The details of the suffering endured may take up most of the verses. But the psalm eventually moves beyond pouring out all the woes of the heart to turning those woes over in trust to God, whose wisdom and enduring love are beyond all imagining. It ends with praise of God.

The ancient Jews prayed fervently for an end to suffering and injustice, just as modern-day people do. The psalms of lament voice the deep pain people are suffering, but in the process they recall God's goodness and justice, God's mercy and kindness, power and awe. This is the God who has rescued the people over and over, who has worked wonders for them. This is the God who can turn the impossible into the possible and real! This is the God who has never abandoned them, and never will. Through pouring out their pain and entrusting themselves to God's care, those who pray these psalms are consoled and gradually transformed. They become centered in God. No matter what the circumstances of their life, they know their hope is in God.

Read Psalm 42.

A Theme Song of Tears and Trust

In ancient times a Jew might have gone to the Temple with a great sorrow or suffering, asking for a prayer that would help present the concern to God. The Temple priest, then, would give the person a particular psalm that fit his or her needs, encouraging the person to recite and memorize it, and to make it like a heartfelt theme song that could be prayed at home any time of the day or night.

Suppose, for instance, that a man living in Judah in about 350 B.C.E. becomes widowed when his wife dies giving birth. He is grief stricken for months and cannot seem to go ahead with life. His small piece of land lies neglected; he cannot care for his children. At the Temple the priest encourages the man to pray every day what we now know as Psalm 77 and to let it become a part of him. The man does so faithfully. Slowly, over weeks and months, his deadened heart comes alive again. But he is changed from before his grief began. His eyes radiate a quiet hope now, even when he is having a hard day. He has gradually put his trust in God, and allowed God to become the center of his life.

Read Psalm 77.

Why So Brutally Honest?

Although psalms of lament are among the most numerous and the favorite of the Psalms, they contain some features that people find troubling. For one thing many of the lament psalms convey some shocking emotions—things that might seem out of place in a book of prayer, let alone in the inspired word of God. Why are these messages there?

The lament psalms let out anger at God, blame and question God, rage at enemies, cry in despair and a desire for revenge. For instance, recall Psalm 137, the sad song of the exiles in Babylon, about longing for Jerusalem. If you check out verses 7 to 9, which are usually not recited or sung in worship, the psalmist wishes that the Babylonians' babies would be smashed against the rocks.

Why are the Psalms so blunt? Why do they seem to hold nothing back when it comes to negative emotions? Are they even disrespectful to God at times?

Consider the opening words of Psalm 22, which may be familiar to you as the words Jesus says (in Matthew's and Mark's Gospels) while dying on the cross: "My God, my God, why have you forsaken me?" (Psalm 22:1). One might wonder: Is the psalmist accusing God of abandoning him?

The language of the Psalms is not business-as-usual, nice, cover-up talk. It includes the most raw emotions. It is honest. The greatest gift one can bring to God is the gift of one's whole self—honest, true, uncensored, even flawed with sin. But to feel negative emotions and bring them to God is not the same as acting on those emotions. Just because the psalmist says to God, "I wish that such-and-such person was dead!" does not mean the psalmist may go out and kill such-and-such person, or cause anyone else to do so. The desire for revenge shows that the psalmist is only human, not perfect.

Expressing the awful feelings to God is only part of the movement of a psalm of lament. Pouring out the complaint is meant to help the person let go of the feelings and entrust them to God's care, not hold onto them. The complaint of a psalm always alternates with sentiments of trust, praise, and gratitude, as the burden is given over to God. Check out the rest of the verses of Psalm 22 (the psalm Jesus cried from the cross). The psalm moves back and forth from fright and desperation to soaring gratitude, trust, and praise of God. Above all else, praise has the last word.

Read Psalm 22.

What About Those Enemies?

The psalmists see plots and snares everywhere. Certainly a great many real enemies had to be contended with in the ancient times when the Psalms were composed. Enemies of Israel attacked its towns and raided them for spoils. Empires tried to dominate the Israelites and subject them to slavery and persecution. Greedy people tried to exploit others, sometimes right within their own community. And even a few gossipy neighbors, just as today, were prone to destroying others' reputations.

Today, too, evil is in the world. We can recognize it as "the enemies"—injustice, war, oppression, greed, addiction, abuse, violence, disregard of human life, and cruelty. But unlike the ancients, who saw enemies as completely "out there" in other persons, groups, and empires, we know now that so much of "the enemy" is within ourselves as well. Modern psychology has pointed out the human tendency to project onto other people whatever we do not like in ourselves. Thus we may notice and call attention to faults in others that are actually our own worst tendencies. One way to discover our own faults is to pay attention to what traits in others really irritate us. These are probably things we cannot stand in ourselves.

So when in the Psalms we pray about the enemies who are out to take our life, to ensnare us, to torment us, we may certainly have some particular people in mind. We may also be thinking of some oppressive, cruel systems that cause injustice and misery for poor people in the world; we would be right to consider them enemies. But we also need to be aware that the enemy is not all "out there"—that some of what we find evil in the world really resides within us as well. We may be greedy or selfish; we may want to control others; we may want to make our-selves look good or be successful at the expense of others.

God does not want to smash the enemies "out there"; God wants to transform them by love. Likewise, God does not want to smash the sinful tendencies within us but to transform them by love. First, however, we must be aware of what those tendencies are and give them over with trust to God. That is part of praying the psalms of lament with a sincere heart.

Read Psalm 64.

Psalms of Thanks and Praise: Celebrating Who God Is

With the psalms of thanks and of praise, the spotlight moves off the needs of the person praying to shine on God, the source of all goodness. These psalms come from an attitude of humility, one that acknowledges, "*I* am not the source of the universe. *You* are, God."

Psalms of thanks and of praise are similar to each other and often do overlap, because God can be thanked and praised almost in the same breath. However, psalms of thanks most often express gratitude to God for answering some specific prayer (perhaps a psalm of lament) and for rescuing the person or the community from a terrible situation. Psalms of praise, on the other hand, tend to be more general, focusing on the goodness, power, and majesty of God, not on a particular request that God answered.

Both kinds of psalms have similar elements:
1. an introductory word or statement of praise
2. the reason for the praise, or what the person who is praying is grateful for
3. another statement of praise

A Spirit of Gratitude

The spirit of gratitude is expressed in Psalm 30:

> I will extol you, O LORD, for you have drawn me up,
>> and did not let my foes rejoice over me.
> O LORD my God, I cried to you for help,
>> and you have healed me.
> O LORD, you brought up my soul from Sheol,
>> restored me to life from among those gone down to
>>> the Pit.
>
> Sing praises to the LORD, O you his faithful ones,
>> and give thanks to his holy name.
> For his anger is but for a moment;
>> his favor is for a lifetime.
> Weeping may linger for the night,
>> but joy comes with the morning.

(Vv. 1–5)

> You have turned my mourning into dancing;
>> you have taken off my sackcloth
>> and clothed me with joy,
> so that my soul may praise you and not be silent.
>> O LORD my God, I will give thanks to you forever.

(Vv. 11–12)

Even when we do not feel grateful, we can pray a psalm of thanks, trying to be open to its spirit. Little by little we may find ourselves growing in gratitude.
Read Psalms 23, 34, 136.

Psalm 30, like a number of others, refers to "Sheol" and the "Pit," as a place from which the psalmist was rescued. The ancient Jews for the most part did not believe in an afterlife of heaven or hell. Rather, they thought that all who died, whether good or bad, entered a shadowy underworld, Sheol, which in their belief was a void (the Pit). Formless, lifeless, completely removed from God's presence, the inhabitants of Sheol were basically in a state of nonexistence. It was a terrible condition, and much to be dreaded.

When the psalmist says the Lord brought her or him up from Sheol, we do not know just what that means. The psalmist could have been near death from illness. To make the psalm our own, though, we do not need to have been dying. We can substitute for Sheol and the Pit our own experiences with the small deaths of everyday life—rejection, humiliation, failure, loss. Then we can pray the psalm in gratitude for God's bringing us through those deaths into new life and hope again: "You have turned my mourning into dancing" (v. 11).

Letting Loose with Praise

With wonder and jubilation, God is praised in Psalm 47, and everyone is invited to join in the celebration:

> Clap your hands, all you peoples;
>> shout to God with loud songs of joy.
> For the LORD, the Most High, is awesome,
>> a great king over all the earth.
> He subdued peoples under us,
>> and nations under our feet.
> He chose our heritage for us,
>> the pride of Jacob whom he loves.
>
> God has gone up with a shout,
>> the LORD with the sound of a trumpet.
> Sing praises to God, sing praises;
>> sing praises to our King, sing praises.
> For God is the king of all the earth;
>> sing praises with a psalm.

(Vv. 1–7)

Why is God praised? Two themes come up over and over in the Psalms:
- God's wonderful deeds and goodness to the people, again and again
- the beauty and intricacy of all creation, which God has brought into existence and sustains with love
  Read Psalms 96, 100, 139.

Becoming a Song of Praise

The sense of wonder and awe so apparent in the psalms of praise may not come easily to us. For small children, wonder seems to come naturally. At a certain point in growing up, a more matter-of-fact way of looking at the world tends to take over. The phrase "What you see is what you get" expresses this attitude, a kind of flat numbness to the wonder of the world. There is nothing else beyond the obvious—no mystery, no unseen loving power at work in our life and in the universe, no glory shining within each leaf, each person. That attitude is so opposite from the sense of wonder that fills the Psalms.

Perhaps the psalms of praise can help us to see things we have never seen before. As we pray these songs of praise over a long time, maybe we will become a song of praise, joining with all creation in a hymn to our Creator.

> Make a joyful noise to the LORD, all the earth;
>   break forth into joyous song and sing praises.
> .   .   .   .
>
> Let the sea roar, and all that fills it;
>   the world and those who live in it.
> Let the floods clap their hands;
>   let the hills sing together for joy
> at the presence of the LORD, for he is coming
>   to judge the earth.
> He will judge the world with righteousness,
>   and the peoples with equity.
>
> (Psalm 98:4–9)

"Everything I Ever Needed to Know . . ."

As inspired writings the Psalms are a loving gift from God to us, for they show us the way to a genuine relationship with God. To paraphrase a well-known essay about learning in kindergarten everything needed for life, we can say,

"Everything I ever needed to know about prayer, I learned in the Book of Psalms."

With the Psalms as our teacher, what lessons can we learn about relating to God? Here are a few:

- Let your prayer grow out of your everyday experiences. Offer God the stuff of your life.
- Don't be afraid to share with God what is in your heart, no matter how negative you feel. Pouring yourself out in all honesty to God is the beginning of a real relationship—and God can handle it.
- Give your burdens over to God in trust that God will know what to do with them. In trusting God you will be transformed because you will become centered in God.
- See God's hand at work in your life, now and in your past. Tell God how grateful you are for the ways God has been loving you.
- Cultivate a sense of wonder and awe. Be amazed by things. Resist becoming jaded. Let the mystery of God stir your imagination.
- Celebrate with all your heart.

> Praise the LORD!
> Praise God in his sanctuary;
>   praise him in his mighty firmament!
> Praise him for his mighty deeds;
>   praise him according to his surpassing greatness!
>
> Praise him with trumpet sound;
>   praise him with lute and harp!
> Praise him with tambourine and dance;
>   praise him with strings and pipe!
> Praise him with clanging cymbals;
>   praise him with loud clashing cymbals!
> Let everything that breathes praise the LORD!
> Praise the LORD!

(Psalm 150)

Questions for Reflection and Discussion

1. If we live long enough, we have wounds that we live with. Our own words seem to fail us as we pray about these losses and hurts. Recollect two or three of your most lasting wounds. For each one find a psalm that expresses your sorrow and your need for God's healing. Pray the psalm when you need to do so.

2. Find three metaphors about God in the Psalms that you find comforting or disturbing. Ponder your reactions.

3. Consider each of these questions:
   • What messages did you receive as a child about how to pray to God, about what words to use?
   • How do you feel now about being completely honest with God?
   • If a person is not able to be honest in relationships with other people, is it possible to have an honest relationship with God?

4. If you were composing your own psalm of praise and thanks, what would you include? Use Psalms 136, 147, and 148 as your guides.

EPILOGUE

God's Love Story Fulfilled in Jesus

In the course of this book, we have reflected on the marvelous stories and characters of the Old Testament, the ups and downs of the biblical people's journey with God, the passionate teachings of the prophets on justice and faithfulness, and the beautiful, moving prayer that expressed Israel's struggle to walk in God's ways.

In the Bible we meet the living God who reaches out to us in love through the great Story of our salvation. At the close of the Old Testament, there is a sense of expectant longing for God's love to be fully realized in the world. There is an urgency to have God's Reign of justice and peace over all the earth become a reality.

In the New Testament, the story of God's love for humankind is fulfilled. The Reign of God is inaugurated on earth with the coming of Jesus.

An incident told in one of the Gospels provides a link between the Old Testament and the New. Picture the scene:

It is about ninety years since the Roman Empire has taken over the region of Palestine. The Jews live as an oppressed people, subjugated by a mighty dictatorship in the very land God promised to Abraham and his descendants so long ago.

Many Jews have put their hopes and dreams in the coming of a messiah, one anointed by God to save them from oppression and misery. Prophets have spoken and written of such a messiah for hundreds of years, and now the people's expectation of a savior has reached a fever pitch.

One day in a town called Nazareth in Galilee (the northern district of Palestine), a young man who was raised in the town enters the local synagogue for Sabbath worship.

> He stood up to read, and the scroll of the prophet Isaiah was given to him. He unrolled the scroll and found the place where it was written:
> "The Spirit of the Lord is upon me,
>   because he has anointed me
>   to bring good news to the poor.
> He has sent me to proclaim release to the captives
>   and recovery of sight to the blind,
>   to let the oppressed go free,
> to proclaim the year of the Lord's favor."
> And he rolled up the scroll, gave it back to the attendant, and sat down. The eyes of all in the synagogue were fixed on him. Then he began to say to them, "Today this scripture has been fulfilled in your hearing." (Luke 4:16–21)

In this dramatic moment, the young man, Jesus of Nazareth, identifies himself as the one fulfilling the prophetic message of Isaiah 61:1–2.

Of course, the four Gospels go on to tell of Jesus' ministry among the people. As a preacher, teacher, and healer, Jesus proclaims God's mercy and all-embracing love and calls them to love as God does. Although his message is not a rallying call for rebellion, the authorities are threatened by him. Eventually Jesus is arrested, tortured, and crucified, dying a criminal's death on a cross.

Could this poor victim of the Roman Empire possibly be the Messiah?

Three days after Jesus' death and burial, his followers encounter him risen from the dead! They begin to grasp that all God's promises to Israel have been fulfilled in Jesus (whom they call the Christ, meaning "the anointed," "the messiah"). They come to recognize that Jesus was more than any messiah they could have dreamed of. They believe that the man who walked the earth with them and suffered and died for them was also the Son of God, now risen from the dead in glory. They see that God was revealed to them fully through Jesus, and that God's holy spirit will be with them forever to help them be faithful witnesses to the love of God in Christ Jesus. The New Testament records the inspired faith testimonies of those early followers of Jesus.

One of the New Testament writings, the Letter to the Hebrews, proclaims this sacred belief: "Long ago God spoke to our ancestors in many and various ways by the prophets, but in these last days he has spoken to us by a Son" (1:1–2).

The Story of God's boundless love for us began with Creation and it culminated in Jesus, the fulfillment of all God's loving promises. So the Old Testament and the New Testament form one continuous story, and Christians cannot appreciate one without the other.

May the study of the Old Testament you have undertaken in this book enrich your mind and make ready your heart for all that God pours out to you in love as you walk your journey of life.

Index

L

M

Y

Z

Acknowledgments *(continued)*

The scriptural quotes on pages 136, 142, and 211 are from the New American Bible with revised New Testament. Copyright © 1986, 1991 by the Confraternity of Christian Doctrine, 3211 Fourth Street NE, Washington, DC 20017. All rights reserved.

All other scriptural quotations in this book are from the New Revised Standard Version of the Bible. Copyright © 1989 by the Division of Christian Education of the National Council of the Churches of Christ in the United States of America. All rights reserved.

The abbreviation NJB in this book refers to the New Jerusalem Bible.

The quotation on page 21 is from *The Writings of Martin Buber,* edited by Will Herberg (Cleveland: World Publishing Company, 1956), page 275.